Yung Wing

容　閎　著

徐鳳石　惲鐵樵　譯

My
Life
in China
and America

西學東漸記

商務印書館

西學東漸記 *My Life in China and America*

作　　者：容　閎

譯　　者：徐鳳石　惲鐵樵

責任編輯：黃振威

封面設計：張　毅

出　　版：商務印書館（香港）有限公司

　　　　　香港筲箕灣耀興道 3 號東廣場 8 樓

　　　　　http://www.commercialpress.com.hk

發　　行：香港聯合書刊物流有限公司

　　　　　香港新界荃灣德士古道 220-248 號荃灣工業中心 16 樓

印　　刷：永經堂印刷有限公司

　　　　　香港新界荃灣德士古道 188-202 號立泰工業中心第 1 座 3 樓

版　　次：2021 年 1 月第 1 版第 1 次印刷

　　　　　© 2021 商務印書館（香港）有限公司

　　　　　ISBN 978 962 07 4612 3

　　　　　Printed in Hong Kong

目錄

編輯説明

　　本書中文部分根據 1915 年商務印書館出版的《西學東漸記》，英文部分
則為 1909 年 Henry Holt and Company 出版的 *My Life in China and America*。
為保留原書歷史面貌，編者僅修正若干錯字、統一全書體例和重新整理標
點部分，其他則一仍其舊。另外，編者加入了少量註釋，以便讀者了解書中
內容。

第一章
幼稚時代

1828 年 11 月 17 日，予生於彼多羅島（Pedro-Island）之南屏鎮，鎮距澳門西南可四英里。澳門，葡萄牙殖民地也。島與澳門間，有海峽廣半英里許。予第三，有一兄、一姊、一弟。今兄弟若姊，俱已謝世，惟予僅存。

1834 年，倫敦婦女會議在遠東提倡女學。英教士古特拉富之夫人（Mrs. Gutzlaff）遂於是時蒞澳，初設一塾，專授女生。未幾復設附塾，兼收男生。其司事某君，予同里而父執也，常為予父母道古夫人設塾授徒事。其後予得入塾肄業，此君與有力焉。惟是時中國為純粹之舊世界，仕進顯達，賴八股為敲門磚，予兄方在舊塾讀書，而父母獨命予入西塾，此則百思不得其故。意者通商而後，所謂洋務漸趨重要，吾父母欲先着人鞭，冀兒子能出人頭地，得一翻譯或洋務委員之優缺乎？至於予後來所成之事業，似為時世所趨，或非予父母所及料也。

1835 年，隨父至澳門，入古夫人所設西塾，予見西國婦女始此，時纔七齡。當時情形，深印腦中，今雖事隔數十年，猶能記憶。古夫人軀幹修長，體態合度，貌秀而有威，眼碧色，深陷眶中，唇薄頤方，眉濃髮厚，望而知為果毅明決之女丈夫。時方盛夏，衣裳全白，飄飄若仙，兩袖圓博如球，為當年時製。夫人御此服飾，乃益形其修偉。予睹狀，殊驚愕，依吾父肘下，逡巡不前。雖夫人和顏悅色，終惴惴也。我生之初，足跡不出里巷，驟易處境，自非童稚所堪。迨後思家之念稍殺，外界接觸漸習，乃覺古夫人者和藹仁厚，視之若母矣。予於學生中，齒最稚，乃益邀夫人憐憫。入塾後即命居女院中，不與男童雜處，蓋特別優待也。

予兒時頗頑劣，第一年入塾時曾逃學，其事至今不忘。古夫人之居予於女院，本為優遇，予不知其用意。男生等皆居樓下層，能作戶外運動。而予與諸女生，則禁錮於三層樓上，惟以露台為遊戲場。以為有所厚薄，心不能甘。常課餘潛至樓下，與男生嬉。又見彼等皆許自由出門，散步街市，而予等猶無此權利，心益不平。乃時時潛出至埠頭，見小舟艤集，忽發異想，思假此逃出藩籠，以復我自由之舊。同院女生，年事皆長於予。中有數人，因禁閉過嚴，亦久蟄思啟，故於予之計劃，深表同情。既得同志六人，膽益壯。定計予先至埠頭，僱定蓋篷小船，乘間脫逃。翌晨早餐後，古夫人方就膳，予等七人遂於此時潛行出校，匆匆登舟，向對岸進發。對岸為彼多羅島，予家在也。謂同伴六人先至予家小住，然後分別還鄉。在予固自以為計出萬全，不謂渡江未半，追者踵至。來船極速，轉瞬且及。予乃惶急，促舟子努力前進，許渡登彼岸時，酬以重金。但予舟只二櫓，來舟則四櫓。舟子知勢力懸殊，見來舟手巾一揮，即戢耳聽命，而予等七人束手受縛矣。放豚入笠，乃施懲戒。古夫人旋命予等排列成行，巡行全校。且於晚課後，課堂中設一長桌，命七人立其上一小時。予立中央，左右各三人，頭戴尖頂紙帽，胸前懸一方牌大書「逃徒」，不啻越獄罪囚也。予受此懲創，羞愧無地。而古夫人意猶未足，故將果餅、橙子等分給他生剝食，使予等饞涎欲流，絕不一顧。苦樂相形，難堪滋甚，古夫人洵惡作劇哉！

古夫人所設塾，本專教女生。其附設男塾，不過為瑪禮孫學校（Morrison School）之預備耳。瑪禮孫學校發起於 1835 年，至 1839 年成立。未成立時，以生徒附屬古夫人塾中，酌撥該校經費，以資補助。是予本瑪禮孫校學生而寄生於此者。憶予初入塾時，塾中男生，合予共二人耳。後此塾逐漸擴張，規劃益宏。夫人乃邀其姪女派克司女士（Miss Parkes）姊妹二人，來華襄助。派女士之兄海雷派克司（Mr. Harry Parkes）即 1864 年 [1] 主張第二次之鴉片戰爭者，因其於此事著異常勞績，故英皇錫以勳爵云。予於此短期內，得親炙於派克司女士二人，亦幸事也。

1　編者按，原文如此，與史實有出入。

其後此塾因故停辦，予等遂亦星散。古夫人攜盲女三人赴美，此三女乃經予教以凸字讀書之法。及予輟教時，彼等已自能誦習《聖經》及《天路歷程》二書矣。派克司姊妹則一嫁陸克哈醫士（Dr. William Lockhart），一嫁麥克來穿傳教士（Rev. MacClatchy），仍受倫敦傳道會之委任，在中國服務甚久云。

予既還家，從事漢文。迨 1840 年夏秋之交，方鴉片戰爭劇烈時，適予父逝世，身後蕭條，家無擔石。予等兄弟姊妹四人，三人年齒稍長，能博微資。予兄業漁，予姊躬操井臼，予亦來往於本鄉及鄰鎮之間，販賣糖果，兢兢業業，不敢視為兒戲。每日清晨三時即起，至晚上六時始歸，日獲銀幣二角五分，悉以奉母。所得無多，僅僅小補。家中揩挂，惟長兄是賴耳。予母得予等臂助，尚能勉強度日。如是者五閱月，而嚴冬忽至，店舖咸停製糖果。予乃不得已而改業，隨老農後，芸草阡陌間。予姊恆與予偕。相傳古有盧斯（Ruth）者，割禾無所獲，遇波亞士（Boaz，亦人名）時時周給之，予惜無此佳遇。幸予粗通西文，窘迫時竟賴以解厄。予之能讀寫英文，農人本不之知。予姊告之，乃忽動其好奇心，招予至前曰：「孺子，試作紅毛人之語。」予初忸怩不能出口，後予姊從旁慫恿謂：「汝試為之。彼農或有以犒汝。」農人欣然曰：「老夫生平從未聞洋話。孺子能言者，吾將以禾一巨捆酬汝勞，重至汝不能負也。」予聞此重賞，膽立壯，乃為之背誦二十六字母。農人聞所未聞，咸驚奇詫異。予為此第一次演說時，稻田中之泥水深且沒脛。演說既畢，獲獎禾數捆，予與予姊果不能負，乃速返家邀人同往荷歸。予之拉雜英文，早年時即著此奇效，是則始願所不及。時予年十二歲，即古時盧斯之獲六斛，其成績亦不予過矣。

刈禾時期甚短，無他事足述。其後有一比鄰，向在天主教士某處，為印刷書報工人。適由澳門請假歸，偶與予母言教士欲僱用童子摺疊書頁，僅識英字母及號碼無誤即得，程度不必過高。予母告以此事予能為之，乃請其介紹於教士。條約既定，別母赴澳門就新事，月獲工資四元五角，以一元五角付膳宿費，餘三元按月匯寄堂上。然予亦不遽因此致富。可四閱月，忽有夢想不到之人來函招予，而上帝又似命予速往勿失時機者。函蓋來自霍白生醫生（Dr. Hobson）。醫生亦傳道者，其所主任之醫院，距予執業之印刷所僅一英里。予在古夫人西塾時數見之，故稔識其人。此次見招，初不解其故，以為霍氏欲予從其學醫也。繼乃知古夫人赴美時，其臨別之末一語，即托予於霍白生，謂必訪得予所在，俟瑪禮孫學校開課時送予入校云。霍氏負此宿諾，無日或忘。蓋覓予不得，已數月於茲。相見時霍氏謂予：「瑪禮孫學校已開課，汝亟歸家請命，必先得若母允汝入塾，然後捨去汝業，來此伴余數月，使予得熟知汝之為人，乃可介紹汝於該校教習也。」時予母方深資予助，聞言意頗不樂，然卒亦從予請，命予往澳門辭別天主教教士。該教士雖沉靜緘默，四月之中從未與予交一語，然亦未嘗吹毛求疵，故予去時頗覺戀戀。予辭出後，逕往醫院，從霍醫生終日杵臼丁丁，制藥膏丸散。霍氏巡行醫院，撫視病人時，則捧盆隨其後。如是者二閱月，霍君乃引予至瑪禮孫學校，謁見校長勃朗先生（Rev. S. R. Brown）。

第二章
小學時代

　　瑪禮孫學校於 1839 年 11 月 1 日開課，主持校務者為勃朗先生。先生美國人，1832 年由耶路大學（Yale University）畢業，旋復得名譽博士學位。乃於是年（1839 年）2 月 19 日偕其夫人蒞澳，以其生平經驗從事教育，實為中國創辦西塾之第一人。予入是校，在 1841 年，先我一年而入者已有五人：黃君勝、李君剛、周君文、唐君傑與黃君寬也。校中教科，為初等之算術、地文及英文。英文教課列在上午，國文教課則在下午。予惟英文一科，與其餘五人同時授課；讀音頗正確，進步亦速。予等六人為開校之創始班，予年最幼。迨後 1846 年之 12 月，勃朗先生因病歸國，六人中竟半數得附驥尾，亦難得之時會也。

　　瑪禮孫學校何由而來乎？讀者宜急欲知之矣。1834 年 8 月 1 日，瑪禮孫博士（Dr. Robert Morrison）卒於中國，其翌年 1 月 26 日，乃有傳單發佈於寓澳之西人，提議組織瑪禮教育會，以紀念其一生事跡，並議建設學校，及設施他種方法，以促進中國之泰西教育。至瑪禮孫博士之來中國，乃為英國傳道會所委派。彼為中國之第一傳道師。博士於 1807 年 1 月 31 日由倫敦啟程，經大西洋而至紐約，改乘帆船名「屈利亥登」（Trident）者而至中國。原擬在澳門登陸，因為天主教士之嫉忌，不果，乃折至廣州。後因中外適起交涉，中政府與西商感情頗惡，乃往麻拉甲（Malacca）暫時駐足，以植基礎。於是從事著作，成第一部之華英字典，分訂三冊，並以耶教《聖經》譯成漢文，以供華人披閱。又有第一信徒名梁亞發者，助其宣講，為傳道界別開生面，成效卓著。此後寓華之教士，咸奉瑪禮孫所著之字典及其所譯之《聖經》，以為圭臬。瑪禮孫博士既在中國成如許事業，其名永垂不朽，允宜建一大學以紀念之。乃所建者只區區一塾，規模偏小，且因經費僅僅恃僑寓西商，時虞匱乏。以瑪氏之豐功偉烈，而紀念之成績，乃不過如是，庸非一憾事哉！

1840 年鴉片戰爭起，其後結果，即以香港讓於英人。瑪禮孫學校遂於 1842 年遷於香港某山之巔，高出海平線幾六百英尺。山在維多利亞殖民地（Victoria Colony）之東端。登山眺望，自東至西，港口全境畢現。即此一處，已足見香港為中國南部形勝，無怪外人垂涎。且港口深闊，足為英國海軍根據地。有此特點，故此島終不我屬，卒為英國有也。瑪禮孫學校既設於山頂，其後此山遂亦以瑪禮孫得名云。

1845 年 3 月 12 日，威廉麥克（William Macy）先生來港，為瑪禮孫學校之助教。是校自澳門徙此以來，大加擴張，學生之數已達四十餘人。新增三班，教授一人之力，不能兼顧，故須延聘教習，相助為理。麥先生之來校，適當其會。勃朗先生則仍專心校務，毫無間斷。直至次年秋間回美，乃以麥先生繼之。蓋其時麥先生已有一年之經驗矣。

勃朗與麥克二君之品性，大相懸殊。勃先生一望而知為自立之人，性情態度沉靜自若，遇事調處秩序井然。其為人和藹可親，溫然有禮，且常操樂觀主義，不厭不倦，故與學生之感情甚佳。其講授教課，殆別具天才，不須遠證，而自能使學生明白了解。此雖由於賦性聰敏，要亦閱歷所致。蓋當其未來中國、未入耶路大學之前，固已具有教育上之經驗矣。故對於各種學生，無論其為華人、為日人或為美人，均能審其心理而管束之。知師莫若弟，以才具論，實為一良好校長。其後先生回國，任阿朋學校（Auburn Academy）之監院，後往日本亦從事教育，皆功效大著，足證是言之不謬也。至於助教麥克先生，亦為耶路大學之畢業生。第未來中國之先，未嘗執教鞭，故經驗絕少。而於中國將擇何種事業，亦未有方針。然其天性敏捷，德行純懿，思想卓犖，使君自不凡也。

1850 年瑪孫學校解散，麥克與其母返美，復入耶路大學聖教科學道，1854 年復經美國公會派至中國傳道。其時予已畢業於耶路大學，準備回國，乃與之偕歸。自桑得阿克（Sandy Hook）啟程以至香港，計歷百五十四日之久，始達目的地。長途寂寂，無聊殊甚，當於第六章中詳之。

　　1846 年冬，勃朗先生回國。去之前四月，先生以此意佈告生徒，略謂己與家屬均身體羸弱，擬暫時離華，庶幾遷地為良，並謂對於本校，感情甚深，此次歸國，極願攜三五舊徒，同赴新大陸，俾受完全之教育。諸生中如有願意同行者，可即起立。全堂學生聆其言，爽然如有所失，默不發聲。其後數日間，課餘之暇，聚談及此，每為之愀然不樂。其欣欣然有喜色者，惟願與赴美之數人耳，即黃勝、黃寬與予是也。當勃先生佈告遊美方針時，予首先起立，次黃勝，次黃寬。第予等雖有此意，然年幼無能自主。歸白諸母，母意頗不樂。予再四請行，乃勉強曰諾。然已淒然淚下矣。予見狀，意良不忍，竭力勸慰之曰：「兒雖遠去，尚有兄弟與姊三人，且長兄行將娶婦，得有兄嫂承歡膝下，不致寂寞。母其善自珍攝，弗念兒也！」母聞予言，為之首肯。由今思之，殆望予成器，勉強忍痛也。嗚呼！

　　予等均貧苦，若自備資斧，則無米安能為炊？幸勃朗先生未宣言前，已與校董妥籌辦法。故予等留美期內，不特經費有着，即父母等亦至少得二年之養贍。既惠我身，又及家族，仁人君子之用心，可謂至矣。資助予等之人，本定二年為期限，其中三人之名，予尚能記憶。一為蓄德魯特君（Andrew Shortrede），蘇格蘭人，香港《中國日報》（China Mail）之主筆。其人素鯁居，慷慨明決，有當仁不讓之風。一為美商李企君（Ritchie）。一為蘇格蘭人康白爾君（Campbell）。其餘諸人，惜不相識，故無從記其名姓。此外又有阿立芬特公司（The Olyphant Brothers）者，為美國紐約巨商兄弟三人所設，有帆船一艘名「亨特利思」（Huntress），專來中國運載茶葉，予等即乘是船赴美。蒙公司主人美意，自香港至紐約不取船資，亦盛德也。此數君者，解囊相助，俾予等受完全之教育，蓋全為基督教慈善性質，並無他種目的。今則人事代謝，已為古人，即稱道其名，亦已不及。然其後裔聞之，知黃寬、黃勝與予之教育，全為其先人所培植，亦一快心愜意事也。

第三章
初遊美國

　　1847 年 1 月 4 日，予等由黃浦首途，船名「亨特利思」，帆船也，屬於阿立芬特兄弟公司，前章已言之。船主名格拉司彼 (Captain Gillespie)。時值東北風大作，解纜揚帆，自黃浦抵聖希利那島 (St. Helena)，波平船穩。過好望角時，小有風浪，自船後來，勢乃至猛，恍若惡魔之逐入。入夜天則黑暗，濃雲如幕，不漏星斗。於此茫茫黑夜中，仰望桅上電燈星星，搖蕩空際，飄忽不定，有若墟墓間之燐火。此種愁慘景象，印入腦際，迄今猶歷歷在目。惟彼時予年尚幼，不自知其危險，故雖扁舟顛簸於驚濤駭浪中，不特無恐怖之念，且轉以為樂。竟若此波濤洶湧，入予目中，皆成為不世之奇觀者。迨舟既過好望角，駛入大西洋，較前轉平靜。至聖希利那島稍停，裝載糧食淡水。凡帆船之自東來者，中途乏飲食料，輒假此島為暫時停泊之所。自舟中遙望聖希利那島，但見火成石焦黑如炭，草木不生，有若牛山濯濯。予等乘此停舟之際，由約姆司坦 (Jamestown) 登陸，遊覽風景。入其村，居民稀少，田間植物則甚多，濃綠芸芸，良堪娛目。居民中有我國同胞數人，乃前乘東印度公司船以來者，年事方盛，咸有眷屬。此島即拿破崙戰敗被幽之地，拿氏遂終老於此。其墳在島之浪奧特 (Longwood) 地方，予等咸往登臨，撫今弔古，根觸余懷。墳前有大柳樹一，乃各折一枝，攜歸舟中，培養而灌溉之，以為異日之紀念。後抵美國，勃朗先生遂移此柳枝，植諸紐約省之阿朋學校中。勃朗即在此校任教授數年，後乃往遊日本。迨 1854 年予至阿朋學校遊覽時，則見此枝已長成茂樹，垂條萬縷矣。

　　舟既過聖希利那島，折向西北行，遇「海灣水溜」(Gulf Stream)，水急風順，舟去如矢，未幾遂抵紐。時在 1847 年 4 月 12 日，即予初履美土之第一日也。是行計居舟中凡九十八日，而此九十八日中，天氣清朗，絕少陰霾，洵始願所不及。1847 年紐約之情形，絕非今日（指 1909 年）。當時居民僅二十五萬乃至三十萬耳，今則已成極大之都會，危樓摩天，華屋林立，教堂塔尖，高聳雲表，人煙之稠密，商業之繁盛，與倫敦相頡頏矣。猶憶 1845 年予在瑪禮孫學校肄業時，曾為一文，題曰〈意想之紐約遊〉。當爾時搦管為文，詎料果身履其境者。由是觀之，吾人之意想，固亦有時成為事實，初不必盡屬虛幻。予之意想得成為事實者，尚有二事：一為予之教育計劃，願遣多數青年子弟遊學美國；一則願得美婦以為室。今此二事，亦皆如願以償。則予今日胸中，尚懷有種種夢想，又安知將來不一一見諸實行耶？

予之勾留紐約，為日無多。於此新世界中第一次所遇之良友，為巴脫拉脫夫婦二人（Mr. and Mrs. David E. Bartlett）。巴君時在紐約聾啞學校教授，後乃遷於哈特福德（Hartford），仍為同類之事業。今巴君已於 1879 年逝世，其夫人居孀約三十年，於 1907 年春間亦溘然長逝矣。巴夫人之為人，品格高尚，有足令人敬愛。其宗教之信仰尤誠篤，本其慈善之懷，常熱心於社會公益事業。影響所及，中國亦蒙其福。蓋有中國學生數人，皆為巴夫人教育而成有用之材。故巴夫人者，予美國良友之一也。

自紐約乘舟赴紐海紋（New Haven），以機會之佳，得晤耶路大學校長譚君（President Day of Yale University），數年之後，竟得畢業此校，當時固非敢有此奢望也。予等離紐海紋後，經威哈斯角（Warehouse Point）而至東溫若（East Windsor），逕造勃朗夫人家。勃夫人之父母，爾時尚存，父名巴脫拉脫（Rev. Shubael Bartlett，與前節之巴君為另一人），為東溫若教堂之牧師。予等入教堂瞻仰，即隨眾祈禱，人皆怪之。予座次牧師之左，由側面可周矚全堂，幾無一人不注目予等者。蓋此中有中國童子，事屬創見，宜其然也。予知當日眾人神志既專注予等，於牧師之宣講，必聽而不聞矣。

巴牧師乃一清教徒（Puritan，清教徒為耶穌教徒之一派，最先來美洲者），其人足為新英國省清教徒之模範（按新英國省 New England States 為美國東部之數省，紐約省亦在其內），宣講時語聲清朗，意態誠懇。聞其生平兢兢所事，絕不稍稍草率。凡初晤巴牧師者，每疑其人嚴刻寡恩，實則其心地甚仁厚也。惟以束身極謹，故面目異常嚴肅，從未聞其縱笑失聲，尤無一諧謔語。每日起居有定時，坐臥有常處，晨興後則將《聖經》及祈禱文置於一定之處，端正無少偏。舉止動作，終年如一日。總其一生之行事，殆如時計針之移動，周而復始，不爽晷刻。故凡與巴牧師久處者，未見巴牧師之面，咸能言巴牧師方事之事，歷歷無少差也。

巴牧師之夫人，則與其夫旨趣大異。長日歡樂，時有笑容，遇人接物尤藹吉，每一啟口，輒善氣迎人，可知其宅心之仁慈。凡牧師堂中恆多教友，酬酢頗繁。巴牧師有此賢內助，故教友咸樂巴君夫婦。牧師年俸不過四百美金，以此供衣食猶虞其不足，乃巴夫人且不時款享賓客。余不解其點金何術，而能措置裕如。後乃知巴牧師有田園數畝，歲入雖微，不無小補。又其幼子但以禮（Daniel）尤勤於所事，以所得資歸奉父母。牧師得常以酒食交歡賓客，殆賴有此也。後予在孟松中學及耶魯大學肄業時，每值假期，輒過巴牧師家。

第四章
中學時代

　　予在東溫若，小住勃朗家一星期，乃赴馬沙朱色得士省（Massachusetts），入孟松學校（Monson Academy）肄業。彼時美國尚無高等中學，僅有預備學校，孟松即預備學校中之最著名者。全國好學之士，莫不負笈遠來肄業此校，為入大學之預備。按孟松在新英國省中，所以名譽特著，以自創設以來，長得品學純粹之士，為之校長。故當予在孟松時，其校長名海門（Rev. Charles Hammond），亦德高望重，品學兼優者。海君畢業於耶路大學，夙好古文，兼嗜英國文藝，故胸懷超逸，氣宇寬宏。當時在新英國省，殆無人不知其為大教育家。且其為人富自立性，生平主張儉德，提倡戒酒。總其言行，無可訾議，不愧為新英國省師表。以校長道德文章之高尚，而學校名譽亦頓增。自海門來長此校，日益發達，氣象蓬勃，為前此未有云。而斯時中國人入該校者，惟予等三人耳。海校長對於予等特加禮遇，當非以中國人之罕覯，遂以少為貴，而加以優禮，蓋亦對於中國素抱熱誠，甚望予等學成歸國，能有所設施耳。

　　在孟松學校之第一年，予等列英文班中，所習者為算術、文法、生理、心理及哲學等課。其生理、心理兩科，則為勃朗女師（Miss Rebekah Brown）所授。美國學校通例，凡行畢業禮時，其畢業生中之成績最優者，則代表全體，對教師來賓而致謝詞。勃朗女師嘗為此致謝詞之代表者，畢業於霍來克玉山女校（Mt. Holyoke School）之第一人也。後與醫學博士麥克林（Dr. A. S. McClean）結婚，遂寓於斯丕林費爾（Springfield）。勃朗女師之為人，操行既端正，心術仁慈，尤勇於為善，熱心於教育。夫婦二人，待予咸極誠摯。每值放假，必邀予過其家。及予入耶路大學肄業，處境甚窘，賴渠夫婦資助之力尤多。歸國後，彼此猶音問不絕。及再至美國，復下榻其家。斯不林費爾有此良友，令人每念不忘。1872年予攜第一批留學生遊美時，即賃屋鄰麥博士，公暇期常得與吾友把晤也。

勃朗君（此指勃朗牧師）之至美也，以予等三人托付於其老母。母字[1]余等殊周到，每餐必同食。惟勃君有妹已媔，挈子三人，寄居母家，遂無餘室可容予等。乃別賃一屋，與勃朗對門而居。

方予遊學美國時，生活程度不若今日之高。學生貧乏者，稍稍為人工作，即不難得學費。尚憶彼時膳宿、燃料、洗衣等費，每星期苟得一元二角五之美金，足以支付一切。惟居室之灑掃拂拭，及冬令熾炭於爐、劈柴生火諸瑣事，須自為之。然予甚樂為此，藉以運動筋脈，流通血液，實健身良法也。予等寓處去校約半英里，每日往返三次，雖嚴寒雪深三尺，亦須徒步。如此長日運動，胃乃大健，食量兼人。

於今回憶勃朗母夫人之為人，實覺其可敬可愛，得未曾有。其道德品行，都不可及。凡知媼之歷史者，當能證予此言不謬。計其一生艱苦備嘗，不如意之事，十有八九，然卒能自拔於顛沛之中。嘗自著一詩自況，立言幽閒沉靜，怡然自足，如其為人。

校長海門君之志趣，既如前所述。其於古詩人中，尤好莎士比亞（William Shakespeare）；於古之大演說家，則服膺威白斯特（Daniel Webster），於此可想見其所學。其教授法極佳，能令學生於古今文藝佳妙處，一一了解而無扞格。每日登堂授課，初不屑於文法之規則，獨於詞句之構造及精義所在，則批卻導窾，評釋無遺。以彼文學大家，出其為文之長技，用於演講，故出言咸確當而有精神。大教育家阿那博士（Dr. Arnold）之言曰：「善於教育者，必能注意於學生之道德，以養成其優美之品格，否則僅僅以學問知識授於學生，自謂盡其能事，充乎其極，不過使學生成一能行之百科全書，或一具有靈性之鸚鵡耳，曷足貴哉？」海君之為教授，蓋能深

1　編者按，疑為「侍」。

合阿那博士所云教育之本旨者也。予在孟松學校時，曾誦習多數英國之文集，皆海君所親授者。

在孟松之第一年，予未敢冀入大學。蓋予等出發時，僅以二年為限，1849年即須回國也。三人中，以黃勝齒為最長。1848年秋，黃勝以病歸國，僅予與黃寬二人。居恆晤談，輒話及二年後之方針。予之本志，固深願繼續求學。惟1849年後，將恃何人資助予等學費，此問題之困難，殆不啻古所謂「戈登結」(Gordian Knot)，幾於無人能解者，則亦惟有商之於海門校長及勃朗君耳。幸得二君厚意，允為函詢香港資助予等之人。迨得覆書，則謂二年後如予二人願至英國蘇格蘭省愛丁堡大學習專門科者，則彼等仍可繼續資助云云。予等蒙其慷慨解囊，歷久不倦，誠為可感。嗣予等互商進止，黃寬決計二年後至蘇格蘭補此學額。予則甚欲入耶路大學，故願仍留美。議既定，於是黃寬學費，已可無恐。予於1849年後，藉何資以求學，此問題固仍懸而未決也，亦惟有泰然處之，任予運命之自然，不復為無益之慮。

此事既決，予於1849年暑假後，遂不更治英國文學，而習正科初等之書。翌年之夏，二人同時畢業。黃寬旋即妥備行裝，逕赴蘇格蘭入愛丁堡大學。予則仍留美國，後亦卒得入耶路大學。予與黃寬二人，自1840年同讀書於澳門瑪禮孫學校，嗣後朝夕切磋，共筆硯者垂十年，至是始分袂焉。

黃寬後在愛丁堡大學習醫，歷七年之苦學，卒以第三人畢業，為中國學生界增一榮譽，於1857年歸國懸壺，營業頗發達。以黃寬之才之學，遂成為好望角以東最負盛名之良外科。繼復寓粵，事業益盛，聲譽益隆。旅粵西人歡迎黃寬，較之歡迎歐美醫士有加，積資亦富。於1879年逝世，中西人士臨弔者無不悼惜。蓋其品行純篤，富有熱忱，故遺愛在人，不僅醫術工也。

第五章
大學時代

　　予未入耶路大學時,經濟問題既未解決,果何恃以求學乎?雖美國通例,學生之貧乏者,不難工作以得學費。然此亦言之非艱行之惟艱,身履其境,實有種種困難,而捨此更無良策。計予友在美國人中可恃以謀緩急者,惟勃朗及海門二君。勃朗即攜予赴美者,海門則予在孟松學校時,嘗受其教育者也。予既無術自解此厄,乃乞二人援手。彼等謂予:「孟松學校定制,固有學額資送大學,蓋為勤學寒士而設。汝誠有意於此,不妨姑試之。第此權操諸校董,且願受其資助者,須先具志願書,畢業後願充教士以傳道,乃克享此利益。」予聞言爽然若失,不待思索,已知無補額希望,故亦決意不向該校請求。數日後,諸校董忽召予往面議資遣入學事。是殆勃朗與海門二君,未悟予意,已預為予先容矣。校董之言正與勃朗、海門同,謂畢業後歸國傳道則可,第具一志願書存查耳。此在校董一方面,固對予極抱熱誠。而予之對於此等條件,則不輕諾。予雖貧,自由所固有。他日竟學,無論何業,將擇其最有益於中國者為之。縱政府不錄用,不必遂大有為,要亦不難造一新時勢,以竟吾素志。若限於一業,則範圍甚狹,有用之身,必致無用。且傳道固佳,未必即為造福中國獨一無二之事業。以吾國幅員若是其遼闊,人苟具真正之宗教精神,何往而不利。然中國國民信仰果何如者?在信力薄弱之人,其然諾將如春冰之遇旭日,不久消滅,誰能禁之?況志願書一經簽字,即動受拘束,將來雖有良好機會,可為中國謀福利者,亦必形格勢禁,坐視失之乎!余既有此意,以為始基宜慎,則對於校董諸人之盛意,寧抱歉衷,不得不婉辭謝之。嗣海門悉予意,深表同情。蓋人類有應盡之天職,決不能以食貧故,遽變宗旨也。

人生際會，往往非所逆料。當予卻孟松校董資助時，為 1850 年之夏，勃朗方至南部探視其姊，順道訪喬治亞省薩伐那婦女會 (The Ladies Association in Savannah, Ga.) 之會員。談次偶及予事，遂將得好消息以歸。尤幸者，勃朗之歸，適逢其會。設更晚者，則予或更作他圖，不知成如何結果矣。渠對於予之意見，亦深以為然，因語余薩伐那婦女會會員，已允資助。此豈前此夢想所及者？遂束裝東行，赴紐海紋 (New Haven)，逕趨耶路大學投考，居然不在孫山之外。蓋予於入大學之預備，僅治拉丁文十五月，希拉文十二月，算術十閱月。於此短促之歲月中，復因孟松左近地方新造鐵路，築路之際，學校不得不暫時停輟，而予之學業遂亦因以間斷。同學之友，學程皆優於余。竟得入穀，事後追思，不知其所以然。余之入耶路大學，雖尚無不及格之學科，然在教室受課，輒覺預備工夫實為未足，以故備形困難。蓋一方面須籌畫經費，使無缺乏之虞；一方面又須致力所業，以冀不落人後也。尚憶在第一年級時，讀書恆至夜半，日間亦無餘暇為遊戲運動。坐是體魄日就羸弱，曾因精力不支，請假赴東溫若休息一星期，乃能繼續求學焉。

至第二年級，有一事尤足困予，則微積學是也。予素視算術為畏途，於微積分尤甚。所習學科中，惟此一門，總覺有所捍格。雖日日習之，亦無絲毫裨益，每試常不及格。以如是成績，頗懼受降級之懲戒，或被斥退。後竟得越過此難關，則賴有英文為助。美國大學制，每級分數班，每班有主任教員，專司此班中學生功課之分數。學生欲自知其分數多寡者，可問主任教員。予班之主任教員，曰白洛及 (Blodget)，乃教拉丁文者。予在二年級時，自愧分數過少，至不敢向教員探詢，私意或且降級。幸英文論說頗優，第二、第三兩學期連獲首獎，故平均分數，猶得以有餘補不足。自經兩次獲獎，校中師生異常器重，即校外人亦以青眼相向。然余未敢略存自滿心，以予四學年中平均分數之少，捫心慚汗。若因人之譽己而趾高氣揚，抑自欺之甚矣。

第二學年之末及第三學年，學費漸充裕。以校中有二、三年級學生，約二十人，結為一會，共屋而居，另倩一人為之司飲膳。予竭力經營，獲充是職。晨則為之購辦蔬餚，飯則為之供應左右。後此二年中予之膳費，蓋皆取給於此。雖所獲無多，不無小補。薩伐那婦女會既助予以常年經費，阿立芬公司亦有特捐相助。此外予更得一職：為兄弟會管理書籍。兄弟會者，校中兩辯駁會之一也。會有一小藏書樓，予以會員之資格，得與是選，博微資焉。

第四學年，兄弟會中仍舉予為司書人，每歲酬予美金三十元。予既得此數項進款，客囊乃覺稍裕，不復以舉債為生。若例以小村落中之牧師，每年薪俸所入，亦不過兩、三百金。彼且以贍養八口之家而無缺乏，則予以個人而有此，又有婦女會贈予以襪履等物，更不必自耗囊金。於此猶云不足，則亦過矣。

予於 1854 年畢業。同班中畢業者，共九十八人。以中國人而畢業於美國第一等之大學校，實自予始。以故美國人對予感情至佳。時校中中國學生，絕無僅有，易於令人注目。又因予嘗任兄弟會藏書樓中司書之職二年，故相識之人尤多。同校前後三級中之學生，稔予者幾過半。故余熟悉美國情形，而於學界中交遊尤廣。予在校時，名譽頗佳。於今思之，亦無甚關係。浮雲過眼，不過博得一時虛榮耳。

予當修業期內，中國之腐敗情形，時觸予懷，迨末年而尤甚。每一念及，輒為之怏怏不樂，轉願不受此良教育之為愈。蓋既受教育，則予心中之理想既高，而道德之範圍亦廣，遂覺此身負荷極重。若在毫無知識時代，轉不之覺也。更念中國國民，身受無限痛苦、無限壓制。此痛苦與壓制，在彼未受教育之人，亦轉毫無感覺，初不知其為痛苦與壓制也。故予嘗謂知識益高者，痛苦亦多，而快樂益少。反之，愈無知識，則痛苦愈少，而快樂乃愈多。快樂與知識，殆天然成一反比例乎！雖然持此觀念以論人生之苦樂，則其所見亦甚卑，惟怯懦者為之耳。此其人必不足以成偉大之事業，而趨於高尚之境域也。在予個人而論，尤不應存此悲觀。何也？予既遠涉重洋，身受文明之教育，且以辛勤刻苦，倖遂予求學之志，雖未事事能如願以償，然律以普通教育之資格，予固大可自命為已受教育之人矣。既自命為已受教育人，則當旦夕圖維，以冀生平所學，得以見諸實用。此種觀念，予無時不耿耿於心。蓋當第四學年中尚未畢業時，已預計將來應行之事，規劃大略於胸中矣。予意以為，予之一身既受此文明之教育，則當使後予之人，亦享此同等之利益，以西方之學術，灌輸於中國，使中國日趨於文明富強之境。予後來之事業，蓋皆以此為標準，專心致志以為之。溯自 1854 年予畢業之時，以至 1872 年中國有第一批留學生之派遣，則此志願之成熟時也。

第六章
學成歸國

　　自予畢業耶路大學，屈指去國之日，忽忽十年。[1] 予之初志，所望甚奢，本欲延長留學年限，冀可學成專科。蓋當予在耶路大學時，校中方創一雪費爾專門學院（Sheffield Scientific School），院長為諾德君（Prof. Norton）。予修業時，曾入此院附習測量科，擬為將來學習工程之預備。設予果能學成專科以歸國者，自信予所企望之事業，將益易於着手也。惜以貧乏，不能自籌資斧。助予之友，又不願予久居美國。彼蓋目予為中國有用之人材，慮予久居不歸，「樂不思蜀也」。於是捐棄學習專科之奢願，而留學時期，於以告終。美人中勸予歸國最力者，其一為白禮特（Perit），其人執業於美國某東方公司中；其二為阿立芬特兄弟公司之主人翁。所謂阿立芬特公司，即八年前曾以帆船載予來美而不取值者。此數人之見解皆甚高尚，其所以慫惥予歸中國，非有私意存於其間；蓋欲予歸國後熱心傳道，使中國信仰上帝，人人為耶穌教徒耳。

　　有麥克教士者，於 1845 年至香港代勃朗為瑪禮孫學校教員，於前第二章中已言之。迨後瑪禮孫學校解散，麥克乃重歸美國，復入耶路為學生。兹復經美國教會派往中國傳道，遂於 1854 年 11 月 13 日，與予同乘紐約某公司帆船名「歐里加」（*Eureka*）者，自紐約首途。時值冬令，為過好望角最惡劣之時會。蓋隆冬之際，東北風極大，凡帆船向東方行，必遇逆風，無可倖免，而歐里加船此時正依此航路以進行也。此船本為運貨以赴香港者，舟中乘客，除予及麥克外，實無第三人。起程之日，適彤雲密布，嚴寒襲

1　編者按，原文如此。應為八年。

人。舟又停泊於東河（East River）中流，不能傍岸，予等乃覓小舟以渡。當登舟時，回顧岸旁，不見有一人揮巾空際，送予遠行者。及舟既起碇，岸上亦無高呼歡送之聲，此境此情，甚蕭條也。船初行，先以他船拖至桑得阿克（Sandy Hook），迨出口後乃解纜自行。正值逆風迎面而來，勢殊猛烈。風篷不能扯滿，則張半帆，旁行斜上，曲折以進。船中載貨極少，即欲覓一壓艙之重物，亦不可得。以故衝擊風浪中，顛簸愈甚。滄海一粟，如明星倒影水中，蕩漾不定。此航路之惡，為夙昔所著稱，固非自今日始也。由桑得阿克以至香港，幾無平穩之一日。計水程凡一萬三千海里，船行歷一百五十四日乃達目的地。予生平航海不為不多，然寂寞無聊，則未有如此行之甚者。船主名輝布（Whipple），籍隸費拉特爾費亞（Philadelphia）城。為人粗獷無文，以口吃故，舉止尤躁急。每日於船中所為，令人可笑之事極多，而於晨間則尤甚。彼每晨必登甲板，自船首至船尾，來回急走，以測候天空氣象。有時忽驟止其步，駐足癡立，對逆風吹來之方向，仰首矚天，筋漲面赤，眼珠幾欲突出。暴怒之極，則伸兩手盡力自搔其髮，一若與此煩惱絲有無窮夙憾，必欲根根拔而去之者。如是往來跳躍，嚙齒有聲。或以足與甲板鬥其堅，力蹬不已。口中作種種褻語，對天漫罵，謂天公之作此逆風，蓋有意與之為難，阻其進行也。顧船主雖毒罵，而口吃乃期期不可辨，其狀可笑亦復可憐。予初見其狂暴如瘋，頗生憐憫之念。迨後見其無日不如是，乃覺其人可鄙，殊不足憐惜。彼每次向天示威之後，必至力盡筋疲，乃於甲板上獨據胡牀，枯坐歷數小時。舟中雖無人願與之接談，而彼固怡然自得，恆力搓其兩手，自語自笑，狀若無辜之瘋人。長途中凡其舉動，非瘋非慎。船中水手，司空見慣，不以為奇。雖外貌不敢顯輕侮之色，而心中固無不匿笑其為人也。舟行之際，一切調度，全由大副一人指揮。此大副之專制，不啻海中一暴君。幸水手皆為挪威及瑞典兩國之人，故尚肯服從其命令。若在美國人遇此野蠻無人理之事，必不能堪，或且起暴動以為對待矣。蓋此船主、大副之役使水手，有如牛馬，日夜無少停。途中所得暫事休息者，惟船行至熱帶時，適風波平靜之數日耳。予稽旅行之日記冊，計自解纜後約行兩星期，始至馬加撒海峽（Macassar Strait），舟中人殆無一不生厭倦之心。過海峽後，船主乃揚言於眾曰：「予此行所以不幸而遇逆風者，以舟中有約拿其人在也。」（相傳約拿為古時先知，運最蹇。一日航海遇暴風，舟且覆，同舟者拈鬮以求罪人，適得約拿，舉而投諸海，風乃立止云。）語時故使予友麥克聞之，其意蓋以約拿況麥克也。予友聞是言，絕不介意，惟對予目笑而存之。時予方與麥克談論舟過海峽事，乃語麥克曰：「設以予司此船者，過此海峽不過十日足矣。」語時亦故高其聲浪，使船主聞之。一則報復其語侵麥克，一則使彼自知其航術未精也。

當隆冬之際，設行舟不過好望角，而繞亨角（Cape Horn）以進，利便實甚。蓋如是則可得順風，不獨縮短航海之期，且可省船主無數氣力。但予以乘客資格，亦莫知其內容真相。該公司駛行此船，既無甚貨物，又必逆東北風而行，豈其於經濟上有特別之目的耶？若以予意，則必經亨角遵新航路以行，而予又可藉此耳目一新矣。

船近香港時，有領港人至船上。船主見其為中國人，乃倩予為舌人，詢其近處有無危險之暗礁及沙灘。予默念此暗礁與沙灘者，中國語不知當作何辭，久思不屬，竟莫達其意。幸領港人適解英語，乃轉告予以暗礁、沙灘之中國名詞。噫，此領港人者，竟為予回國後之第一國語教授，不亦異乎！船主及麥克等見予狀，咸笑不可仰。予自念以中國人而不能作中國語，亦無詞以自解也。

登陸後予第一關懷之事，為往視予友蓄德魯特。蓄德魯特者，《中國日報》（China Mail）主筆。予在孟松學校時，彼曾以資助予一年有餘，蓋予之老友也。把晤後，彼即邀予過其家，小作勾留。旋赴澳門，省視吾母。予去家日久，慈母倚閭懸念，必至望眼欲穿矣。予見母之日，以一時無從易中國衣，乃仍西裝以進。是時予已鬍矣，若循中國習慣，則少年未娶者，不應若是早鬍也。予見母無恙，胸中感謝之心，達於極點，轉無一語能出諸口。質言之，予此時喜極欲涕，此種狀況，實非語言筆墨所能形容於萬一。母見予立現一種慈愛之色，以手撫摩予身且遍，謂此十年[2]中思見兒而不可得也。予知母尚未悉予旅美之詳情，乃依坐膝下，告之曰：「母乎！兒方經一五、六閱月可厭之長期旅行也。然今幸無恙，已得抵家省母矣。兒自離膝下，前後已有八年。此八年中，在在皆遇良友，能善視兒，故兒身常健無疾病。兒在校肄業，常思藉此時學習，以為將來效力祖國之預備。守此宗旨，八年如一日。當未入大學之前，又曾先入一預備學校。於預備學校畢業後，乃入耶路大學。耶路大學在美國為最著名大學之一，校內所訂課程，必四年乃能畢業，此兒所以久客異鄉。今既畢業於該校，遂得一學士學位。美國之學士，蓋與中國之秀才相仿。」語次隨出一羊皮紙以示母，且告之曰：「此即畢業文憑也。凡得畢業於耶路大學者，即在美國人猶視為榮譽，況兒以中國人而得與其列耶？」予母聞言，乃詢予此文憑與學位，可博獎金幾何？蓋予母固未知其效用如何也。予乃告母曰：「此非可以得獎金者。第有文憑，則較無文憑之人，謀事為易。至大學之給學位，亦非有金錢之效用。惟已造就一種品格高尚之人材，使其將來得有勢力，以為他人之領袖耳。大學校所授之教育，實較金錢尤為寶貴。蓋人必受教育，然後乃有知識，知識即勢力也。勢力之效用，較金錢為大。兒今既以第一中國留學生畢業於耶路大學，今後吾母即為數萬萬人中第一中國留學生畢業於美國第一等大學者之母。此乃稀貴之榮譽，為常人所難得。兒此後在世一日，必侍奉吾母，俾母得安享幸福，不使少有缺乏也。」予之為此大言不慚，非敢自矜自滿，不過欲博吾母歡心耳。母聞予言果甚樂，面有笑容。旋謂予曰：「吾見兒已蓄鬚，上有一兄尚未蓄鬚，故吾意汝去鬚為佳。」予聞母言，即如命趨出，召匠立薙之。母見予狀，樂乃益甚。察其意以為吾子雖受外國教育，固未失其中國固有之道德，仍能盡孝於親也。予此時胸中愛母之忱，恨未能剖心相示。此後予每盡力所能及，以奉予母，頤養天年。迨 1858 年予母棄養，壽六十有四；計

2　編者按，原文如此。

去予失怙時，凡二十四[3]年。予母逝時，予適在上海，未能見一面，實為終天遺憾。

1855 年予居粵中，與美教士富文（Vrooman）君同寓，地名「鹹蝦欄」，與行刑場頗近。場在城外西南隅，鄰珠江之濱。予之寓此，除補習漢文而外，他無所事。以予久居美洲，於本國語言，幾盡忘之，至是乃漸復其舊。不及六月，竟能重操粵語，惟唇舌間尚覺生硬耳。至予之漢文，乃於 1846 年遊美之前所習者，為時不過四年。以習漢文，學期實為至短，根基之淺，自不待言。故今日之溫習，頗極困難，進步極緩。夫文字之與語言，在英文中雖間有不同之點，究不若中國之懸殊特甚。以中國之文字而論，爛煌華麗，變化萬端，雖應用普及全國，而文字之發音，則南北互異，東西懸殊。至於語言，則尤龐雜不可究詰。如福建、江蘇、安徽等省，即一省之中，亦有無數不同之方言。每值甲、乙兩地人相遇，設各操其鄉談，則幾如異國之人，彼此不能通解。此乃中國語言文字上特別困難之處，為各國所無者。

當予在粵時，粵中適有一暴動，秩序因之大亂。此際太平天國之軍隊，方橫行內地，所向披靡，而粵亂亦適起於是時。顧粵人之暴動，初與太平軍無涉。彼兩廣總督葉名琛者，於此暴動發生之始，出極殘暴之手段以鎮壓之，意在摧殘方苞之花，使無萌芽之患也。統計是夏所殺，凡七萬五千餘人。以予所知，其中強半皆無辜冤死。予寓去刑場才半英里，一日予忽發奇想，思赴刑場一覘其異。至則但見場中流血成渠，道旁無首之屍縱橫遍地。蓋以殺戮過眾，不及掩埋。且因驟覓一遼曠之地，為大壙以容此眾屍，一時頗不易得，故索任其暴露於烈日下也。時方盛夏，寒暑表在九十度或九十度以上，致刑場四圍二千碼以內，空氣惡劣如毒霧。此累累之陳屍，最新者暴露亦已二、三日。地上之土，吸血既飽，皆作赭色。餘血盈科而進，匯為污池。空氣中毒菌之彌漫，殆不可以言語形容。據此景象，加以粵省人煙之稠密，在理當發生極大之瘟疫，乃竟得安然無恙，寧非怪事？後聞於城西遠

3　編者按，疑為十八年。容閎父逝於 1840 年。

僻處覓得一極大溝渠，投屍其中，任其自然堆疊，以滿為度，遂謂盡掩埋之能事矣。當時有往觀者，謂此掩埋之法，簡易實甚。擲屍溝中後，無需人力更施覆蓋。以屍中血色之蛆，已足代赤土而有餘，不令羣屍露少隙也。此種情形，非獨當時觀者酸鼻，至今言之，猶令人欲作三日嘔。人或告予，是被殺者有與暴動毫無關係，徒以一般虎兒郎胥役，敲詐不遂，遂任意誣陷置之死地云。似此不分良莠之屠戮，不獨今世紀中無事可與比擬，即古昔尼羅 (Nero) 王之殘暴，及法國革命時代之慘劇，殺人亦無如是之多。罪魁禍首，惟兩廣總督葉名琛一人實尸其咎。葉為漢陽人。漢陽於太平軍起事時即被佔據，遂遭兵火之劫。人謂葉在漢陽本有極富之財產，此役盡付焚如，故對於太平軍恨之切齒。而太平軍之首領，又多籍隸兩廣，於是葉乃遷怒於兩廣人民。1854 年，既攫得兩廣總督之權位遂假公濟私，以報其夙怨，粵人乃無辜而受其殃矣。葉之戮人，不訊口供，捕得即殺，有如牛羊之入屠肆。此殺人之惡魔，天所不容，其罪惡滿盈之一日，且不旋踵而至，彼固猶在夢中也。未幾，葉因事與英政府釀成大交涉，為英兵所擄，幽之印度極邊杳無居人之處。遂於此荒涼寂寞之區，苟延殘喘，以度其含垢忍辱之餘生，不特為全國同胞所唾罵，抑亦為全世界人所鄙棄也。

　　予自刑場歸寓後，神志懊喪，胸中煩悶萬狀，食不下咽，寢不安枕。日聞所見種種慘狀，時時纏繞於予腦筋中。憤懣之極，乃深惡滿人之無狀，而許太平天國之舉動為正當。予既表同情於太平軍，乃幾欲起而為之響應。及後深思靜慮，乃覺此舉魯莽，究非妥善之策；不若仍予舊有計劃，先習國語與漢文，俟其嫺熟，乃依一定之方針，循序而進，庶可達予夙昔之希望也。

第七章
入世謀生

　　前章言予習國文既極困難，未可遂云有得。而於中國語言，則漸復舊觀，談話無虞扞格。於時頗思於社會中得一職守，此非僅為家人衣食，欲有所藉手，達於維新中國之目的，謀食亦謀道也。

　　有美教士曰派克（Parker）者，彼邦醫學博士，奉美教會之命來華傳道，懸壺於粵有年。此時方為美政府之特別委員，暫代公使事。時吾華尚無各國全權公使；北京之應設公使與否，在磋商中，國際上尚未有互派公使之條約。派克博士之於外交，非有特別經驗，其於律學亦非專門；徒以其旅華日久，習中國之語言風俗，故美政府以此任之。予有友曰歇區可克（Mr. M.N. Hitchcock），亦美人，與派克有舊，乃紹介予為派克處書記。予前在古夫人小學時，已耳派克博士名。渠亦畢業於耶路大學者，因與予有同校之誼，頗相得。其辦事地點在粵之省垣，惟夏季則至澳門避暑焉。予在派克處，事少薪薄，月十五金耳。予樂就之，意本不在金錢，欲藉派克力，識中國達官，庶幾得行予志。顧派克雖攝公使，乃非近水樓台。與予之計劃甚左。三月後遽自行辭職，赴香港習法律。香港有老友蓄德魯特君，遇予素厚，因主[1]其家。無何，蓄薦予於香港高等審判廳為譯員，月薪七十五金。處境略裕，乃稍稍放膽，潛心治法律。英國審判廳制度，律師資格凡兩種：曰小律師（Solicitors），專司收集證據、抄閱公文及摘述案情始末，以備辯護之材料，而己不出庭；曰大律師（Barristers），則出庭司辯護者。予從予友蓄德魯特之言，學習第一種律師事業。余之為此，可謂鑄錯。蓋香港為英國之殖

1　編者按，疑為「住」。

民地，予以中國人而律師於此，是以外人侵入英國法律團體，損彼利益，分我杯羹，必召英律師之惡感。以余之魯鈍，未計及此，一誤也。又予所師事者，乃一尋常律師。此時有一總律師，思羅致予於門下，乃捨此就彼，二誤也。一時失檢，有此二誤。他日之離香港，即種因於此矣。

因第一着之誤，致香港律師合羣力以拒予。一時新聞界，惟予友蓄德魯特主筆之《中國日報》差無貶詞，餘皆連篇累牘，肆意攻擊。若輩以為予於中西文字，皆所擅長，設於香港律師界得佔一席，則將來凡涉於華人訴訟事件，必為予個人壟斷，英律師且相將歸國。故對於予之學法律，出全力以拒之。因第二着之誤，又得罪於總律師。其人曰安師德（Anstey），曾欲就其權力所及，為予辟一實習律師之途。因上書英政府，請允中國人之在香港者，苟試驗及格，有充律師之權利，並草擬章程，附於請願書後。按法定手續，此舉必須經英國議會之通過，乃成為殖民地之單行法，則其事之不易可知。旋竟邀英政府之允准，著為定律，是總律師之所以為予盡力者，不可為不至。顧予乃不就籠絡，事後始知，予誠為負負。予既另事律師派森（Parson）為師，總律師則大恚，每相值於法庭翻譯時，輒事事苛求予短，不復如前之謙和。於是予以一身，受雙方衝擊，覺在香港已無立足餘地。抑不獨予處境困難，予師派森亦復日坐針氈，身為眾矢之的，而無可抵抗。彼乃不得不自謀，取消予學律之合同。予既受此排擠，自念戀戀於此殊非計，不如辭職，去而之他。予去未久，派森亦以他故棄其香港事業，買棹歸英。

今回憶在港時短期歷史，轉覺學律未成，為予生幸事。使當日果成一香港律師，則所成事業，必甚微末。且久居英國殖民地，身體為所拘束，不能至中國內地，與上流社會交遊。縱使成一著名律師，博得多金，亦安所用之？余既去香港，於 1856 年 8 月，乘一運茶船北赴上海。名「佛羅稜司」（Florence），乃自美國波司頓（Boston）來者，船主名都瑪勒司克（Dumaresque），此船為所自有。船之名，即船主女公子名也。憶 1855 年予自美歸國時，所乘「歐里加」船之船主，以較今日之都船主，不可同日語。都之為人，仁厚而通達，彬彬有禮。彼聞予名後，即極表歡迎，立以由港至上海之船票贈予，不取值。此行程期僅七日，船未抵岸，而予與船主二人，已於此短期內成莫逆交矣。

予抵上海未久，於海關翻譯處謀得一職，月薪七十五兩，折合墨銀可百元。因中國向無銀元，墨西哥銀幣輸入遂流行也。此職之薪金，固已較香港高等法庭譯員為優，即所事亦不若彼繁重可厭。惟予性好勞動，轉嫌太簡易耳。此時辦公時刻外，頗多餘暇，在寓讀書。如是者三月，旋覺此事於予，亦不相宜。使予果願獨善其身，為一潔己奉公之人，則絕不應混跡於此。蓋此間有一惡習，中國船上商人與海關中通事，咸通聲氣，狼狽為奸，以圖中飽。予既知此，乃深惡其卑鄙，不屑與伍，以自污吾名譽，乃決意辭職，而苦無詞。某日予逕訪總稅務司，故問之曰：「以予在海關中奉職，將來希望若何？亦能升至總稅務司之地位乎？」彼告予曰：「凡中國人為翻譯者，無論何人，絕不能有此希望。」予聞言退出，立作一辭職書投之。書謂予與彼受同等教育，且予以中國人為中國國家服務，奈何獨不能與彼英人享同等之權利，而終不可以為總稅務司耶？予書入後，總稅務司來 (Mr. Lay) 君，初不允予請，面加慰留，令勿去職，且誤會予之此舉為嫌俸薄，故以辭職相要挾，因許月增予俸至二百兩。噫！彼固以為中國人殆無一不以金錢為生命者，寧知眾人皆醉之中，猶有能以廉隅自守，視道德為重、金錢為輕者耶？且予之為此，別有高尚志趣，並不以得升總稅務司為目的。予意凡欲見重於人者，必其人先能自重。今海關中通事及其餘司一職者，幾無一不受賄賂。以予獨處此濁流中，決不能實行予志，此辭職之本意也。辭職書中，亦不明言及此。四閱月後，卒離去海關，而另覓光明磊落之事業。

同事諸友，見予棄此二百兩厚俸，圖不可必之事，莫不目予為痴，是燕雀不知鴻鵠也。予之操行差堪自信者，惟廉潔二字。無論何往，必保全名譽，永遠不使玷污。予非不自知，歸國以來，未及一年，已三遷其業。若長此見異思遷，則所希望之事業，或且如幻燈泡影，終無所成。又非不自覺予之希望過奢，志向過高，頗難見諸實行也。第念吾人競存於世界，必有一定之希望，方能造成真實之事業。予之生於斯世，既非為哺啜而來；予之受此教育，尤非易易。則含辛茹苦所得者，又安能不望其實行於中國耶！一旦遇有機會，能多用我一分學問，即多獲一分效果，此豈為一人利益訐，抑欲謀全中國之幸福也！予於所事，屢次中綴，豈好為變遷哉？

第八章
經商之閱歷

　　予離海關後，至某英商公司為書記。此公司專收中國絲茶者。予之入此，不過暫借枝棲。然雖相處僅數月，獲益良多，於商家內幕及經商方法，已略知梗概，於他日事業，關係實多。該公司自余就事六閱月，而停止營業，予乃重為失業之人。此時如投身大海中，四顧茫茫，不知方針當何向。計予為書記，六閱月中，值意外之事二，是亦不可不紀。

　　某星期四之夕，予自蘇州河邊禮拜堂行禱禮歸，經四川路。見有西人成羣在前，人各手[1]一中國紙燈，高舉過頂，晃蕩不定。行路則左傾右斜，作折線而前，且行且唱，亦有狂呼者，狀似甚樂。道旁中國人見之，皆四竄奔走，若有虎狼追逐者。予行既近，與之相距約百碼。此時頗有騎虎之勢，即欲退避，亦已無及。予僕本執燈為予導，此時乃退匿予後。予告以無恐，迤邐前進。不數武[2]，三四被酒[3]西人已迎面至。一人奪予僕手中燈，一則舉足思蹴予；顧被酒已甚，足方舉，身已搖搖欲仆。予見其醉態蹣跚，亦不與較，惟避而過之。旋見在後有清醒者，乃目睹其伴侶之行為，不加勸止，且顧而樂之。予乃竚立與語，先告以予名，並詢以適欲蹴予及奪僕燈者之名。彼等初不肯吐實，繼予力言縱知其人，必不與之為難。彼乃告予其中一人名，及在某船中所操之業。嘻，異矣！彼所告之人名，蓋即「歐里加」船中大副也。此船非他，即於 1855 年載予歸國者，今此船又適為予所處之公司運貨。予乃於翌晨作一函，致其船主，詳告一切。船主閱函其怒，擲示大副。大副讀

1　　編者按，疑脫一「持」字。
2　　編者按，即「不數步」。
3　　編者按，醉酒之意。

未竟，色立變，急奔登岸，向予謝罪。予仍遇以和藹之色，婉言告之曰：「君當知美人之在中國，固極受中國人之敬禮者。故凡美人之至中國，尤當自知其所處地位之尊貴，善自保惜，不宜有強暴行為以自喪其名譽，而傷中國人感情。予之作此函，非欲與君為難，第欲藉此以盡予之忠告耳。」大副聞言，備道感愧。並邀予至其船中，杯酒言歡，訂為朋友。予謝之，旋自去。此事遂和平了結。

二月後，又值一意外事。此事迥不如前，其結果乃令人不適。當予所處公司停止貿易，所有什物盡付拍賣。是日中外人士來者夥多，予亦廁人叢中駢肩立。適有一體量高六尺餘、雄偉無倫之蘇格蘭人，立於予後。覺有人弄我髮辮，一回顧則彼郰瞞[4]者以棉花搓成無數小球繫予辮上，以為戲樂。予初不怒，僅婉請其解去。彼交叉兩手於胸，若不聞者，一種傲慢之態，令人難堪。予仍不怒，惟申言之。彼忽驟舉拳擊予頰，勢甚猛，特未見血耳。予勃然不復能忍，以彼偉岸，予長才及其肩，鬭腕力寧有幸者？然當時不暇計勝負，即以其人所施者反之，遽以拳衝其面。拳出至迅，且有力。彼不及防，受創，唇鼻立破，流血被面。此蘇格蘭人殆體育家，孔武有力，予之右腕旋被執不能少動。予方思以足力蹴其要害，適公司主人自旁來，極力解散，彼乃自人叢中擠出。時有人大聲謂予曰：「若欲鬭耶？」予即應之曰：「否，予固自衛。君友先犯予，傷予頰，殊無賴。」予發此言，聲色俱厲，故使眾人皆聞之。旋退入別室，任他人之論短長，充耳不聽。後有友告予，謂是日英國領事亦在眾中，目睹此事，曾發評論，謂：「此中國少年，血氣太盛。設彼不自由施行法律（指還擊）者，固可至英國領事公署控此蘇格蘭人。今既已報復，且又於眾辱之，此其所為已甚，不能更控人矣。」此蘇格蘭人者，予前於道中嘗數遇之，故能省識。自互毆後，不出現者一星期。人言彼方閉戶養傷，殆非事實。蓋以被創於一短小之中國人，並受侮辱之辭，故無顏遽出耳。此事雖瑣細無謂，而於租界中頗引起一般人之注意。事閱數日，

4　編者按，似指外國人之意。

外人猶引為談助。更有多數中國人，因聞予為此事，異常推重。蓋自外人闢租界於上海以來，侵奪我治外法權。凡寄居租界之中國人，處外人勢力範圍之內，受彼族淩侮，時有所聞。然從未有一人敢與抵抗，能以赤手空拳，自衛其權利者。此實由於中國人賦性柔和，每受外人無禮之待遇，輒隱忍退讓，不敢與較。致養成一般無意識外人之驕恣，喧賓奪主，不復以平等遇我同胞也。予意他日中國教育普及，人人咸解公權、私權之意義，爾時無論何人，有敢侵害其權利者，必有膽力起而自衛矣。近如日人之戰勝俄國，亦足使中國人眼界為之一廣，不再忍受無禮之待遇。即外人之以強權蠶食我邊疆，擴充其勢力，我國人亦豈能常聽其自由行動乎？國人夜郎自大，頑固性成，致有今日受人侮辱之結果。歐洲各強國，甚且倡瓜分中國之議。幸美政府出而干涉，乃不得實行。今中國人已稍稍知其前此之非，力圖自振，且自慈禧太后及光緒帝逝世後，時局又為之一變。究竟中國前途若何，此時尚難逆料也。

自公司閉歇後，予乃為第四次失業之人。第予本不希望以商業終身者，故雖失業，亦不甚措意。予自歸國以來，二年中於漢文一道，已略窺門徑，遂不汲汲於謀事。此後惟譯書自食，以度此優遊之歲月，無拘無束，亦殊自由。縱不得多金，固大可藉此以多識商學界上流人物，推廣交遊，以遂予之第一目的。予藉譯書之機會，遂得識一洋公司中之華經理。此公司在上海實為首屈一指，其行主亦極負一時之盛名。中外商人，無不與之契洽。1857年，行主不幸逝世，一時商界中人無不深為哀悼，乃撰一長篇誄文，詳述死者一生事業，以為紀念。該公司中人得此誄文，則聘二人以譯成英文。任此譯事者，一為英國領事公署中書記官，其兄即曾著《中國內亂記》者，其一則予也。予之得獲此職，實賴該公司華經理之推薦。初不意予所為文，竟博外人之稱許，謂較英署書記所譯者為佳也。予為此事，不獨為公司經理所賞識，即中國商界中人，聞同胞中有人能以長篇誄辭譯成精確之英文，優勝於英人手筆，咸引以為榮譽。自予文入選為墓銘，勒之碑石，而本國人中，遂稍稍知予之微名。第此番之博聲譽，與前次迥乎不同。前以毆人稱，今則人人知予為曾受西國教育之中國學生也。

　未幾，又有一事，需予臂助。其時黃河決口，江蘇北境竟成澤國，人民失業無家可歸者，無慮千萬，咸來上海就食。滬上紳商界中負時譽者，聞予名，乃倩予撰一西文募捐啟，向旅滬外人勸募。不數日，竟得西人捐款二萬元。中國慈善會董事見成效之速，樂乃無極。後復由董事具名，予為作函，報告外人以收到捐款之數目，並謝其慷慨解囊之誼。此函旋經滬上某某兩西報登出，故予為譯事三閱月，而上海之中國人，幾無一不知予為美國畢業生矣。予之譯事，所以能奏此成效而博此名譽者，皆予友曾繼甫（譯音）之力也。曾君文學極佳。人咸敬而重之。因其在公司日久，故信用尤著。其所往來皆國中名儒碩學，又以身居商界，故凡中國大資本家及殷實之商家，無論在申或居他埠，亦無不與之相識。予前此所譯之誄文及募捐啟，皆彼所紹介者。曾君後又介予於中國之著名大算學家李君壬叔[5]，予因李君又得識曾公國藩。曾公蓋中國之軍事家及政治家，予之教育計劃，後亦卒賴曾公力為提倡，乃得實行。予嘗謂世上之事，殆如蛛網之牽絲，不能預定交友之中，究何人能解吾畢生之結。即如予之因曾（繼甫）而識李，因李而識曾（文正），因曾而予之教育計劃乃得告成。又因予之教育計劃告成，而中西學術萃於一堂。充類至義之盡，將來世界成為一家，不可謂非由此濫觴。則又如蛛網之到處牽連，不知何處為止境也。

　予因曾繼甫，旋識寶順公司（Dent & Co.）之西經理。經理遇予頗厚，欲命予至日本長崎為其分公司之買辦。時日本與各國通商尚未久也。予則婉辭不就此職，且實告以故，謂：「買辦之俸雖優，然操業近卑鄙。予固美國領袖學校之畢業生，故予極重視母校，尊之敬之，不敢使予之所為於母校之名譽少有辱沒。以買辦之身份，不過洋行中奴隸之首領耳。以予而為洋行中奴隸之首領，則使予之母校及諸同學聞之，對予將生如何之感情耶？人雖有時困於經濟，不得不屈就賤役，為稻粱謀，第予之貧乏尚未至此。設君

5　編者按，即李善蘭。

果任予以事者，則予甚願為公司代表，至內地一行。如是則予不至以金錢之故而犧牲尊貴之身份。予苟得代表公司以收買絲茶，無論或給常薪，或給用費，似較任奴隸首領為佳也。」予言時，予友曾君亦在座。曾君粗解英語，於予言雖知之不詳，固已得其概略。予語畢，乃先辭出，以待彼二人協商。曾君後出語予，謂繪白（Webb，即該公司之經理）評予曰：「容某雖貧，傲骨殊稜稜。天下貧骨之與傲骨，乃往往長相伴而不相離也。」談判後數日，曾君告予，謂繪白已決計派予至產茶區域，調查裝茶之情形云。

第九章
產茶區域之初次調查

　　1859 年 3 月 11 日，予等乘一小艇，俗名「無錫快」者，由滬出發，從事於產茶各區域之調查。所謂「無錫快」，乃一種快艇之名，因在運河流域中無錫縣所創造，故有是稱。無錫距蘇州甚近。蘇州為名勝之區，與杭州齊名，居民繁庶，物產豐饒，而以絲織品為尤著。蘇屬城鄉市鎮間居民往來，咸藉「無錫快」為交通利器。其制大小不一，舟中裝設頗佳，便利安適，使乘客無風塵之苦。又有一種專供官紳富商僱乘者，則船身較大，裝飾尤華麗。此種舟皆平底，值順風時，其行甚速。惟遇逆風，則或繫繩於桅，令人於岸上牽之，或搖櫓以進。搖櫓為中國人長技，尋常之舟，後舵兩旁有櫓，左右舷有鐵樞紐，櫓着其上。搖時一櫓需四人。櫓身為平面之板，於船尾處在水中左右搖曳，借水力以推舟，速率極大。惟近年中國通行汽船，操此業者為汽船所奪。故江蘇一帶河面上，民船已漸歸淘汰。從前美國 1850 年及 1860 年間，向有帆船駛至東印度及中國，往來裝運貨物；今則海面航業，已為郵船所奪，其事如一轍也。

　　予等舟行三日，至杭州。杭州為浙江省垣，地勢頗不平，正西及西南、東北，皆有高山。全城面積，可三、四英方里。南北較長於東西，為長方形。城之西有湖曰西湖，為著名名勝。湖面平如鏡，底為沙泥，水澄碧，游魚可數。由城腳迄西山之麓，皆西湖範圍。傍湖之山，高入霄漢，綿亘直至城北，有若天然堡壘為城屏障者。錢塘江亦在城西，去城約二英里。江水發源於徽州東南高山中，蜿蜒而下，以趨入杭州灣。去城東約四十英里之處，山水由高處下衝入河中，水勢湍激，波濤澎湃，聲如萬馬奔騰。錢塘江中於一定之時間，有所謂「錢塘潮」者，潮頭高至八、九英尺，亦巨觀也。當 12、

13 世紀時，宋代君主曾建都於此，故杭州之名著於歷史。風景絕佳，有多數之公私建築物，如巨寺、高塔、橋樑、陵寢等，能令此特別之天然景物益增其靈秀。獨惜自宋以後，歷時既久，美麗之建築物多半頹廢失修，致令杭州昔日之榮譽漸以湮沒。國家多難，恐未易遽復舊觀也。

3 月 15 日，予等離杭州，溯錢塘江而上。有地名江頭，去杭城東約二英里，亦甚繁盛。河中帆檣林立，商船無慮千數，大小不一，長約五十尺至百尺，闊約十尺至十五尺，吃水不過二、三尺，亦皆平底，咸取極堅緻彎曲之木材為之。因錢塘江之潮流曲折迂迴，其底又多礁石，無逆流順水，恆遇極猛烈之激湍，時虞顛覆。故非有極堅固之質，不克經久受衝擊也。舟中以板隔成小室，室各設牀榻以備乘客之需。若遇裝貨時，則此隔扇及牀榻可以拆卸，騰出空地以容貨物。全舟若裝配完全，上蓋以穹形之篷，乃成圓筒式，狀如一大雪茄。此類船多航行杭州、常山間。浙江與江西接壤處，交通多水道，其裝運貨物，大半即用此船。常山為浙省繁盛商埠。江西境亦有巨埠曰玉山，與常山相去僅五十華里。二埠間有廣道，坦坦蕩蕩，闊約三十英尺，花崗石所鋪，兩旁砌以碧色之卵石，中國最佳路也。兩省分界處，有石制牌坊，橫跨路中，即以是為界石。兩面俱鐫有四大字曰「兩省通衢」，以鮮明之藍色塗之。此坊蓋亦著名之古物，可見其商務之盛，由來舊也。當予等自常山至玉山時，漢口、九江、蕪湖、鎮江等處，猶未闢為通商口岸，汽船之運貨至內地者絕少。而此兩省通衢，苦力運貨，項背相望，耶許相應答也，每日不下數千人。自遊歷家之眼光觀之，饒有趣味。而在中國愛國之士見之，亦足引起其懷古之思。

於揚子江中，行舟可直達四川邊境之荊州。全航路之長，約三千英里，六、七省之商務賴以交通。設中國無歐西各國之干涉，得完全行使其主權，則揚子江開濬後，其利益實未可限量，予敢云全世界中人必有三分之一分此幸福也。彼西人者，何不與中國以時機，俾得自行解決其國內問題耶？又如工人問題，自有歐西之汽船、電氣及各種機械輸入中國以來，中國工界乃大受其影響，生計事業幾已十奪其九。非謂不當輸入中國，第當逐漸推行，假以時日，俾人民得徐圖他項事業，以恢復元氣，不宜驟然盡奪其所業也。

3月15日晨五時，予等自江頭起碇。適值順風，揚帆而卜，一日間幾行一百英里。暮十時，舟泊七龍（按浙省無地名七龍者，或為七里瀧之誤）。遙望錢塘江之東岸，其露出水面者，岩石層次，歷歷可辨，殆全為紅砂岩所砌成。岸上隨處皆見有紅砂岩所造之屋。四圍山嶺，晚景尤佳。浙江多佳山水，故隨處皆入畫。

翌日由七龍首途，值大雨如注，舟仍前進不息。下午泊於蘭谿，是日約行四十英里。蘭谿亦浙省大市場，兩湖所產之工夫茶，咸集此間，由此經杭州以至上海。城中只有一街，長至六英里。其著名土產，為極佳之火腿，全國聞名。予等因阻雨，在蘭谿小住半日。日落後，天色漸霽，遂於夜半十二鐘時復行，至衢州。衢州為浙省之州城，去年（1858年）3月間，為太平軍所困，歷四月，圍乃解，幸尚無大損失云。在衢州旅館中一宿，即趲赴蕭山。蕭山去此可三十英里，因關役查驗繁苛，輿人腳夫亦難驟覓多人，登岸至不便。抵蕭山後，旋復乘肩輿赴玉山。當晚預僱漁舟，備翌晨赴廣信。廣信去玉山，亦三十英里。既過玉山，已行入江西境界。此新航路乃向西北行，順流而下，掠鄱陽湖南岸而至南昌。南昌為江西省會，城垣外觀頗壯麗。惜予無暇遊覽，且不及調查太平軍戰後之狀況若何也。

既過南昌，航路則轉向，西南趨湘潭。湘潭即予等最後之目的地。途中歷數城，以於歷史及商業上無大關係，故略之。湖南之省會曰長沙。予過長沙時，適在夜間。迨4月15日之晨，乃抵湘潭。湘潭亦中國內地商埠之巨者。凡外國運來貨物，至廣東上岸後，必先集湘潭，由湘潭再分運至內地。又非獨進口貨為然，中國絲、茶之運往外國者，必先在湘潭裝箱，然後再運廣東放洋。以故湘潭及廣州間，商務異常繁盛。交通皆以陸，勞動工人肩貨往來於南風嶺者，不下十萬人。南風嶺地處湘潭與廣州之中央，為往來必經之孔道。道旁居民，咸藉肩挑背負以為生，安居樂業，各得其所。迨後外洋機械輸入，復經國際戰爭及通商立約等事，而中國勞動界情勢，乃為之一變。此不僅擾亂中國工業制度，且於將來全國之經濟、實業、政治上，皆有莫大影響也。

予等乃各依其所指定之地點，分往各處收買生茶，以備運往上海裝箱。留湘潭約十日。十日後，擬更赴湖北之荊州，以調查華容地方所產之黃絲。

4月26日，離湘潭北行，趨予等所欲赴地點。翌晨八時至湖南長沙。是日適空氣潮濕，同人中感覺煩瞞[1]不歡，乃相約入城遊覽。城中情形，與他處略同，建築街衢等，皆齷劣穢污，無可觀者。明日乘舟復行，遂過洞庭湖，渡揚子江，入荊河口，以達華容。計離湘潭後，水程十日，所經處尚有太平景象。居居各安農業，禾黍滿望，叱犢時聞。予於此見二村童，共騎一驢，沿途笑語，意至歡樂，他處未見有此也。抵華容後，因覓旅館不得，遂寄榻於某絲行中。行裝甫卸，即有地方保甲二人，來詢旅客姓名職業。行主知其故，即為予等代述來意。彼聞為誠實商人，非為匪徒作偵探者，遂滿意而去，任予等自由動作，不復來相擾矣。予既宣布來意，旋有無數商人，送種種黃絲來，以備選購。是日得各種絲樣，約六十五鎊，裝運上海。

兩星期後，各收拾行裝，準備歸計。經漢口後，又赴轟家市（譯音）。轟家市屬長沙，亦產茶區域也。自5月26日離華容，於6月5日抵漢口，寓一中國旅館中。天氣既炎熱潮濕，所居復湫隘異常，殊少清新空氣，至為不適。三日後，有委員三人來查詢，一如在華容時。示以在華容所購之黃絲，及其包皮上所蓋由華容至漢口沿途稅卡之戳。彼等見此，知非匪徒偵探，遂去不復相擾。

漢口當時尚未通商，惟此事已經提議，不久且實行。當太平軍未起事之前，漢口本一中國最重要之商埠。1856年，太平軍佔據武昌時，漢口、漢陽亦同時失陷。以是漢口之一部，盡被焚毀，頓成一片焦土。當予至時，商業已漸恢復，被焚之區，亦重新建築。第所建房屋，類皆草率急就。若以今日（1909年）之漢口言之，沿岸一帶，貨棧林立，居屋櫛比，類皆壯麗之西式建築，大有歐西景象，非昔比矣。故在今日中國之有漢口，殆如美國之

1　編者按，疑為「悶」字。

有芝加哥及聖魯意二城。予知不久漢口之商業發達，居民繁盛，必將駕芝加哥、聖路易而上之。予等勾留數日，遂重渡揚子江，趨聶家市產黑茶之地。

6月30日離漢口，7月4日至聶家市及楊柳洞（譯音），於此二處，勾留月餘。於黑茶之製造，及其裝運出口之方法，知之甚悉，其法簡而易學。予雖未知印度茶之制法如何，第以意度之，印茶既以機器製造，其法當亦甚簡。自1850年以後，中國人頗思振興茶業，挽回利權，故於人工之制茶法，亦已改良不少。究印度所以奪我茶業利權之故，初非以印茶用機器製造，而華茶用人工製造之相差。蓋產茶之土地不同，茶之性質，遂亦因之而異。印茶之性質強烈，較中國茶味為濃，烈亦倍之。論葉之嫩及味之香，則華茶又勝過印茶一倍也。總之印茶烈而濃，華茶香而美。故美國、俄國及歐洲各國上流社會之善品茶者，皆嗜中國茶葉。惟勞動工人及尋常百姓，乃好印茶，味濃亦值廉也。

8月下旬，所事既畢，共乘一湖南民船以歸。船中滿載裝箱之茶，以備運滬。於8月29日，重臨漢口，計去初次離漢時且兩月矣。此行不復過湘潭，經漢口後，即自揚子江順流而下，至九江，過鄱陽湖。鄱陽湖之南岸，有地曰河口。自河口以往，乃遵三月間所經之原路，9月21日抵杭州。由杭州復乘「無錫快」，於9月30日抵上海。溯自3月以迄10月，凡歷七閱月之旅行，藉此機緣，予得略知內地人民經太平軍亂後之狀況。凡所歷沿途各地，大半皆為太平軍或官軍所駐紮者，外狀似尚平靜。至於各地人民，經太平軍及官軍搶掠之後，究竟受何影響，則無人能知其真象矣。惟有一事，令予生無窮之感慨。予素閱中國記載及旅行日記等書，莫不謂中國人口之眾，甲於全球。故予意中國當無地不有人煙稠密之象。乃今所見者，則大抵皆居民稀少，與予夙昔所懷想者，大不相符，是則最足以激刺予之腦筋者也。此種荒涼景象，以予所經之浙江、江西、湖南、湖北四省為尤甚。當予遊歷時，為春、夏兩季，正五穀播種、農事方殷之際，田間陌上，理應有多數之驢馬牛畜，曳鋤相接。乃情形反是，良可怪也。

予自內地歸後，10月間復有英友某君，倩予至紹興收買生絲。紹興去杭州西南約二十英里，所產絲頗著名。予在紹興收絲約兩月，忽患瘧，不得已中途輟業。紹興城內污穢，不適於衛生，與中國他處相彷彿。城中河道，水黑如墨。以城處於山坳低濕之地，雨水咸瀦蓄河內，能流入而不能洩出。故歷年堆積，竟無法使之清除。總紹興之情形，殆不能名之為城，實含垢納污之大溝渠，為一切微生物繁殖之地耳，故瘧疾極多。予幸不久即愈，甫能離榻，即急急去之。

第十章

太平軍中之訪察

　　1860 年，有二美教士，不憶其名，一中國人曰曾蘭生，擬作金陵遊，探太平軍內幕，邀予與偕。予欣然諾之。太平軍中人物若何，其舉動志趣若何，果勝任創造新政府以代滿洲乎？此余所亟欲知也。是年 11 月 6 日，予等共乘一「無錫快」，自上海首途。時適東北風大作，船順風行頗速，天氣復晴朗。同行諸人，興致殊高。適攜有美國國旗，眾人乘興，遂以插船首，迎風招颺，顧而樂之。既念此舉殊疏，或誤認吾舟謂有國際關係，而加以盤詰，則徒生枝節，乃急捲而藏之。吾儕此行，擬先至蘇州，本應道出松江。因聞松江方駐有官軍炮艇，恐為所攔阻，不聽向前，或被遞送還上海，亦殊不便，乃繞道避之。舟離上海三十英里中，沿途居民安堵，不顯有政治上擾亂情狀。田家操作自若，方收穫也。然予赴內地調查產茶時，蘇州已為太平軍佔領。蘇滬密邇，故上海租界中西人咸揣惴，惟恐太平軍來佔據租界，乃嚴為戒備。松江各河中亦炮艇密佈，西人守衛隊亦遠出租界線之外嚴密巡邏矣。

　　11 月 9 日之晨，船抵蘇州。沿途暢行無阻，絕未遇一官軍，或一太平軍。當此戰爭緊急之際，而巡邏疏略如是，中國人事事不經意，於此可見一斑。予等抵蘇州之婁門，先至一軍站。站中有護照，欲赴城內者，必先於此領照，乃得入，出城時仍須繳還之。予等欲入城謁其主將，乞介紹書，俾得直赴金陵，沿途無阻。乃以二人留站守候，先遣二人面軍站長，問四人可否同時入城。二人去時，有該地警察長，特派一人伴之行。去一小時而返，謂站長已允所請。於是予等同入。時城中民政長方公出，遂往謁軍事首領劉某。其人軀幹高大，身着紅衣，有驕矜氣，望而可知為淺陋無根柢者。彼詢予等赴南京目的，雖反復盤詰，禮遇尚優。旋授一函介紹予等於丹陽主將，並繕一護照，謂持此暢行於無錫、常州間，可無留難。劉復紹介予等晤四西人。四人中二美人，一英人，一法人。法人自謂為法國貴族，因在本國喪失其資財，故來中國以圖恢復。英人則自稱係英國副將。其二美國人，一為醫士，一則販賣槍彈者，因索值過昂，尚未成議云。之數人者，其所謂貴族、副將、醫士、商人云云，初莫辨其真偽。其為冒險而來，各懷所欲，則無疑也。予聞劉頌讚美歌，口齒頗伶俐。日暮返舟，復遣人以雞、羊等物相饋遺，以故此行食品頗充裕。11 月 11 日晨抵無錫。既至，出護照示關吏，果得彼等禮遇。其地之主將某，設筵相款。宴罷，復贈種種乾、鮮水果，且親至舟中送行。予等與談論甚久，後亦頌讚美歌作終結，與蘇州劉某所頌者同。

11 月 12 日，離無錫赴常州。自蘇至丹陽，舟皆行運河中。河之兩岸，道路猶完好。途中所見皆太平軍。運河中船隻頗少，有時經日不遇一舟。運河兩傍之田，皆已荒蕪，草長盈尺，滿目蒿萊，絕不見有稻秧麥穗。旅行過此者，設不知其中真象，必且以是歸咎於太平軍之殘暴。殊不知官軍之殘暴，實無以愈於太平軍。以予等沿途所見，太平軍之對於人民，皆甚和平，又能竭力保護，以收拾人心。其有焚掠肆虐者，治以極嚴之軍法，非如紂之不善，盜跖之率徒為暴。然則仁與不仁，其成敗之代名詞歟？抵常州，日已暮。自無錫至此，沿途房屋，看[1] 空無人居。偶遇一二老叟，提小筐售物。筐中所貯橘、蛋、糕餅、菜蔬、魚肉等零星食品，見舟來，輒追呼求售。觀其狀，似因年老不能遠逃，故藉此以延喘息。然皆愁苦萬狀，窮蹙無生趣矣。13 日晨六鐘，復解維趨丹陽行。丹陽居民，對於太平軍較有信用，商不輟業，農不綴耕，無荒涼景象。而太平軍之對於人民，亦未聞有虐遇事，相處甚得也。是日之晨，途中見有兵千人。傍晚已望見丹陽雉堞，因暮色蒼茫，故寄宿舟中。翌日破曉入城，謁其地主將。先以蘇州所得之介紹書投入。後知此主將亦劉姓，彼適他出，有副官秦某（疑即天官秦日昌）出迎，

1　　編者按，疑多一「看」字。

蓋文職也。為人和藹可親，禮貌周至。予等與談，偶詢以太平軍中宗教信仰。秦君自謂對於耶穌教之觀念，皆得諸其首領洪秀全。其言曰：

「吾等所崇拜之天主，即在天之父。天父之外，復有耶穌及聖靈。三位一體，合成真人，是曰上帝。耶穌教分為二派，一曰舊派，一曰新派，太平軍則棄新派而從舊派，吾等之天王，曾至天上面謁天父。天父命其降世行道，掃除一切罪惡，指引一切迷路，毀滅偶像及其他一切邪教之迷信，曉諭百姓，使人人咸知天主之真體，其責任蓋甚重大也。天王之至天上，其為靈魂御空而行，抑為肉體白日飛昇，則非吾等所能知。但天王自言，天王之尊，猶不能與天主相提並論。世人之當崇拜天主，乃為宗教上之崇拜。至天王之受世人敬禮，不過猶世上皇帝之尊榮，為臣民者對其君上，當極其尊敬而已。天王之位，錫自天主，與耶穌為兄弟行。此所謂兄弟者，非謂其為同父共母所生，第因天王與耶穌，皆為上帝先後所派之天使，命其至世界上普渡眾生，為世人贖罪。天王唧此使命在耶穌後，故當兄事耶穌耳。至太平軍中之教規，有所謂飲三杯茶者，乃表感謝上帝之心，初不含贖罪意義。其數之以三者，亦與三位一體之教旨無關，即一杯二杯，本無不可。而必捨一捨二而擇三者，則以三之數乃中國人素來崇尚，如古語稱天地人為三才等是也。若言贖罪，則無論何等供養祭獻，絕不能贖吾人罪孽於毫末。此權蓋盡操諸耶穌之手，世人但盡其真心懺悔之忱，則耶穌自能為之救贖，否則雖祭奉亦無益。即天王自己，亦長日兢兢業業，惟恐或得罪於天主云。」

秦某言次，又論及戰爭時軍民必分處之故。謂中國亙古以來，無論何代，依向來之習慣，凡遇戰爭時，人民必退處田野，軍士則駐守城中。所謂攻城略地，能攻克一城，則城外之地可唾手得也。又言自蘇至此，運河兩旁荒涼之況，其故有三：一為張玉良軍隊退敗時所焚燒，一為土匪所搶掠，一為太平軍之自燬也。當忠王（即李秀成）在蘇州時，嘗竭力欲禁搶掠之風，懸重賞以募奇才。謂有能出力禁絕焚掠之事者，立酬鉅金，並頒以爵位。又下令三通：一不許殘殺平民，二不許妄殺牛羊，三不許縱燒民居。有犯其一者，殺無赦。迨後忠王至無錫，曾有一該地長官縱任土匪焚燬民居，忠王乃戮此長官以警眾。忠王與英王（即陳玉成）之為人皆極聰穎，不獨擅於軍旅之事，文學亦極優長云。

秦某又言攻略各地之情形，及 1860 年春間官軍圍攻金陵之失敗。語次並出一函相示，函為徽州某主將所發，內云「曾國藩已受大創，現方為太平軍所困，四面受敵。」據其函中所言，似曾國藩已戰歿陣中矣。秦某復謂：「張玉良攻金陵敗退後，已受傷咯血，現在杭州養疴，一時不能復出。運河一帶，居揚子江之北者，皆入太平軍掌握。而忠王、英王，則居上游，方謀取湖北。石達開經略四川、雲。貴等省。鎮江近方被圍，更有西王率軍駐紮於此，以指揮江南全境」云云。當日太平軍勢力所及蓋如此。

是日於秦處晚餐，入夜歸宿舟中。明日復入城，謁劉主將，又不值。僅晤其中軍某，因請其設法護送予等至南京。中軍允諾，屬以所乘舟可暫留丹陽，彼能善為守護，勿使有失。歸途出此再乘之，固甚便也。翌晨（16 日），予等遂徒步出丹陽。行十五英里，至一鎮曰寶堰，其地去句容六英里。鎮中覓宿頗不易，土人皆貧苦不支，對於外來之客，尤懷疑懼。費幾許唇舌，僅於隘巷中得空屋，無几案牀榻，以稻藁席地而已。次晨，居停老婦以餉客，瀕行酬以銀一圓。九鐘，抵句容。城門盡閉不得入。蓋此時適有謠傳，謂太平軍敗於鎮江，將來此暫避，故句容戒嚴。予等聞此大失望，美教士至欲折回上海。余意必至南京，持論久之，乃復前進。幸離句容不遠，覓得肩輿及騾，乃不復退縮。

11 月 18 日抵南京。予先至，候於南門外。餘人齊集，乃同行入城。城中勞白芝教士（Rev. Roberts）已遣僕數人，迎候於途，遂至勞君寓所。寓近干王洪仁（疑為洪仁玕之誤）軍署。勞白芝，美教士舊友也。既晤勞君後，彼等殷勤話舊，予則先退至己臥室。長途僕僕，頗覺勞頓，因略盥洗，即休息。予晤勞君時，未發一語，亦未嘗告以予之姓名。但前在古夫人小學肄業時，曾晤其人，故一見即能識之。渠此時所衣為黃緞官袍，足華式笨履，舉步遲緩，益形龍鐘。勞氏在南京果身居何職，予實未詳。洪秀全之宗教顧問歟？抑太平天國之國務卿耶？

翌日，予等謁干王。干王為洪秀全之姪。(按干王洪仁玕與洪仁達同輩，於洪秀全為兄弟行，此處云云，恐誤。) 1856 年，予在香港曾識其人。當時彼方為倫敦傳道會職員，任中國牧師，其主教為萊克博士 (Dr. Legge)。萊克博士，即著名善譯中國古文者。予曩在香港晤干王時，干語予，將來願於金陵得再相見，今果然矣。干王本名洪仁[2]，迨至金陵與其叔共事，晉爵至王位，乃曰干王，殆取干城之義歟？干王接見予等，極表歡迎，尤樂於見予。寒暄後，即詢問予對於太平軍之觀念若何，亦贊成此舉而願與之共事否？予告以此來初無成見，亦無意投身太平軍中，妄思附驥，第來探視故人，以慰數年來晦明風雨之思耳。干王復固問，余曰：「實無他目的，但得略悉金陵實在情形，一釋傳聞之疑，於願已足。惟此次自蘇至寧，途次頗有所感觸，願貢其千慮一得之愚。」因言七事：一、依正當之軍事制度，組織一良好軍隊。二、設立武備學校，以養成多數有學識軍官。三、建設海軍學校。四、建設善良政府，聘用富有經驗之人才，為各部行政顧問。五、創立銀行制度，及釐訂度量衡標準；六、頒定各級學校教育制度，以耶穌教聖經列為主課。七、設立各種實業學校。

此其大略。至若何實行，自非立談所能罄。倘不以為迂緩，而採納予言，願為馬前走卒。余之此言，蓋度德量力，自謂能盡力於太平軍者祇此耳。

越二日，干王復邀予等為第二次談判。既入見，干王乃以予所言七事，逐條討論。謂何者最佳、何者最要，侃侃而談，殊中肯綮。蓋干王居外久，見聞稍廣，故較各王略悉外情。即較洪秀全之識見，亦略高一籌。凡歐洲各大強國所以富強之故，亦能知其秘鑰所在。故對於予所提議之七事，極知其關係重要。第善善不能用，蓋一薛居州無能為役，且此時諸要人皆統兵於外，故必俟協議，經多數贊成，乃可實行也。

又數日，干王忽遣使來，贈予一小包揪。拆而視之，則中裹一小印，長

2　編者按，疑欠一「玕」字。

四英吋，寬一英吋，上鐫予名。又有黃緞一幅，鈐印十三，上書予官階，曰「義」字。按太平軍官制，王一等爵，義字四等爵。予睹此大惑不解。干王以此授予，意果何居？其以是為干旌之逮歟？然未先期得予同意，不可謂招以其道。豈謂四等榮銜，遂足令人感激知己，抑亦隘矣。予每見太平軍領袖人物，其行為品格與所籌劃，實未敢信其必成。乃商之同伴諸人，決計返璧。更親至干王府，面謝其特別之知遇。且告之曰：「無論何時，太平軍領袖諸君，苟決計實行予第一次談判時提出之計劃，則予必效奔走。無功之賞，則不敢受。君果不忘故人，願乞一護照，俾予於太平軍勢力範圍中，無論何時得自由來去，則受賜多矣。」干王知不可強，卒從予請。遂於 12 月 24 日發出護照，並為予等代備糧食與馬，送至丹陽。予等共乘原舟遣歸，於翌年 1 月初旬安抵上海。途中追憶太平軍起事情形，及彼中人物之舉動，以為與中國極有關係，當於下章詳之。

第十一章
對於太平軍戰爭之觀感

革命之在中國，固數見不鮮。聞者疑吾言乎？則試一翻中國歷史。其中所謂二十四朝，非即二十四次革命寫真耶？顧雖如此，戰國而外，中國之所謂革命，類不過一姓之廢興，於國體及政治上，無重大改革之效果。以故中國兩千年歷史，如其文化，常陳陳相因，乏新穎趣味，亦無英雄豪傑，創立不世偉業，以增歷史精神。太平軍戰爭之起，則視中國前此鼎革，有特異之點，非謂彼果英雄豪傑，以含有宗教性質耳。其魄力至偉，能自僻遠之廣西，由西南蔓延東北，而達精華薈萃之金陵，歷時至十五年之久，亦惟宗教之故。此十五年中，滿洲政府幾無日不處於飄搖風雨之中。然於歷史上究有若何精神，則未易輕許也。

太平軍之大戰爭，以宗教觀念為原質。此觀念來自歐西，耶穌教徒實傳播之。其輸此種子於中國之第一人，為英人瑪禮孫（Morrison）氏，蓋倫敦傳道會所派出者。其後十年，復有美教士勞氏繼踵而起。二氏者，開濬洪秀全知識之功臣也。瑪禮孫善著述，曾譯耶教《聖經》為漢文，而譯《康熙字典》為英文。雖其書未必當，而後之西人來中國傳教者，咸藉為津梁。瑪氏所譯《聖經》，旋經後人加以潤色，《漢英字典》後亦經多人修正，如梅博士（Dr. Medhurst）、文主教（Bishop Boone）、雷博士（Dr. Legge）及勃禮區文（Bridgeman）、威廉姆司（Williams）諸人，先後增訂，經過多人之手，要不能不藉瑪氏所譯者為藍本也。瑪禮孫於中國有一最著名之事業，曾於中國得第一耶教信徒，名梁亞發。其人能本耶教宗旨，著成傳道書數種。洪秀全求道時，即以瑪氏所譯《聖經》，及梁氏所著書，誦習研究。第此等書中，微言奧義，非得人善為解釋，殊難悟澈。時值美國米蘇釐（Missouri）省教士勞白芝君在粵傳道，洪秀全乃時至其處請業，二人遂為莫逆交。迨太平軍起，洪既雄踞金陵，勞氏亦居此處，大抵友而兼師者，故甚清貴。勞苦功高，固宜有此不次之賞。1864 年，官軍既克復金陵，勞氏遂不知所終。

洪秀全為耶穌教徒時，尚醉心科舉之虛榮。曾應小試，不幸鎩羽。乃專心傳道，往來兩粵，宣揚福音於客家 (Hakkas) 族中。所謂「客家」者，兩廣間一種客民，遷徙無常，故俗稱為客家云。洪秀全一生之功業，此時傳道，不過為其宗教經驗之起點，其後革命事業，乃其宗教經驗之結果。

洪秀全於應試落第後，得失心盛，殆成一種神經病。神志昏瞶中，自謂曾至天上，蒙天主授以極重要之職，命其毀滅世界上崇拜之偶像，指引迷途，曉諭世人，使人人咸知天主，信仰耶穌，俾耶穌得為世人贖罪。洪秀全既自以為在天主之前受此重任，故自命為天主之子，與耶穌平等，稱耶穌為兄。蓋昏瞶中構成之幻想，乃自信為真。日至客家中，歷敍其所遭如是。謂世人必須信仰一己，乃能獲上帝之福佑。遂以崇拜上帝之事，蹈狐鳴篝火之嫌，每日瞻禮祈禱，高誦贊美之歌。廣西四境人民聞之，乃大欣動。每日必有多人入教，號召即至。及後人數日增，聲勢日廣。地方官吏對於此一般耶穌教徒，目為異端邪說，妖言惑人，然亦無如之何。

此種人所具耶教之知識，半為西來教士所傳播，半為本地中國信徒所講授。故無論如何，其宗教知識，皆甚淺陋而簡單。顧雖淺陋簡單，而宗教中真實之勢力，則已甚大，足使一般無識愚民，皆成為草野英雄，人人能冒危險，視死如歸。此種特性之潛蓄，於政府欲實行解散該教時，乃大發現。彼等揭竿而起，以抵抗官軍之壓迫。初無槍彈軍火之利器，所持者耰鋤棘矜耳。以此粗笨之農具，而能所向無敵，逐北追奔，如疾風之掃秋葉，皆由宗教上所得之勇敢精神為之。

雖然，太平軍之起，固宗教上之逼迫使然。實則亦非真因，不過爆發之導火線耳。即使當時政府，無此等逼迫之舉動，洪秀全及其屬下諸人，亦未必能安居於中國內地，而專以傳佈宗教為事也。予意當時即無洪秀全，中國亦必不能免於革命。設有人以耶穌教之關係及清政府之操切，為 1850 年革命之原因，則其所見淺陋實甚。惡根實種於滿洲政府之政治，最大之真因為行政機關之腐敗，政以賄成。上下官吏，即無人不中賄賂之毒。美其名曰饋遺，黃金累累，無非暮夜苞苴。官吏既人人欲飽其貪囊，遂日以愚弄人民為能事。於是所謂政府者，乃完全成一極大之欺詐機關矣。

革命事業之開幕於中國，殆如埃及之石人，見者莫不驚奇。埃及石人首有二面，太平軍中亦含有兩種性質，如石人之有二面。凡崇拜天主、信仰救主聖靈、毀滅偶像廟宇、禁止鴉片、守安息日、飯前後戰爭時均祈禱，種種耶教中重大之要旨，太平天國無不畢具。遂使全世界耶教中人，咸逆料滿洲政府必為推翻，洪秀全所稱之太平天國行且建設成立。此天意或將使中國立一震古爍今之世業，而為全世界人所驚心動魄也。耶教中人此種幻想，亦未免感情用事，過於信任太平軍矣。彼曷不細為分析，一研究太平軍之內容耶？

洪秀全之起兵廣西也，馬首東向，沿途收集流亡，聲勢甚壯。中途曾移師直指北京，至天津為官軍所敗，乃折回逕趨南京。所過湖南、江西、安徽等省，旌旗所至，無堅不摧。第自天津敗北，兵力縮減。良由其所招撫，皆無業遊民，為社會中最無知識之人，以此加入太平軍，非獨不能增加實力，且足為太平軍之重累，而使其兵力轉弱。蓋此等無賴之尤，既無軍人紀律，復無宗教信仰。即使齊之以刑，不足禁其搶掠殺人之過惡。其所以受創於天津，亦此等人實尸其咎。銳氣既挫，迨佔據揚州、蘇州、杭州等城，財產富而多美色，而太平軍之道德，乃每下而愈況。蓋繁華富麗，固足以銷磨壯志，而促其滅亡也。

此次革命，雖經十五年劇烈之戰爭，乃不久而霧散煙消，於歷史上曾未留一足為紀念之盛跡。後之讀史至此者，亦不過以為一時狂熱，徒令耶教中人為之失望，於宗教上毫無裨補。即如南京佔據至十年之久，亦不見留有若何之耶教事跡。廣西為其起事之地，亦復如是。至若於中國政治上，則更絕無革新之影響。簡而言之，太平軍一役，中國全國於宗教及政治上，皆未受絲毫之利益也。其可稱為良好結果者惟有一事，即天假此役，以破中國頑固之積習，使全國人民皆由夢中警覺，而有新國家之思想。觀於此後 1894、1895、1898、1900、1901、1904、1905 等年種種事實之發生，足以證予言之不謬矣。

第十二章
太平縣產茶地之旅行

　　南京之行，本希望遂予夙志，素所主張之教育計劃，與夫改良政治之贊助，二者有所藉手，可以為中國福也。不圖此行結果，毫無所得。曩之對於太平軍頗抱積極希望，庶幾此新政府者能除舊布新，至是頓悟其全不足恃。以予觀察所及，太平軍之行為，殆無有造新中國之能力，可斷言也。於是不得不變計，欲從貿易入手。以為有極鉅資財，則藉雄厚財力，未必不可圖成。然畢竟營何種商業，以為致富之資乎？

　　某日予方徜徉某茶肆，值素識之茶商某某亦在品茗，遂相與閒話。談次及予前至兩湖江西各省調查產茶事，已復及南京之行，議論分歧，語乃愈引而愈遠。已而眾茶商言安徽太平縣茶，或謂該處有綠茶百餘萬，已裝箱準備出口，不幸盡落太平軍之手。此時設有人能冒險向彼軍取回者，鉅富可立致。予聞言若有所觸，心識之。眾人旋散，予亦徐步歸寓，且行且思，適間茶商之言，寧非絕好時機乎？第處此亂離時勢，前途之危險與困難，不問可知。又況盜賊橫行，隨在而是。稍有經驗之商人，誰復肯以金錢冒奇險，圖此毫無憑藉之事業耶？然予以為事有可圖，不願坐失時機。因商之予友曾苗（當即第八章所述之曾繼甫），即一年前介紹予往內地採茶者。其人商業經驗極富，交遊亦多，且於我亦非泛泛。曾曰：「此事當深長思之，未敢貿然遽答。君苟能少待者，數日後當有以報命。」已而果然。曾謂予已與公司主人討論至再。予所提議之策，已決定實行矣。

　　此事進行之初步，為余受公司委任赴太平調查，畢竟有無此項茶葉，設有此茶，以鉅金向太平軍中購出，有無危險？購得茶葉後，僱民船運出，更以汽船載之來申，其間有無困難？蓋必如是先期籌備，然後億則屢中也。

自上海赴太平有二途：一由蕪湖直達，一在蕪湖上游百英里處有地曰大通。當時蕪湖至太平縣，在太平軍勢力範圍中，大通則為官軍所駐。由蕪湖入內地，舟行二百五十英里。大通雖較近，然須陸行，殊不便，旅費亦巨。且經大通，沿途有重稅，蕪湖則否。權衡利害，遂決計取道蕪湖。瀕行邀四人為伴。此四人亦業茶，皆太平縣人，故鄉在劫火中已兩年，因避亂來上海者。既首途，溯江上行。途中經大城三，盡為太平軍所佔據。居民甚少，田園荒蕪，蘆葦高且過人。多數市鎮，亦寂無居人。慘淡情狀，不堪屬目。若在平時，此長途所經地方，至少當有五十萬戶，今則不知流離何所。存者才數十人耳，亦復形容枯槁，衣裳垢敝，憧憧往來，生氣蕭索，遠望之幾疑骷髏人行也。舟行一星期，抵一鎮曰山口。於是復遇茶商三人，亦四年前在上海相識者。此三茶商者，在漫天烽火中，可謂碩果僅存。見予等至，如他鄉遇舊，愉快之情，不可言喻。蓋當此時此地而有仍余等，不啻空山中聞足音也。於是於焚燼未盡諸屋中，擇一最完善者居之，作為辦事地點，以從事調查，並邀所遇三茶商相助為理。渠乃示予某處某處，有存茶若干。並謂山口地方，至少必有綠茶五十萬箱。合太平縣全境計之，當不下百五十萬箱，每箱裝茶重可六十磅云。予居此一星期，遂返蕪湖，函上海報告調查情形。略謂由太平縣至蕪湖，水程尚平安。以予意度之，當不至有生命財產之危險。予在太平縣境內，曾親見有無數之綠茶。但能攜款至蕪湖，並僱用數人護送以往，款至太平縣，茶即不難運歸。函外並附茶樣多種。已而上海復書來，謂茶種良佳，命予速往購辦。謂能得幾許者，儘量收購，不厭多也。

公司匯錢既至，予偕同伴諸人，運資赴山口，復由山口裝茶返蕪湖。僕僕道途，往返不知幾次。猶憶某日伴予行者十二人，中有歐洲人六，亦素業茶者，有銀八箱，共四萬兩。爾時市價，每銀一兩，約易墨銀一圓三角三分。故予所攜者，殆合墨銀五萬三千圓。予僱運茶之舟八，分所攜銀為二，擇二大舟之最堅固者載之。同行之人，亦分為兩組。每載銀舟，以三西人三華人守之，並將手槍、腰刀及消防具，所以防意外者。吾儕並舟人計之，人數可四十餘。然雖多，皆不習武事，設遇警實不足恃。可為緩急之助，惟此數西人耳。雖然，此輩大半皆冒險之徒，或為逃亡之水手，不過在上海受公司傭僱，遂來此為護送之人。究竟能否臨難不避，此時亦殊不可必。就中有一英人自言為獸醫，身高六英尺，狀貌雄偉，望之精神曄然。後乃知此人之心志，亦不堅定，則知人之難也。予既部署粗定，遂解維趨蕪湖。舟中諸人，咸鼓其冒險精神，有陳元龍氣概。蕪湖山口適中處，有城曰涇縣，某日至此而泊。城中駐太平軍，其主將曾驗予在南京時所得之護照，並知予曾識彼中權要者。予舟泊於湖之小灣。小灣面積，適可容數舟。載銀二大舟居中，餘舟環之。入夜，以槍械分與眾人，令皆實子彈。又另增傭金，每舟各派一人行夜。分布既畢，始各就寢。就中一年老之茶商及予，睡不成寐。餘人因日間勞倦，頭着枕，已鼾聲動矣。予心既懸懸，不能安寢。臥觀天際，見黑雲片片，飛行甚速。一彎新月，時從雲隙窺人。既而雲益濃厚，月不可見，夜色乃益昏沉，黑暗中一無所覩。依枕無聊，長夜將半，耳際忽聞隱隱有呼嘯聲，由遠漸近。乃大驚，披衣起，醒各舟人。此時聲益近，聽之歷歷可辨，似有數千人同時吶喊。深夜靜野中有此，益覺凄厲。數分鐘後，已見對岸火光熊熊，有無數火捻，閃爍於昏黑可怖之世界中。幸此羣匪與予舟尚隔一河。又幸夜黑，予舟尚未為所見。予等咸知危險即在目前，向同伴商抵禦之策，如臨時會議然。咸謂眾寡懸殊，果對壘者，當以一當千，竟無一人主戰。彼為獸醫之英人，創議盡獻所有勿與抗，發言時已面無人色，戰慄不止。此公可謂虛有其表者。餘人議論歧出，莫衷一是。予等誠不值為此區區四萬兩之銀而犧牲生命，但此金係受他人委託，奈何不設法保護之？慷他人之慨，資寇盜之糧，人且鄙予等為無勇懦夫，誰復以一錢相托者。計必臨難不苟，庶幾捫心自安。乃謂眾：「諸君且勿自擾，匪果來劫，予請挺身與其酋開談判。君等第執槍械，守衛銀箱。鄙意匪眾苟知吾儕為何等人物，並示黃鍛護照，明告若輩，脫果取吾金者，當訴之南京，必追還原物，不虞有絲毫損失。如此或竟倖免，亦未可知。」予發言畢，眾人勇氣得稍振，共坐船頭，靜待其來。默念數分鐘後，不知當得若何結果。人人自危，咸注目對岸火光不少瞬。久之，呼嘯聲漸低，火捻漸分作無數小隊。背予舟方向，徐徐引去。行時每一隊皆小作停頓，乃復前行。如是者約歷兩小時。予莫解其意，或謂殆對岸備有船隻，此輩盜匪分隊登舟也。時已向曉三鐘，天忽雨，果見有無數盜舟紛紛駛去，有數舟且掠予舟旁而過。直至四鐘，乃不復見盜舟蹤跡。予等遇此奇險，竟安然無恙，可謂天幸。設非黑夜天雨，或舟不停泊於灣僻處，則不堪設想矣。迨五鐘後，一切恐懼焦灼之念，盡歸烏有，人人額手相慶，感謝上帝。更二日，遂安抵山口。予於兩星期內，得綠茶十六船，六西人監送至蕪湖，更由蕪湖易舟運上海，是為第一批。其第二批覆十二船，予自護送之。時值盛夏，河水乃乾淺，有數處舟不能行，必掘深河底，乃得通過。予命舟人挖泥，舟人難之。予以身作則，躬自入水掘河，水及予腰。眾乃不復觀望，踴躍將事，河道遂通。

予從事販茶之事，凡六閱月，前後共得綠茶六萬五千箱，然尚不及太平縣所有者十之一。乃予忽膺重疾，蕪湖不得良醫，則就醫上海，纏綿病榻，歷兩月之久始愈。愈後逢知體弱不勝勞劇，遂棄所業，不復為茶商。涇縣夜中遇險事，過後思量，猶為心悸。當時予雖持鎮靜態度，然神經系已受非常震動。意此二月之病，未始不種因於此。吾人處世，以生命為基本。倘果為土匪所得，則一死真等於鴻毛，且余既志在維新中國，自宜大處落墨，若僅僅貿遷有無，事業終等於撈月。太平軍當時因茶葉暢銷，昂其價格。為此手續繁重之事，以博微利，即多金亦屬奢願難償。靜言思之，頓覺前此之非計。不如善自珍攝，留此有用之身。蓋至此而余前此之金錢思想，為二豎子破壞無餘矣。

予於太平縣之役，雖無所獲，然任難事而能堅忍，遇危險而能鎮定，頗受中西商人疾風勁草之知。以故余因病辭職，病癒即為某公司聘予至九江，為茶葉經理人。雖非所願，亦姑就之。半年後，辭職自營商業。計在九江三年，境況殊不惡。而余魂夢不忘之教育計劃，亦於此時獲一機會，有實行之希望焉。

第十二章
與曾文正之談話

　　1863 年，余營業於九江。某日，忽有自安徽省城致書於余者，署名張世貴。張寧波人，余於 1857 年於上海識之，當時為中國第一炮艦之統帶，該艦屬上海某會館者。嗣升遷得入曾文正公幕中。余得此書，意殊驚詫。蓋此人於我初無若何交誼，僅人海中泛泛相值耳。地則勞燕，風則馬牛，相隔數年，忽通尺素，而書中所言，尤屬可疑。彼自言承總督之命，邀余至安慶一行，總督聞余名，亟思一見，故特作此書云。當時總督為曾公國藩，私念此大人物者，初無所需於予，急欲一見胡為？予前赴南京，識太平軍中渠帥。後在太平縣，向革軍購茶，豈彼已有所聞歟？憶一年前湘鄉駐徽州，為太平軍所敗，謠言總督已陣亡。時予身近戰地，彼遂疑予為奸細，欲置予於法，故以甘言相誘耶？雖張君為人，或不至賣友，然何能無疑？躊躇再三，擬姑復一函，婉辭謝卻。余意暫不應召，俟探悉文正意旨，再決從違。故余書中，但云辱荷總督寵召，無任榮幸，深謝總督禮賢下士之盛意，獨惜此時新茶甫上市，各處訂貨者多，以商業關係，一時驟難捨去，方命罪甚，他日總當晉謁云云。

　　兩閱月後，張君之第二函至，囑予速往，並附李君善蘭（即壬叔）一書。李君亦予在滬時所識者。此君為中國算學大家，曾助倫敦傳道會中教士惠來（Rev. Wiley）翻譯算學書甚夥。中有微積學，即予前在耶路大學二年級時，所視為畏途，而每試不能及格者也。予於各科學中，惟算學始終為門外漢，此予所不必深諱者。李君不僅精算學，且深通天文，此時亦在曾文正幕府中，因極力揄揚予於文正。謂曾受美國教育，1857 年賴予力捐得鉅款賑災，且謂其人抱負不凡，常欲效力政府，使中國得致富強。凡此云云，來書中皆詳述之。書末謂總督方有一極重要事，欲委予專任，故勸駕速往。並謂某某二君，以研究機器學有素，今亦受總督之聘，居安慶云。予得此書，疑團盡釋，知前此之淺之乎測丈夫也。遂復書，謂更數月後，准來安慶。乃曾文正欲見予之心甚急，七月間予復得張君之第三函及李君之第二函。兩函述文正之意，言之甚悉。謂總督欲予棄商業而入政界，居其屬下任事。予初不意得此機緣，有文正其人為余助力，予之教育當不患無實行之時。若再因循不往，必致坐失事機。乃立覆一書，謂感總督盛意，予已熟思至再，決計應召來安慶。惟經手未完事件，必須理楚。種種手續，當需一月之摒擋。最遲至8月間，必可首途矣。此書發後，張、李二君遂不復來書相催。是為予預備入政界之第一步。

　　曾文正為中國歷史上最著名人物，同輩莫不奉為泰山北斗。太平軍起事後，不久即蔓延數省。曾文正乃於湖南招練團勇，更有數湘人佐之。湘人素勇敢，能耐勞苦，實為良好軍人資格，以故文正得練成極有紀律之軍隊。佐曾之數湘人，後亦皆著名一時。嘗組織一長江水師艦隊，此艦隊後於揚子江上，大著成效。當時太平軍蔓延於揚子江兩岸，據地極廣，而能隔絕其聲援，使之首尾不相顧者，則艦隊之功為多也。不數年，失陷諸省，漸次克復。太平軍勢力漸衰，範圍日縮，後乃僅餘江蘇之一省，繼且僅餘江蘇一省中南京一城。迨 1864 年，南京亦卒為曾文正軍隊所克復。平定此大亂，為事良不易。文正所以能指揮若定，全境肅清者，良以其才識道德，均有不可及者。當時七、八省政權，皆在掌握。凡設官任職、國課軍需，悉聽調度，幾若全國聽命於一人。顧雖如是，而從不濫用其無限之威權。財權在握，絕不聞其侵吞涓滴以自肥，或肥其親族。以視後來彼所舉以自代之李文忠 (鴻章)，不可同日語矣。文忠絕命時，有私產四千萬以遺子孫。文正則身後蕭條，家人之清貧如故也。總文正一生之政績，實無一污點。其正直、廉潔、忠誠諸德，皆足為後人模範。故其身雖逝，而名足千古。其才大而謙，氣宏而凝，可稱完全之真君子，而為清代第一流人物，亦舊教育中之特產人物。是即 1863 年秋間，予得良好機緣所欲往謁者也。

予既將九江商業結束後，遂乘民船於 9 月間抵安慶，逕赴文正大營，得晤故人張世貴、李善蘭、華若汀[1]、徐雪村等（譯音）。此數人皆予上海舊交相識，見予至，意良欣慰。謂總督自聞予歷史後，此六閱月之內，殆無日不思見予一面。張、李二君之連發數函，亦即以此。今予既至，則彼等之勸駕已為有效，推轂之力，當不無微勞足錄云。予問總督之急欲見予，豈因予以中國人而受外國教育，故以為罕異，抑別有故歟？彼等咸笑而不言，第謂君晤總督一、兩次後，自能知之。予察其狀，似彼等已知總督之意，特故靳不以告予。或者總督之意，即彼等所條陳，未可知也。

抵安慶之明日，為予初登政治舞台之第一日。早起，予往謁總督曾公。刺入不及一分鐘，閽者立即引予入見。寒暄數語後，總督命予坐其前，含笑不語者約數分鐘。予察其笑容，知其心甚忻慰。總督又以銳利之眼光，將予自頂及踵，仔細估量，似欲察予外貌有異常人否。最後乃雙眸炯炯，直射予面，若特別注意於予之二目者。予自信此時雖不至忸怩，然亦頗覺坐立不安。已而總督詢予曰：「若居外國幾何年矣？」予曰：「以求學故，居彼中八年。」總督復曰：「若意亦樂就軍官之職否？」予答曰：「予志固甚願為此，第未習軍旅之事耳。」總督曰：「予觀汝貌，決為良好將材。以汝目光威稜，望而知為有膽識之人，必能發號施令，以駕馭軍旅。」予曰：「總督獎譽逾恆，良用慚悚。予於從軍之事，膽或有之，獨惜無軍事上之學識及經驗，恐不能副總督之期許耳。」文正問予志願時，予意彼殆欲予在其麾下任一軍官以御敵。後聞予友言，乃知實誤會。總督言此，第欲探予性情近於軍事方面否耳。及聞予言，已知予意別有所在，遂不復更言此事。後乃詢予年事幾何？曾否授室？以此數語，為第一次談話之結束。計約歷三十分鐘。語畢，總督即舉茶送客。予亦如禮還報，遂興辭出。舉茶送客，蓋中國官場之一種禮節。凡言談已盡，則舉杯示意，俾來客得以興辭也。予既出，歸予室。關懷之舊友，咸來問訊，細詢予見總督時作何狀。予詳告之，諸友意頗愉快。

1 　編者按，即華蘅芳。

余見文正時為 1863 年，文正已年逾花甲，[2] 精神奕然，身長約五尺八、九英吋，軀格雄偉，肢體大小咸相稱。方肩闊胸，首大而正，額闊且高，眼三角有稜，目皆平如直線。凡尋常蒙古種人，眼必斜、顴骨必高。而文正獨無此，兩頰平直，髭鬚甚多，鬢髮直連頰下，披覆於寬博之胸前，乃益增其威嚴之態度。目雖不巨，而光極稅利，眸子作榛色，口闊唇薄，是皆足為其有宗旨有決斷之表證。凡此形容，乃令予一見即識之不忘。

文正將才，殆非由於天生，而為經驗所養成者。其初不過翰林，由翰林而位至統帥，此其間蓋不知經歷幾許階級，乃克至此。文正初時所募之湘勇，皆未經訓練之兵。而卒能以此湘軍，克敵致果，不及十年而告成。當革軍勢力蔓延之時，實據有中國最富庶之三省。後為文正兵力所促，自 1850 年至 1865 年，歷十五年之凶患，一旦肅清，良非細故。溯自太平軍起事以來，中國政府不特耗費無數金錢，且二千五百萬人民之生命，亦皆犧牲於此政治祭台之上。自此亂完全肅清後，人民乃稍稍得喘息。中國之得享太平，與滿政府之未被推翻，皆曾文正一人之力也。皇太后以曾文正功在國家，乃錫以爵位，為崇德報功之舉。然曾文正之高深，實未可以名位虛榮量之。其所以成為大人物，乃在於道德過人，初不關其名位與勳業也。綜公生平觀之，後人謚以文正，可謂名副其實矣。

今更回述予在安慶之事：當時各處軍官，聚於曾文正之大營中者，不下二百人，大半皆懷其目而來。總督幕府中亦有百人左右。幕府外更有候補之官員、懷才之士子，凡法律、算學、天文、機器等等專門家，無不畢集，幾於舉全國人才之精華，匯集於此。是皆曾文正一人之聲望道德，及其所成就之功業，足以吸引之羅致之也。文正對於博學多才之士，尤加敬禮，樂與交遊。予來此約兩星期，在大營中與舊友四人同居，長日晤談，頗不寂寞。一日，予偶又詢及總督招予入政界之意。諸友乃明白告予，謂彼等曾進言於總督，請於中國設一西式機器廠，總督頗首肯，議已成熟，惟廠之性質

2　按，此處有誤，當時曾國藩只是五十多歲。

若何，則尚未決定耳。某夕諸友邀予晚餐，食際即以此機器廠問題為談論之資。在座諸君，各有所發表，既乃詢予之意見。蓋諸友逆知總督第二次接見予時，必且垂詢及此，故欲先知予之定見若何也。予乃告之曰：「予於此學素非擅長，所見亦無甚價值。第就予普通知識所及，並在美國時隨時觀察所得者言之，則謂中國今日欲建設機器廠，必以先立普通基礎為主，不宜專以供特別之應用。所謂立普通基礎者無他，即由此廠可造出種種分廠，更由分廠以專造各種特別之機械。簡言之，即此廠當有製造機器之機器，以立一切製造廠之基礎也。例如今有一廠，廠中有各式之車牀、錐、銼等物。由此車牀、錐、銼，可造出各種根本機器。由此根本機器，即可用以製造槍炮、農具、鐘錶及其他種種有機械之物。以中國幅員如是之大，必須有多數各種之機器廠，乃克敷用。而欲立各種之機器廠，必先有一良好之總廠以為母廠，然後乃可發生多數之子廠。既有多數子廠，乃復拼而為一，通力合作。以中國原料之廉、人工之賤，將來自造之機器，必較購之歐美者價廉多矣。是即予個人之鄙見也。」諸友聞言，咸異常欣悅。謂願予於總督詢及此事時，亦能如是以答之。

數日後，總督果遣人召予。此次談論中，總督詢予曰：「若以為今日欲為中國謀最有益最重要之事業，當從何處着手？」總督此問，範圍至廣，頗耐吾人尋味。設予非於數夕前與友談論，知有建立機器廠之議者，予此時必以教育計劃為答，而命之為最有益最重要之事矣。今既明知總督有建立機器廠之意，且以予今日所處之地位，與總督初無舊交，不過承友人介紹而來。此與予個人營業時，情勢略有不同，若貿然提議予之教育計劃，似嫌冒昧。況予於予之朋友，尤當以恪守忠信為惟一之天職。予胸中既有成竹，故對於此重大問題，不至舉止失措。以予先期預備答辭，能恰合總督之意見，欲實行時即可實行也。於是予乃將教育計劃暫束之高閣，而以機器廠為前提。予對總督之言，與前夕對友所言者略同，大致謂應先立一母廠，再由母廠以造出其他各種機器廠。予所注意之機器廠，非專為製造槍炮者，乃能造成制槍炮之各種機械者也。槍炮之各部，配合至為複雜，而以今日之時勢言之，槍炮之於中國，較他物尤為重要，故於此三致意焉。總督聞言，謂予曰：「此事予不甚了了，徐、華二君研此有素，若其先與二君詳細討論，後再妥籌辦法可耳。」

予辭出後，即往晤諸友。諸友亟欲知予此談之結果，聞予所述情形，咸極滿意。自此次討論後，諸友乃以建立機器廠之事，完全托付於予，命予徵求專門機器工程師之意見。二星期後，華君若汀告予，謂總督已傳見彼等四人，決計界予全權，先往外國探詢專門機器工程師，調查何種機器於中國最為適用。將來此種機器應往何國採購，亦聽予決定之。

建立機器廠之地點，旋決定為高昌廟。高昌廟在上海城之西北約四英里，廠地面積約數十畝。此機器廠即今日所稱「江南製造局」，其中各種緊要機器工程，無不全備者也。自予由美國採購機器歸國以來，中國國家已籌備千百萬現金，專儲此廠，鳩工製造，冀其成為好望角以東之第一良好機器廠。故此廠實乃一永久之碑，可以紀念曾文正之高識遠見。世無文正，則中國今日，正不知能有一西式之機器廠否耳？

第十四章
購辦機器

　　自予與曾督第二次晤談，一星期而有委任狀命予購辦機器，另有一官札授予以五品軍功。軍功為虛銜，得戴藍翎。蓋國家用兵，以此賞從軍有功之人，為文職所無。文職官賞戴花翎，必以上諭頒賜，大員不得隨意賞其僚屬。又有公文二通。命予持以領款。款銀共六萬八千兩，半領於上海道，半領於廣東藩司。余籌備既畢，乃稟辭曾督，別諸友而首途。

　　予此行抵上海，為 1863 年 10 月。其時適有一美國機械工程師名哈司金（Haskins）者，為上海某洋行運機器來華。事畢，方欲挈妻子返美。而予不先不後，適於此時抵滬，得與其人相值，時機之巧，洵非意料所及者。予既識哈司金，遂以購機器事委其主任，與訂立合同。二人皆取道香港，經蘇彝士地峽（Isthmus of Suez）以達倫敦，本可同行。惟哈司金偕其眷屬乘法公司輪船，而予則乘英公司船。哈以行期已迫，匆匆別，期會於紐約。船既放洋，途中惟至新加坡略一停泊，遂過印度洋，由錫蘭（Ceylon）地方登陸，易舟更過孟加拉海灣（Bay of Bengal），於埃及之開羅（Cairo）城登陸。爾時蘇彝士河（Suez Canal）之工程，方開鑿未竣，於是予乃由開羅乘火車，過蘇彝士地峽，赴亞立山大（Alexandria）城，復由亞立山大乘舟至法國之馬塞（Marseilles）。馬塞為法國南方第一海口，哈司金已由此乘舟逕赴英國。予則於馬塞上岸，乘火車赴巴黎，作十日遊。巴黎之公園、教堂及各處繁盛之區，遊覽殆遍。此世界著名繁華都會，予得大擴眼界，略知其梗概焉。十日後，遂於法國加來司（Calais）地方，乘舟過英吉利海峽（English Channel）至英國之多爾維（Dover），由多爾維改乘火車抵倫敦，是為予初次身履英倫之一日。藉此良好機會，使予得睹世界第一大都會，於願良足。予在倫敦，曾往惠特維爾司機器廠（Whitworth's Machine Shop）參觀，無意中遇一十年前在中國所識之西友，其名曰克里司特（Christy）。予居倫敦一月，乃乘哥拿脱（Cunard）公司之汽船過大西洋，於 1864 年春初抵紐約。予畢業耶路大學，於今十年。予之同班諸學友，將於 7 月暑假時，開十週[1] 紀念聯合會。此時方在正二月間，聞會期尚遠。哈司金因須預備機器圖樣、訂貨條款及估價單等，故已偕眷先予至紐約。予以哈氏諳練可恃，遂以選擇機器等事，畀以全權。當此 1864 年時，正南北美戰爭之末年，美國國內多數機器廠，皆承造國家急需之要件，工作忙迫異常，而以新英國省中為尤甚。以故外來購機器者，急切驟難成議。幸得哈司金素識各廠，乃克於馬沙朱色得士省非支波克（Fitchberg, Mass.）城中，與樸得南公司（Putnane & Co.）訂約，承造此項機器。然亦須半年後，方能造成運回中國云。

予乘此六閱月休息之暇，遂至紐海紋赴耶路大學，參與同班所開之十週紀念聯合會。舊雨重逢，一堂聚話，人人興高采烈，歡樂異常。雖自畢業分袂後，十載於茲，而諸同學之感情，仍不減當年親密。予乃有緣得躬與其盛，何幸如之！此會宗旨，既專以聯絡舊情，作賞心之樂事，故予於胸中所懷，隻字不道。況此時南北美戰爭尚未結束，美人以國事方殷，亦無暇他顧。故於予此次來美所任之事，咸未注意，幾無一知之者。第予自念今茲所任購辦機器之事，殆為一種應經之階級，或由此將引予日夕懷思之教育計劃，以漸趨於實行之地也。高會既終，友朋星散，予亦興盡而返。抵非支波克後，對於南北美戰爭，忽有感觸。因余曩曾入美籍，美國實余第二祖國也。因囑哈司金暫居此，主持一切，告以將赴華盛頓投效美政府，盡六閱月之義務。設於此六月內發生意外事，致予一時不能遽歸，則此機器裝運回國之事，當若何處置，擬悉以奉托。哈氏忻然允予請，乃以種種應需之要件，如訂貨單、提貨單、機器價值單，以及保險裝運等費，——交付哈氏。並告以若何手續，點交與曾督所派駐申之委員。籌備既畢，旋即束裝就道。

1　編者按，指十週年。

時有斯不林非爾（Springfield）地方之總兵名彭司（Brigadier-General Barnes）者，方在華盛頓任將軍之職，專司義勇隊事務。總兵有子曰威林（William），為香港[2] 著名律師，曾與予同時肄業於耶路大學者也。1863 年，彭總兵至紐海紋探視其子時，予於耶路大學圖書館中，與有一面之素。此時探得彭君之辦公處，在威拉旅館（Willard Hotel）中，予乃逕往謁之，告以來意。因言：「雖他無所能，然若任予以軍差之職，傳遞軍書於華盛頓及最近之大營間，供六閱月之馳驅，至所幸願。且此六月內，予當自備資斧，不敢耗美國國帑。」又言曩在耶路曾晤總兵，總兵亦尚能憶之。乃詢予現任何事。予告以自耶路畢業後，向居中國。此來因奉曾大帥國藩之命，至美購辦機器，以為中國建設機器廠之預備。刻已於非支波克城由樸得南公司訂約承造，另有一美國機械工程師，監督其事。因此項機器製造，須六月後方能告竣，故予甚願藉此餘暇，得略盡義務，以表予忠愛美國之誠也。彭總兵聞言甚悅，且極重視此事，乃謂予曰：「鄙人極感君之美意，但君現受中國國家重任，故鄙意君宜仍回非支波克，調度一切，以免貽誤。此間傳遞軍書，以及趨赴前敵，尚不乏健兒也。」予聞總兵言，知其意已決，遂亦不更置辭再以為請。予此意雖未獲實行，而自問對於第二祖國之心，可以盡矣。

2　編者按。根據英文版，應為三藩市。

第十五章
第二次歸國

　　予所購辦之機器，直至 1865 年春間始成，由輪船裝運，自紐約而東，繞好望角直趨上海，予則不復循來時舊路。蓋予之願望，此生至少環遊地球一次。今既得有機會，大可藉此遊歷，以擴眼界，以是決計由舊金山 (San Francisco) 西行。此時太平洋鐵路公司，築路由芝加哥 (Chicago) 過鄂馬哈 (Omaha) 以達舊金山，工程猶未完竣。故予此行，只能繞道，先乘一沿海輪船，由紐約以至巴拿馬地峽 (Isthmus of Panama)，過地峽後，更換船，沿墨西哥海岸，以達舊金山 (San Francisco)。

　　抵舊金山後，遲兩星期以待船。由此間赴上海，例橫過太平洋。惟爾時駛往遠東之郵船，尚未組成大公司，且須美國國家津貼，以故東行之船極少。予欲另覓他舟不可得，不得已乃乘一南多克 (Nantucket) 之三桅船。船資由舊金山至橫濱，每人須美金五百元。是行乘客並予凡六人，船名「亞衣得老及司」(*Ida de Rogers*)，年齡頗老大。船身長約一百五十英尺，艙中既未裝貨，亦無壓重之石，所載惟一艙淡水耳。船上人役，為船主及船主夫人並一六齡之幼子，此外更有大副一人、水手三人、廚役及中國侍者各一人。此船即船主所自有。船主名諾登 (Norton)，為南多克人。南多克地方出產之航海家，目力甚近，所見不出五步。迨一及金錢，則眼光尤小，錙銖必較。又不獨於金錢為然，凡與人交涉，無論事事物物，較及錙銖，利人之事，一毛不拔。船主諾登，足為此種人之代表。予於此行，本極乏味，乃有機會得以研究南多克種人之行為，不可謂非閱歷也。有金門 (Golden Gate) 口者，為舊金山出口必由之路。當未過金門時，予等每日之佳餚為鹹鯖魚，鹹而腥，不堪下箸。而船主視為珍品，若畢生食之不厭者，遂無日不以是飼客。奈予等口之於味,偏不同嗜。而尤劣者為舟中庖人之烹調法,於是余等每飯如仰藥矣。庖人為船主於舊金山臨時僱來承乏者,其是否素操此業,實未可知。凡烹鹹鯖魚,未入鑊時,法當先浸以水,令其味稍淡。今乃無需此繁重手續,而以速成為工。又不獨於鯖魚為然,即所食玉粟粉制之餅,亦多不熟者,故予等每食不飽。而船主家庭之風趣,亦有令人見而作惡者。船主每發言,非最穢褻者不出諸口。船主夫人雖無之,而於其夫之褻辭穢語,亦處之泰然,有若司空見慣。其幼子年可六齡,箕裘克紹,且能跨竈[1],種種穢辭,習之極純熟,不顧而唾,其父母聞之則大慰,殆以為能充宗;時或回顧乘客,冀邀旁觀之稱譽。乘客中有英人某,一日方口啣煙鬥立於旁,聞是兒口出種種穢言,不能復耐,因顧船主夫婦曰:「此兒佳哉,口齒玲瓏若百舌[2],微賢夫婦教育不及此。」船主聞言大樂,對客頻頷其首,初不知客之嘲已也。其妻亦信以為真,則左右顧盼,大有自矜之色。凡此怪狀,無日不觸於耳目,即欲逃避,亦苦無術。因舟小艙狹,甲板上竟無六尺餘地,容人着足,惟餐室尚涼爽,為全舟最佳處,故予等長日居此中,以觀可厭之醜劇,無可如何也。行程未及半,泊於檀香山 (Honolulu) 極北之小島,以裝淡水,並添備糧食。予等咸乘此機會紛紛登岸,至田野間散步,神氣為之一舒。遊行竟日,日暮乃返舟。忽見船主購有多數之火雞及雛雞,畜之前艙。予等見此,以為船主購此享客。是殆前此長食鹽鯖魚,船主或亦抱歉,故備此蓋愆者,不覺食指之動。迨明日就食,餐桌之上,果有嫩雞,深幸期望之不虛。乃異味之嘗,只此一次,翌晨即復原狀。火雞之肉,則永不出現。怪之,私詢廚役,始知此雞船主之販賣品,以備售之橫濱云。船主之計劃良得,但眾雞不慣風濤,於未抵橫濱之前數日,無一存者,船主逐利之術猶未工也。長途困頓,度日如年。抵橫濱後,亟換英公司汽船以赴上海。

予至上海後,始知一切機器,已於一月前運到,幸皆完全無損。計予離

1　編者按,即兒子比父親更精此道。

2　編者按,一種雀鳥。

中國年餘，大陸已一度滄桑，曾文正已與其弟國荃，克復南京，肅清太平軍之大亂矣。時文正方駐徐州，調度諸軍以平捻匪。徐州在運河上游，為江蘇最北之地。捻匪乃當日安徽之一股土匪也。

余往徐州謁文正，同行者為華君若汀。舟自揚子江仙女廟地方，入運河而抵揚州，棄舟陸行，乘騾車，經三日達徐州。曾督對於予之報告，極為嘉許，乃以予購辦機器之事，專摺請獎。中國官場之常例，專奏之效力極大。以予毫無官職之人，遂得特授五品實官，此亦特例。其奏章略言：「容某為留學西洋之中國學生，精通英文。此行歷途萬里，為時經年，備歷艱辛，不負委託，庶幾宏毅之選，不權通譯之材。擬請特授以候補同知，指省江蘇，盡先補用，以示優異，而勵有功。」

曾督幕府中辦奏稿者，於予未離徐州前，即錄此稿示予，以得曾督識拔為賀。故予於稟辭時，即面謝曾督之提攜，謂願將來有所成就，不敢以不舞鶴遺羊公羞也。

予留徐三日，即來上海。十月間奉到曾督札文，謂保奏五品實官，已蒙核准。於是予以候補同知之資格，在江蘇省行政署為譯員，月薪二百五十金。若以官階論，當日之四品銜候補道，無此厚俸也。

此時任上海道者為丁日昌，與予交頗投契。丁之居官，升遷甚速，由上海道而鹽運司，而藩司，未幾竟升為江蘇巡撫。予亦藉丁之力，旋得加銜而帶花翎。當丁任鹽運司時，予曾隨至揚州。在揚州六個月，譯哥爾頓（Colton）所著之《地文學》（*Geography*）一書。六月後仍回上海，就譯員之舊職。公餘多暇，復譯派森（Parson）著之《契約論》（*On Contracts*），予以為此書與中國甚有用也。此時予幸得一中國文士，助予譯事。其人不獨長於文墨、精於算學，且於中國政界事務亦甚諳練。彼旋勸予勿譯此書，謂縱譯畢，亦恐銷路不廣。因在中國法庭中，因契約而興訴訟者極少。即或有之，而違背契約之案件，亦自有中國法律可援，外國之法律，實不合於中國情勢云。1867年，文正得李文忠襄助，平定捻匪，乃至南京就任兩江總督。未抵任前，先於所轄境內巡行一週，以視察民情風俗。而尤注意者，則其親創之江南製造局也。文正來滬視察此局時，似覺有非常興趣。予知其於機器為創見，因導其歷觀由美購回各物，並試驗自行運動之機，明示以應用之方法。文正見之大樂。予遂乘此機會，復勸其於廠旁立一兵工學校，招中國學生肄業其中，授以機器工程上之理論與實驗，以期中國將來不必需用外國機械及外國工程師。文正極贊許，不久遂得實行。今日製造局之兵工學校，已造就無數機械工程師矣。

第十六章
予之教育計劃

　　予自得請於曾文正，於江南製造局內附設兵工學校，向所懷教育計劃，可謂小試其鋒。既略著成效，前者視為奢願難償者，遂躍躍欲試。曾文正者，於余有知己之感，而其識量能力，足以謀中國進化者也。當日政界中重要人物，而與余志同道合者，又有老友丁日昌。丁為人有血性、好任事，凡所措施，皆勇往不縮。當丁升任江蘇巡撫，予即謁之於蘇州公署，語以所謂教育計劃。丁大贊許，且甚注意此事，命予速具詳細說帖，彼當上之文相國，請其代奏。文祥滿人，時方入相，權力極偉也。予聞丁言，驚喜交集，初不意蘇州之行，效力如是。於是亟亟返滬，邀前助予譯書之老友（南京人），倩其捉刀，將予之計劃，撰為條陳四則，寄呈丁撫，由丁撫轉寄北京。略謂：

　　一、中國宜組織一合資汽船公司。公司須為純粹之華股，不許外人為股東。即公司中經理、職員，亦概用中國人。欲鞏固公司之地位，並謀其營業之發達，擬請政府每年撥款若干以津貼之。其款可由上海鎮江及其他各處運往北京之漕米項下，略抽撥數成充之。漕運舊例，皆運米而不解銀，每年以平底船裝運，由運河駛赴北京。故運河中專為運漕而設之船，不下數千艘。運河兩岸之居民，大半皆藉運漕為生。但因運法不善，遂致弊端百出。水程迢迢，舟行紆緩，沿途侵蝕，不知凡幾。值天氣炎熱，且有生蛀之患。以故漕米抵京，不獨量數不足，米亦朽敗不可食。官廳旋亦知其弊，後乃有改用寧波船，由海運至天津，更由天津易平底船以運京。然寧波船之行駛亦甚緩，損失之數，與用平底船等。愚意若汽船公司成立，則平底船及寧波船皆可不用，將來漕米即逕以汽船裝運。不獨可免沿途之損失，即北方數百萬人民仰漕米以為炊者，亦不至常食朽糧也。（此後招商局輪船，即師此法以運漕。）

二、政府宜選派穎秀青年，送之出洋留學，以為國家儲蓄人材。派遣之法，初次可先定一百二十名學額以試行之。此百二十人中，又分為四批，按年遞派，每年派送三十人。留學期限定為十五年。學生年齡，須以十二歲至十四歲為度。視第一、第二批學生出洋留學，著有成效，則以後即永定為例，每年派出此數。派出時並須以漢文教習同往，庶幼年學生在美，仍可兼習漢文。至學生在外國膳宿入學等事，當另設留學生監督二人以管理之。此項留學經費，可於上海關稅項下，提撥數成以充之。

三、政府宜設法開採礦產以盡地利。礦產既經開採，則必兼謀運輸之便利。凡由內地各處以達通商口岸，不可不建築鐵路以利交通。故直接以提倡開採礦產，即間接以提倡鐵路事業也。（按中國當時尚無良好礦師，足以自行開採。人民尤迷信風水之說，阻力多端。予之此策，第姑列之，使政府知中國實有無窮厚利，不須患貧。且以表示予之計劃遠大，冀政府能信任予言也。）

四、宜禁止教會干涉人民詞訟，以防外力之侵入。蓋今日外人勢力之放恣，已漸有入中國越俎代謀之象。苟留心一察天主教情形，即可知予言之非謬。彼天主教士在中國勢力，已不僅限於宗教範圍，其對於奉教之中國人，幾有管轄全權。教徒遇有民刑訴訟事件，竟由教會自由裁判，不經中國法庭訊理。是我自有之主權，已於法律上奪去一部分也。是實不正當手段。若不急謀防範，則涓涓不塞，將成江河，故政府當設法禁止。以後無論何國教會，除關於宗教者外，皆不得有權以管理奉教之中國人。

此條陳之第一、三、四，特假以為陪襯；眼光所注而望其必成者，自在第二條。予友謂予，官廳批答公事，例有准駁。吾與以可駁者，而欲得者乃批准矣。且目的所在，列之第二，乃不顯有偏重之意也。此條陳上後兩閱月，丁撫自蘇馳函告予，謂文相國丁內艱。蓋中國禮制，凡現任職官，遭父母之喪，謂之「丁艱」。丁艱必退職，居喪三年，不得與聞政事。予得此消息，心意都灰，蓋至此而元龍湖海豪氣全除矣。抑塞運之來，天若不厭其酷者。得第二次惡耗，希望幾絕。蓋文祥居喪不三月，亦相繼為古人矣。予目的懷之十年，不得一試，才見萌蘗，遽遇嚴霜，亦安能無快快哉。失望久之。爐餘復熱。自 1868 年至 1870 年，此三年中，無日不懸懸然不得要領。偶因公事謁丁撫，必強聒不已，並懇其常向曾督言此，以免日久淡忘。辦事必俟機會，機會苟至，中流自在，否則枉費推移。余非不知此，然時機者，要亦人力所造也。

已而天津人民忽有仇教舉動，慘殺多數法國男女僧侶，其結果使中國國家蒙極大之不幸。予乃因此不幸之結果，而引為實行教育計劃之機會，洵匪夷所思。然使予之教育計劃果得實行，藉西方文明之學術以改良東方之文化，必可使此老大帝國，一變而為少年新中國。是因仇教之惡果，而轉得維新之善因，在中國國家未始非塞翁失馬，因禍得福也。

天津仇教事，發生於 1870 年春間。所以演成此慘劇者，則以北方人民，類皆強悍而無識、迷信而頑固，遂因誤會以釀成極大之暴動。先是天津有惡俗，貧民無力養其子女者，恆棄之道旁，或沉溺河中。天主教僧侶，憫其無辜，乃專事收育此等棄兒，養之醫院，授以教育，稍長則令其執役於教會之中。此實有益之慈善事業，顧蚩蚩者氓，誤會其意，造為無稽之說，謂教會中人取此棄兒，藏之醫院及教堂中，將其雙目挖去，以配藥劑，或則作為祭祀之供獻品。此等荒唐可哂之謠言，恰合於天津愚民之心理，故一時謠傳極廣。因市虎之訛，竟激起人心之憤。久之又久，禍機乃不可遏，遂不恤孤注一擲，取快一朝，雖鑄錯而不悔也。計是役焚燬天主教醫院及教堂各一所，殺斃教中法國男女僧侶無數。

此暴動發生之際，崇厚適為直隸總督。此人前曾任俄國公使，今甫督直而即值此暴動，可謂大不幸。蓋中國律例，凡地方有變故者，長官須負其責，故崇厚遂因此革職，發配邊遠地方充軍。迨後中國政府，允以巨款賠償被害人之家族，並建還所焚燬之醫院、教堂，更以政府名義發正式公函，向法國道歉，事乃得寢。幸爾時普法戰爭未已，法政府在恐慌中，故未遑以全力對付中國。否則必且借題發揮，肆意誅求，以饜其貪饕，交涉恐未易就範。但此次雖無難堪之要索，然後來中國屬地安南東京之一片土，卒因是不我屬矣。

中國政府當日曾派大臣四人調停，四人為曾文正、丁日昌、毛昶熙，其一人劉姓忘其名。是時捻匪雖漸平，尚未肅清。李文忠身在戎行，未與聞斯役。丁奉派後，電招予為譯員。電至略晚，不及與同行，予乃兼程赴津。抵津後，尚得與聞末後數次之談判。此交涉了結後，欽派之諸大臣，留天津未即散。而予乃乘此時會，十餘年夢想所期者，得告成功焉。

第十七章
經理留學事務所（派送第一批留學生）

　　欽派四大臣中，曾文正實為領袖。當諸人未散時，予乃乘機進言於丁撫，請其向曾督重提教育事，並商諸其他二人。予知丁於三年前已向曾督及此，故曾當已略知此中梗概，丁又素表同情於予，得此二公力助，餘二人當無不贊成矣。一夕，丁撫歸甚晚，予已寢。丁就予室，呼予起，謂此事已得曾公同意，將四人聯銜入奏，請政府採擇君所條陳而實行之。予聞此消息，乃喜而不寐，竟夜開眼如夜鷹，覺此身飄飄然如凌雲步虛，忘其為僵臥牀笫間。兩日後，奏折拜發，文正領銜，餘三人皆署名，由驛站加緊快騎，飛遞入京。此時曾督及餘人皆尚在津沽也。丁撫旋薦陳蘭彬於予，謂將來可副予為中國留學生監督。陳乃中國翰林，在刑部任主事垂二十年。丁撫之薦陳，蓋有深意。嘗謂余：「君所主張，與中國舊學說顯然反對。時政府又甚守舊，以個人身當其衝，恐不足以抵抗反動力，或竟事敗於垂成。故欲利用陳之翰林資格，得舊學派人共事，可以稍殺阻力也。」予聞丁撫此議，極佩其思慮周密。丁撫旋發函召陳，數日後，津中有為曾、丁諸公祖餞者，予及陳蘭彬均在座，丁撫遂為余等介紹。予之與陳，素未識面，今則將為共事之人矣。陳居刑部二十年，久屈於主事末秩，不得升遷，以故頗侘傺不自得，甚願離去北京。居京除刑曹外，亦未任他事，故於世途之經驗甚淺。其為人持躬謙抑，平易近人，品行亦端正無邪，所惜者膽怯而乏責任心耳。即一羽之輕，陳君視之不啻泰山，不敢謂吾力足以舉之。

　　1870 年冬，曾文正辦天津教案事畢，回任兩江。抵南京後，奉到前所上封奏硃批，着照所請。曾督即馳書召予，商此事之進行。至此予之教育計劃，方成為確有之事實，將於中國兩千年歷史中，特開新紀元矣。既抵南京，所商定者凡四事：曰派送出洋學生之額數，曰設立預備學校，曰籌定此項留學經費，曰酌定出洋留學年限。

有種種應辦事宜，勢不能無辦事機關，於是乃有事務所之組織，酌設監督二人、漢文教習二人、翻譯一人。監督即陳蘭彬及予任之。二人之責任，亦復劃清權限。陳君專司監視學生留美時漢文有無進步，予則監視學生之各種科學，並為學生預備寄宿舍等事。至關於經費之出納，則由予二人共主之。此外所聘漢文教員二人，一名葉緒東，一名容雲甫（譯音），翻譯則為曾蘭生。此當日留學事務所組織情形也。

既稍有頭緒，乃議派送之學額並招考章程。旋決定學生人數，照予前次所擬，暫定為百二十人。分四批，每批三十人，按年分送出洋。學生年齡，定為十二歲以上，十五歲以下，須身家清白，有殷實保證，體質經醫士檢驗，方為合格。考試科目為漢文之寫讀，其曾入學校已習英文者，則並須試驗其英文。應考及格後，當先入預備學校，肄習中西文字，至少一年，方可派赴美國留學。當未出洋之先，學生之父兄須簽名於志願書，書中載明自願聽其子弟出洋留學十五年（自抵美入學之日起，至學成止），十五年中如有疾病死亡及意外災害，政府皆不負責。至於學生留學經費及出洋之服裝等，皆由政府出資供給。每批學生放洋時，並派一漢文教習隨同偕往，此規定學額及招考章程之大略也。

予與曾督籌議甚久。議定後乃返上海，為第一步之進行。先於上海設立一預備學校，此校至少須能容學生三十人，因必有此數，方能足第一批派送之定額也。時有久居曾督幕府之劉開成者，奉派為該校校長。劉在曾督幕府，專司奏稿，為曾督第一信任之人，故任以此職。予接見劉君，覺其人實予良好之臂助，即平常相處，亦可稱為益友，對於予之教育，尤抱熱心。後此四批學生，預備期滿，陸續派送，皆由劉君一手料量，始終其事焉。

當 1871 年之夏，予因所招學生未滿第一批定額，乃親赴香港，於英政府所設學校中，遴選少年聰穎而於中西文略有根柢者數人，以足其數。時中國尚無報紙以傳播新聞，北方人民多未知中政府有此教育計劃，故預備學校招考時，北人應者極少，來者皆粵人，粵人中又多半為香山籍。百二十名官費生中，南人十居八九，職是故也。

1871年[1]冬間，曾文正公薨於南京，壽七十有一[2]。曾之逝世，國家不啻壞其棟梁。無論若何，無此損失鉅也。時預備學校開學才數月，設天假以年，使文正更增一齡者，則第一批學生已出洋，猶得見其手植桃李，欣欣向榮。惜夫世之創大業者，造化往往不錫以永年，使得親見手創事業之收效。此種缺憾，自古如斯。然創業之人，既播其種子於世，則其人雖逝，而此種子之孳生繁殖，固已綿綿不絕。故文正種因雖未獲親睹其結果，而中國教育之前途，實已永遠蒙其嘉惠。今日莘莘學子，得受文明教育，當知是文正之遺澤，勿忘所自來矣。文正一生之政績、忠心、人格，皆遠過於儕輩，殆如埃浮立司脫（Mt. Everest）高峰，獨聳於喜馬拉耶（Himalaya）諸峰之上，令人望而生景仰之思。予聞文正臨危時，猶念念不忘教育事業，深望繼己之李文忠，有以竟其未竟之志云。

李文忠雖為曾文正所薦舉以自代之人，顧其性情品格，與文正迥不相侔。其為人感情用事，喜怒無常，行事好變遷，無一定宗旨。而生平大病，尤在好聞人之譽己。其外貌似甚鹵莽，實則胸中城府甚深。政治之才，固遠不逮文正，即其人之忠誠與人格，亦有不可同日而語者。設有燃犀史筆傳之，則其一生行為，如探海燈燭物，秋毫無遁形矣。（鐵樵謹按：文忠事跡俱在，功罪自有定評，不必因此數言，遂累盛德。昔眉山、伊川意見[3]不合，遂以君子而互相水火。是容先生此語，亦未必便為失言。此書悉照原本意思，不敢稍有出入，致失真相，閱者鑒之。）

1872年夏季之末，第一批學生三十人，渡太平洋而赴美國。予先期行，抵美後，即乘火車過華盛頓而至紐約，再由紐約赴斯不林非爾，將於此預先佈置學生住宿諸事。蓋予與彼等，約於此處期會也。當由紐約赴斯不林非爾

1　編者按，此處有誤。曾國藩逝於1872年。

2　編者按，此處有誤。曾國藩生於1811年。

3　編者按，眉山即蘇軾，伊川即程頤。

時，道經紐海紋，遇海德列先生（Prof. James Hadley）。海聞予任此重職，復來美國，班荊道故，不勝歡欣。予告以一人先至之故，海君囑予往謁康納特克省（Connecticut）之教育司，謂渠當能代予籌劃。予如言謁教育司德魯布（Northrop）君，告以來意，請其指示。拿謂當將學生分處於新英國省之各人家，每家二、三人，但須相去不遠，庶便於監視。俟將來學生程度已能入校直接聽講時，乃更為區處。予如其教，即至斯不林非爾覓一適宜之所，以為辦事處。蓋斯不林非爾地處新英國省中心點，居此易於分配學生，使各去予不遠也。況予於 1854 年所識之好友麥克林夫婦（Dr. and Mrs. A. S. McLean）亦居此，公餘之暇，得常與良友把晤，亦人生樂事。後因從教育司拿德魯布及他友之言，乃遷居於哈特福德地方，其地即康納克之省城。此後二年，辦事處皆在哈特福德之森孟納街（Sumner Street）。予雖遷居哈特福德，顧未耘置斯不林非爾，仍以其處為分派學生之中心點。後之學生來美者，皆先至斯不林非爾，然後再分派各處，直至 1875 年乃已。

1874 年，李文忠從留學事務所之請，命予於哈特福德之克林街（Collins Street）監造一堅固壯麗之屋，以為中國留學事務所永久辦公之地。次年春正月，予即遷入此新居。有樓三層，極其宏廠，可容監督、教員及學生七十五人同居。屋中有一大課堂，專備教授漢文之用。此外則有餐室一、廚室一，及學生之臥室、浴室等。予之請於中國政府，出資造此堅固之屋以為辦公地點，初非為徒壯觀瞻，蓋欲使留學事務所在美國根深蒂固，以冀將來中政府不易變計以取銷此事，此則區區之過慮也。而詎知後來之事，乃有與予意背道而馳者。

第十八章
秘魯華工之調查

　　1873 年春，予以謀輸入一種新式軍械於中國，曾歸國一行。此行程途迅速，不敢少延，蓋此時予固有教育職務在身也。予所謂新式軍械，乃格特林（Gatling 人名）新發明之物，為戰爭中利器，炮亦即名「格特林」。予甚願中國有最新式之軍械，猶望中國有新學問之人材也。故特至格特林公司，欲與商訂合同，予願為之經理，專銷此種軍械於中國。初時頗為困難，公司中因未識予之為人，故於予商業上之經驗，未敢遽信。彼蓋未知予於 1860 及 1861 兩年在太平縣販茶之事，固嘗大著成效，冒眾人所不敢冒之險者。後費種種手續，親謁其總理格特林（即創此新炮之人），與之談論此事，幾於唇焦舌敝，始得總理之允諾，託予為中國之經理人，為之推廣新炮銷路。予既歸國，抵天津甫一月，即致電該公司，訂購格特林新炮五十尊，價約十萬美金。公司初頗輕予，今初次即成此大宗交易，實彼等意料所不及。後復陸續訂購不少，於是公司對於予所經理之事業，大為滿意，而對予之態度，遂不復如前之落漠矣。

　　予在津經理軍械貿易時，直督告予，謂有秘魯專使來此，擬與中國訂約，招募華工赴秘魯。命予往謁專使，與之談判此事。予奉命往見，秘魯專使顏色極和霽，歷言華工在秘魯營業若何發達，秘魯政府若何優待，工資之厚為中國所絕無。故彼甚願中政府速與秘魯訂約，鼓勵多數華工赴秘魯，俾此貧困之華人，咸得獲此良好機會，以各謀其生活云云。此種幣重言甘之辭，在他人聞之，鮮不墮其術中，顧予則非其人也。予於華工之事，所見已多，深知此中真相。因以質直之辭告之曰：「販賣華工，在澳門為一極尋常之事，予已數見不鮮。此多數同胞之受人凌虐，予固常目擊其慘狀。當其被人拐誘，即被禁囚室中不令出。及運奴之船至，乃釋出驅之登船。登船後即迫其簽字，訂作工之約，或赴古巴，或赴秘魯。抵埠登岸後，列華工於市場，若貨物之拍賣，出價高者得之。既被賣去，則當對其新主人，再簽字另立一合同，訂明作工年限。表面上雖曰訂年限，實則此限乃永無滿期。蓋每屆年限將滿時，主人必強迫其重簽新約，直欲令華工終身為其奴隸而後已。以故行時，每於中途演出可駭之慘劇。華工被誘後，既悟受人之愚，復受虐待之苦，不勝悲憤，輒於船至大洋四無涯際時，羣起暴動以反抗。力即不足，寧全體投海以自盡。設或竟以人多而戰勝，則盡殺販豬仔之人及船主水手等，一一投屍海中以洩忿。縱船中無把舵之人，亦不復顧，聽天由命，任其飄流。凡此可驚可怖之事，皆予所親聞親見者。予今明白告君，君幸毋希望予能助君訂此野蠻之條約。不惟不能助君，且當力阻總督，勸其毋與秘魯訂約，而為此大背人道之貿易也。」秘魯專使聞予言，大為失望，初時和顏悅色之假面具，猝然收去，代以滿面怒容。即予亦自覺悻悻之色，不可遏止。蓋述此慘無人理之往事，不期而髮指也。因亦不顧秘使之喜怒若何，語畢，遽興辭而出。予對秘使所言，在未曾目擊者，或疑予言不無過甚；不知語語皆真確，無一字虛妄。當 1855 年，予初次歸國時，甫抵澳門，第一遇見之事，即為無數華工，以辮相連，結成一串，牽往囚室。其一種奴隸牛馬之慘狀，及今思之，猶為酸鼻。又某次予在廣州時，曾親獲販豬仔之拐匪數人，送之官廳，拘禁獄中，罰其肩荷四十磅重大木枷兩月，亦令其稍受苦楚也。予即報命直督，告以與秘使談判之言。總督謂予曰：「汝此次返國大佳，否則予亦將電召汝歸矣。今予即命汝至秘魯一行，以調查彼中華工實在之情形。汝其速返哈特福德，部署一切，以備起行。」

　　予勉奉命返至哈特福德，陳蘭彬亦適奉政府之電，派其赴古巴調查華工情形。此雙方進行之舉，蓋亦出於李文忠之意。予乃先陳蘭彬而啟行。行時有二友為予伴，一為吐依曲爾牧師（Rev. Twitchell），一為開洛克博士（Dr. Kellogg），開君即予後日之妻兄。予至秘魯，以迅速之手段，三閱月內即調查完竣，一切報告皆已造齊。返美時，陳蘭彬猶未首途。直俟陳自古巴返，造齊報告後，予之報告書乃與之一併封寄李文忠，以文忠時方掌外交事務也。

予之報告書中，另附有二十四張攝影。凡華工背部受笞、被烙斑斑之傷痕，令人不忍目睹者，予乃藉此攝影，一一呈現於世人之目中。予攝此影，皆於夜中秘密為之。除此身受其虐之數華工外，無一人知之者。此數名可憐之華工，亦由予密告以故，私約之來也。秘魯華工之工場，直一牲畜場。場中種種野蠻之舉動，殘暴無復人理，攝影特其一斑耳。有此確鑿證據，無論口若懸河，當亦無辯護之餘地。

彼秘魯所派之專使，欲與李文忠訂約招募華工者，仍久滯天津，專俟予之調查報告到津，以決訂約之成否。後有友人發函告予，述秘使在津之行為，謂彼初猶堅不承認予之報告，斥為空中樓閣，毫無事實可據。然予已預防其出此，故於報告中密請總督暫秘攝影之片，勿示秘使。俟彼理窮詞遁，專以無證據為言時，然後再出此影以示之，使彼更無一辭之可措。總督果從予言，秘使出不意睹此真確可據之攝影，乃噤不能聲，垂頭喪氣而去。自予報告秘魯調查情形政府遂以華工出洋著為禁令。豬仔之禍，乃不如前此甚矣。

第十九章
留學事務所之終局

　　最後一批學生，於 1875 年秋間抵美。同時偕來者，有新監督區岳良、新翻譯鄺其照，更有漢文教習二人，皆為李文忠所派者。茲數人予曩在中國亦皆識之，而於區、鄺二君交尤熟。此次更動之原因，出於陳蘭彬一人之意。陳以急欲請假回國，遂請政府另派新監督以代其職。又陳於古巴調查華工之役，深得漢文教習葉緒東之臂助，故此次歸國，並欲攜葉偕行。而舊日翻譯曾蘭生，亦以他故，政府命其交卸回國。予於數月前已知有此更動，不以為意也。

　　自陳歸北京三月，中政府忽派陳蘭彬並予同為駐美公使，葉緒東亦得參贊。以常理論，是為遷擢，事屬可喜，然予則不以為榮以為憂。予友皆賀予升遷，蓋亦未就全局之關係一着想。若專就予一身言，以區區留學生監督，一躍而為全權公使，是政府以國士遇我？受知遇而不感激非人情；但以教育計劃言，是予視為最大事業，亦報國之唯一政策。今發軔伊始，植基未固，一旦捨之他去，則繼予後者，誰復能如予之熱心為學生謀幸福耶？況予與諸學生相處既久，感情之親不啻家人父子；予去，則此諸生且如孤兒失撫，是惡可者？默揣再四，乃上書總督，略謂：「過蒙逾格擢升，銘感無既。第公使責任重大，自顧庸朽不堪負荷。擬乞轉請政府收回成命，俾得仍為學生監督，以期始終其事。俟將來留學諸生，學成種種專門學術，畢業歸來，能為祖國盡力，予乃卸此仔肩。如是量而後入，予個人對於祖國，得略盡其天職。且此學生皆文正手植，譬之召伯甘棠，尤願自我灌溉之，俾得告無罪於文正。況政府既已派陳蘭彬為公使，則外交事務以陳獨當一面，必能勝任，固無需予之襄助也。」是書予倩容雲甫屬稿繕就，寄之中國。容雲甫即偕第一批學生來美，與葉緒東同為漢文教習者也。書上後四月，總督有復函來，不准不駁，亦允亦否。蓋命予為副公使而兼監督之任，俾予於留學生方面，仍得有權調度一切也。

新監督區岳良，大約即陳蘭彬所舉薦，此行與一妻二子俱來。區君較陳蘭彬為年少，雖非翰林，固亦中國飽學之文士。其人沉默靜穆，對於一切事物，皆持哲學觀念，不為已甚。其於前人佈置已定之局，絕不願紛更破壞之。觀其所言所行，胸中蓋頗有見地。惜此君任事未久，於 1876 年即辭職歸國。

1876 年，陳蘭彬以全權公使之資格，重履美土，一時攜來僚屬極多。中有一人曰吳子登，予約於二十年前曾在上海識之。其人亦為翰林，第不知何故從未指分各部授職，亦從未得政府之特別差委。聞其人好研究化學，顧所研究亦殊未見其進步。凡與吳交者，咸贈吳以「性情怪僻」四字之考語。當區岳良辭監督職時，陳蘭彬乃薦此性情怪僻者以繼任，李文忠亦竟貿然允陳之情，於是留學界之大敵至矣。吳子登本為反對黨之一派，其視中國學生之留學外洋，素目為離經叛道之舉；又因前與曾文正、丁日昌二人不睦，故於曾、丁二公所創之事業，尤思破壞，不遺餘力。凡此行徑，予初不之知，乃陳蘭彬屬下代理秘魯公使某君告予者。然則陳蘭彬之薦吳繼區，可知陳亦極頑固之舊學派，其心中殆早不以遣派留學為然矣。陳之此舉，不啻表示其自居反對黨代表地位，揎拳擄袖，準備破壞新政，以阻中國前途之進步。甚矣知人之難也。陳既挾此成見，故當其任監督時，與予共事，時有齟齬。每遇極正當之事，大可著為定律，以期永久遵行者，陳輒故為反對以阻撓之。例如學生在校中或假期中之正雜各費，又如學生寄居美人寓中隨美人而同為祈禱之事，或星期日至教堂瞻禮，以及平日之遊戲、運動、改裝等問題，凡此瑣瑣細事，隨時發生。每值解決此等問題時，陳與學生常生衝突，予恆居間為調停人。但遇學生為正當之請求，而陳故靳不允，則予每代學生略為辯護。以是陳疑予為偏袒學生，不無怏怏。雖未至形諸辭色，而芥蒂之見，固所不免，蓋陳之為人，當未至美國以前，足跡不出國門一步。故於揣度物情，評衡事理，其心中所依據為標準者，仍完全為中國人之見解。即其畢生所見所聞，亦以久處專制壓力之下，習於服從性質，故絕無自由之精神與活潑之思想。而此多數青年之學生，既至新英國省，日受新英國教育之陶鎔，且習與美人交際，故學識乃隨年齡而俱長。其一切言行舉止，受美人之同化而漸改其故態，固有不期然而然者，此不足為學生責也。況彼等既離去故國而來此，終日飽吸自由空氣，其平昔性靈上所受極重之壓力，一旦排空飛去，言論思想，悉與舊教育不侔，好為種種健身之運動，跳躑馳騁，不復安行矩步，此皆必然之勢，何足深怪？但在陳蘭彬輩眼光觀之，則又目為不正當矣。

陳蘭彬自赴華盛頓後，與哈特福德永遠斷絕關係。因有以上種種原因，故其平素對於留學事務所，感情極惡。即彼身所曾任之監督職務，亦久存厭惡之心。推彼意想，必以為其一己所受純潔無瑕之中國教育，自經來美與外國教育接觸，亦幾為其所污染。蓋陳對於外國教育之觀念，實存一極端鄙夷之思也。雖然，陳之此種觀念，亦未免自忘其本矣。獨不思彼一生之發跡，固由於此素所厭棄之事耶？設無此留學事務所，則彼亦安能以二十年刑部老主事，一旦而為留學生監督？更安得由留學生監督，一躍而為華盛頓公使？是則此留學事務所者，固大有造於陳蘭彬，不啻為其升官發財之階梯。陳苟能稍稍念木本水源，則不當登高而撤梯。乃不謂其盡忘前事，極力欲破壞予之教育計劃，而特薦吳子登為留學生監督。吳之為陳傀儡，又恰合其身份。蓋捨吳而外，固無人能受陳黑幕中之指揮也。吳既任監督，而留學事務所乃無寧歲矣。

1876 年秋間，吳既任事，對於從前已定之成規，處處吹毛求疵，苛求其短。顧有所不滿意，又不明以告予，惟日通消息於北京，造為種種謠言，謂予若何不盡職、若何縱容學生，任其放蕩淫佚，並授學生以種種不應得之權利，實毫無裨益。學生在美國，專好學美國人為運動遊戲之事，讀書時少而遊戲時多，或且效尤美人，入各種秘密社會，此種社會有為宗教者，有為政治者，要皆有不正當之行為。坐是之故，學生絕無敬師之禮，對於新監督之訓言，若東風之過耳。又因習耶教科學，或入星期學校，故學生已多半入耶穌教。此等學生，若更令其久居美國，必致全失其愛國之心，他日縱能學成回國，非特無益於國家，亦且有害於社會。欲為中國國家謀幸福計，當從速解散留學事務所，撤回留美學生，能早一日施行，即國家早獲一日之福云云。

吳子登日毀予於北京友人及李文忠前，予初毫無聞知。後文忠有書來，以吳報告之言轉告，命予注意。予乃知吳媒蘗予短，因亦作書報文忠。書中略謂：「凡此捕風捉影之談，皆挾私恨者，欲造謠生事，以聳聽聞。予固知造此言者，其人性情乖張，舉止謬妄，往往好為損人不利己之事。似此荒謬之人，而任以重職，實屬大誤。今彼且極力思破壞從前曾文正所創之事業。夫文正之創此留學事務所，其意固將為國家謀極大幸福也。吳子登苟非喪心病狂，亦何至欲破壞此有益於國之事。愚以為若吳子登其人者，只宜置之瘋人院或廢病院中，惡足以任留學生監督，且舉薦吳者實為陳蘭彬，陳亦怯懦鄙夫，生平膽小如鼠，即極細微之事，亦不敢擔負絲毫責任。予之與陳共事，無論外交方面、教育方面，意見咸相左。予今試略舉一事：1873年政府派陳赴古巴調查華工情形，陳奉命不敢遽往，遲至三月後乃首途。且於未行之先，先遣他人為之試探。所遣者為葉緒東及一教員，並有美國律師及通譯各一人。迨諸人調查既竣，事事完備，陳乃至古巴略一周旋，即返美呈報銷差矣。凡冒炎暑任艱巨之事，皆葉緒東一人當之，陳蘭彬特坐享其成耳。今則陳蘭彬已升遷公使，而葉緒東乃僅得參贊。予之為此言，非有所私憾於陳蘭彬而德葉緒東，第見政界中往往有此不平之事，無功受祿轉來不虞之譽，勞苦功高反有求全之毀。總督明察，當知予之所言，非有所掩者。蓋予固甚願辭公使之職，仍退處於監督舊任，俾得專心於教育事業，冀將來收良好之效果。即如某日因事致書於美國國務院，予與陳蘭彬意見不合，致有爭論。爾時予曾語陳謂，無論副使公使何尊榮，皆不在予心目中。予已預備隨時辭職，以便足下獨斷獨行。斯言也，亦足以表明予之心跡矣。」

予為此詳細之報告以覆總督，欲其知予之歷史及陳、吳二人之行為也。至於總督以何言告陳蘭彬，則非予所得知矣。第此後公使館及留學事務所兩處，表面上似覺暫時平靜，並無何等衝突。會有數學生程度已高，予意欲送其入陸海軍學校肄業，乃致書美國國務院，求其允准。美國國務院復書，則以極輕蔑之詞，簡單拒絕予請。其言曰：「此間無地可容中國學生也。」嗟夫，中國之見輕於美人，其由來也漸矣。先是有美國工黨首領某某二人，創議反對華工。太平洋沿海一帶人民咸受其煽惑，即美政府及行政各部亦在其催眠術中，而以美國國會為尤甚。當時有上議院議員名白倫（Blaine）者，最為興高采烈，首先創議反對華人。推白倫之心理，亦非與華人有深仇夙恨，不過其時腦中有欲作總統之妄想，遂假此題目以博譽於工黨，冀得太平洋沿海一帶之選舉票也。自有此議以來，美人種族之見日深，仇視華人之心亦日盛。不獨此次予之請求為其直捷拒絕，即從前 1868 年中政府與美政府所訂勃林加姆（Burlingame）條約亦無端遭其蹂躪，視如無物。此種完全違背公理之舉動，實為外交界從來所未有。而美國國會中人，乃不憚蔑視條約，以為區別種族之預備。故後來禁止華工之議案一經提出，即由國會通過，立見實行。予此次請求之被拒，乃蔑視中國之小焉者耳。

予之所請既被拒絕，遂以此事函告總督。迨接讀總督覆書，予即知留學事務所前途之無望矣。總督覆書，亦言美政府拒絕中國學生入陸海軍學校，實違背 1868 年之條約，惟亦無如之何云。自 1870 年至 1878 年，留學事務所已過之歷史，予已略述如前狀。而此致美政府請求學生入陸海軍學校之一函，亦即為予任學生監督最後所辦之公牘。1878 年以後，則予身之職務，乃專在公使館中矣。

予向美政府請求之事未成，總督意似不憚。吳監督子登聞之，遂又乘風興浪，思設法以破壞此留學事務所。顧吳一人之力猶有未逮，因暗中與陳蘭彬密商，設為種種讒言[1]，以極細微之事，造成一絕大文章，寄之北京。適此時反對黨中有一御史，因美國華工禁約之舉，遂乘機上一封奏，請即解散留學事務所，撤回留學生，以報復美人之惡感。政府閱之，亦未敢貿然准其所

1　編者按，即不實之言。

奏，乃以此事質之總督李文忠、公使陳蘭彬與監督吳子登三人，詢其意見。李文忠此時不願為學生援手，即順反對黨之意而贊成其議。陳蘭彬因曾任留學生監督，此中真象理應洞徹，故政府亦垂詢及之。陳乃以極圓滑之詞答政府，謂學生居美已久，在理亦當召回。其措詞之妙，可謂至極。吳子登則更無猶豫之詞，直捷痛快以告政府，謂此等學生當立即撤回，歸國後並須交地方官嚴加管束云。此三人各陳所見，初無一語詢予。予於此事，已無發言之權。蓋彼等咸疑予懷私見，即有所言，亦不足信也。留學事務所之運命，於是告終，更無術可以輓回矣。此百二十名之學生，遂皆於 1881 年淒然返國。

美國人中，理想高尚、熱心教育、關懷於東西人種之進步者，正復不少。其對於中國解散留學事務所召回留學生之舉動，未嘗不竭全力以爭之，爰即聯名上書於總理衙門（即外務部）反對此事，惟措詞極其和平，態度始終鎮靜耳。其中主張最力者，為予畢生之良友吐依曲爾（Twitchell）君及藍恩（Lane）君。賴彼二人提倡，聯絡多數之大教育家及大學校校長，簽名書中，思有以阻止中國為此退化之事。此書為耶路大學校長樸德（President Porter）手筆，雖後來未獲收效，顧其詞嚴義正、磊落光明，誠不愧為文明人口吻。爰錄其文如下：

　　總理衙門（即外務部）鑒：予等與貴國留美學生之關係，或師或友，或則為其保人。今聞其將被召回國，且聞貴國政府即欲解散留學事務所，予等咸規規自失，且為貴國憂之。今請以某等觀察所及，及得之外界評論者，為貴衙門一陳之。貴國派遣之青年學生，自抵美以來，人人能善用其光陰，以研究學術。以故於各種科學之進步，成績極佳。即文學、品行、技術，以及平日與美人往來一切之交際，亦咸能令人滿意無間言。論其道德，尤無一人不優美高尚。其禮貌之周至、持躬之謙抑，尤為外人所樂道。職是之故，貴國學生無論在校內肄業，或赴鄉村遊歷，所至之處，咸受美人之歡迎，而引為良友。凡此諸生言行之盡善美，實不愧為大國國民之代表，足為貴國增榮譽也。蓋諸生年雖幼稚，然已能知彼等在美國之一舉一動，皆與祖國國家之名譽極有關係，故能謹言慎行，過於成人。學生既有此良好之行為，遂亦收良好之效果。美國少數無識之人，其平日對於貴國人之偏見，至此逐漸消滅。而美國國人對華之感情，已日趨於歡洽之地位。今乃忽有召令回國之舉，不亦重可惜耶？夫在學生方面，今日正為最關重要時期。曩之所受者，猶不過為預備教育，今則將進而求問之精華矣。譬之於物，學生猶樹也，教育學生之人猶農也。農人之辛勤灌溉，胼手胝足，固將以求後日之收穫。今學生如樹木之久受灌溉培養，發芽滋長，行且開花結果矣，顧欲摧殘於一旦而盡棄前功耶？至某等授予貴國學生之學問，與授予敝國學生者不少異，絕無歧視之心。某等因身為師保，故常請貴國所派之監督或其代表來校參觀，使其恍然於某等教授中國學生之方法。惜貴國所派之監督輕視其事，每遇此種邀請，或不親臨，或竟無代表派來也。貴衙門須知此等學生，乃當日由貴政府請求美國國務卿，特別咨送至予等校中，欲其學習美國之語言、文字、學術、技藝，以及善良之禮俗，以冀將來有益於祖國。今學生於科學、文藝等，皆未受有完全教育，是所學未成，予等對於貴國之責任，猶未盡也。乃貴政府不加詳細調查，亦無正式照會，遽由予等校中召之返國。此等舉動，於貴國國體，無乃有虧乎？某等對於貴國，固深望其日躋富強。即美國國人平日待遇貴國學生，亦未嘗失禮。貴政府乃出此種態度以為酬報，揆之情理，亦當有所不安。至於他人之造搖誣衊，謂中國學生在校中肄業，未得其益反受其損等言，此則某等絕對不能承認。何也？苟所謂無益有損者，指其荒蕪中學而言，則某等固不任咎。以某等對於此事，從未負絲毫職務也。況貴政府當日派送學生來美時，原期某得受美國教育，豈欲其緣木求魚，至美國以習中學？今某等所希望之教育雖未告成，然已大有機會，可竟全功。當此事業未竟、功過未定之日，乃預作種種謠言以為誣衊，是亦某等所不樂聞也。某等因對於素所敬愛之貴國學生，見其忽受此極大之損失，既不能不代為戚戚；且敝國無端蒙此教育不良之惡名，遂使美利堅大國之名譽亦受莫大之影響，此某等所以不能安緘默也。願貴衙門三復此言，於未解散留學事務所之前，簡派誠實可恃、聲望素著之人，將此關於學生智育德育上誣衊之言，更從實地調查，以期水落石出，則幸甚幸甚！

第二十章
北京之行與悼亡

　　學生既被召回國，以中國官場之待遇，代在美時學校生活，腦中驟感變遷，不堪回首可知。以故人人心中咸謂東西文化，判若天淵，而於中國根本上之改革，認為不容稍緩之事。此種觀念，深入腦筋，無論身經若何變遷，皆不能或忘也。今此百十名學生，強半列身顯要，名重一時。而今日政府，似亦稍稍醒悟，悔昔日解散留學事務所之非計，此則余所用以自慰者。自中日、日俄兩次戰爭，中國學生陸續至美留學者，已達數百人。是 1870 年曾文正所植桃李，雖經蹂躪，不啻閱二十五年而枯株復生也。

　　當諸學生撤回未久，予亦出使任滿，去美返國。時陳蘭彬已先予一年歸。故事，凡外交官任滿歸國，必向政府報告一次，謂之銷差。予亦循例入都，道出天津，謁直督李文忠。談次及撤回留學生事，文忠忽轉詰予曰：「汝何亦任學生歸國乎？」予聞言，莫知其命意所在，答曰：「此事乃由公使陳蘭彬奉上諭而行，鄙意以為總督及陳蘭彬與吳子登，皆贊成此舉也。予縱欲輓回此事，亦何能為役？且違抗諭旨，則人且目為叛逆，捕而戮之。」文忠曰：「否，予當日亦甚願學生勿歸，仍留美以求學，故頗屬望於汝，謂汝當能阻止學生勿使歸也。」予曰：「當日此舉，總督既未有反對之表示，身居四萬五千里外，安能遙度總督心事？設總督能以一函示予，令勿解散，自當謹遵意旨，惜當日未奉此訓示耳。」文忠怒形如色，忿然曰：「予已知此事之戎首為誰矣。」於是吳子登亦自京來津，約予往晤，以理不可卻，訪之。吳語予，渠在北京，京人士遇之極冷淡；此次謁李文忠，不知何故逢怒，命此後勿再來見，甚怪事也。予察吳狀，似甚狼狽。此為予與彼末次晤談。嗣後此人銷聲匿跡，不復相聞問矣。

既抵京，循例謁政府中各重要人物，如恭親王、慶親王及六部尚書等，耗時幾一月，乃得盡謁諸大老。北京地方遼闊，各達官所居，相去窵遠。往來代步惟騾車，既重且笨。車中坐處，狀類衣箱，其底即輪軸。輪與箱間無彈簧，故行時震動極烈，行亦甚緩。街衢復不平，車轍深至數寸。行路之難，可想而知。道中濁塵撲衣，穢氣刺鼻。漫空漲天者，初非泥砂，乃騾馬糞為車輪馬蹄搗研而成細末，陳陳相因，變為黑色，似塵土也。飛入耳鼻毛孔中，一時不易擦淨。行人皆戴眼紗，頭及兩手，亦有風帽手套等物，以為抵御。水含鹽質，洗濯尤不易去穢。不圖首善之區，而令人難堪如此。

予居京三月，頗欲設法禁止鴉片之輸入，滅絕中國境內之罌粟。乃上條陳於政府，請其採擇施行。旋總理衙門大臣王文韶告予，謂目前殊乏辦理此事之人材，故一時未能實行。於是予此計劃，束之高閣者垂二十五年。直至近數年來，始見此問題於萬國公會中提出討論焉。

1882 年，去京赴滬，居滬者四閱月。得予妻自美來書，謂攖病甚劇，乃急歸視。翌年春間抵美，則病者垂危，喉音盡失。予於途次，頗慮不及面。今猶未為失望，不得謂非上帝厚余。一月後，竟得轉機，尤幸之幸者。予妻體素荏弱，又因予常漫遊，慮或遇不測，恆抑抑不歡。余歸國時，適有美教士某君告予妻曰：「容君此行，殊為冒險，恐中政府或以留學事務所事，置之於法。」女子善懷，聞此不殊青天之霹靂，所以病也。予之返中國，可一年有半。婦已積思成痗，令人增忼儷之好。1883 年之夏，婦病良已，至諾福克 (Norfolk) 避暑，歸時漸復舊狀。醫謂宜遷地調養，庶不復病。因於冬間卜居中於南部喬治亞省之亞特蘭德 (Atlanta, Ga.)，又曾移居紐約省之亞特朗德 (Adirondaks, NY)。但此遷徙之調養，功效亦僅。居亞特朗德久之，1885 年冬，復病胃，飲食銳減，復思遷居他處。予重違其意，乃徙於紐求才省之色末維爾 (Summerville, NJ.)，不幸又感寒疾。居色末維爾約兩月，仍返舊居。1886 年 6 月 28 日，予遂賦哀弦矣。於亞特朗德西帶山公塚 (Cedar Hill Cemetery) 間購地葬之。中年哀樂，人所難堪，吾則尤甚。今老矣，以吾妻留有二子，差幸鰥而非獨。然對子思其母，輒復悽咽。吾二子皆能養志，品行亦佳，無忝耶教人格，此則余引以自慰者。

　　自 1880 年至 1886 年，為餘生最不幸時期。畢生志願，既橫被摧殘（指教育計劃），同命之人，復無端夭折，頓覺心灰，無復生趣。兩兒失母時，一才七齡，一才九齡。計嗣後十年，以嚴父而兼慈母，心力俱付劬勞鞠育之中。予外姑開洛克夫人，助予理家政、撫幼子者凡二年。最難堪之際，賴能勉強支持焉。

第二十一章
末次之歸國

　　1894 年，中日因朝鮮問題，遽起釁端。予頗不值日本，非以祖國之故有所偏袒，其實曲在彼也。日人亦非不自知，特欲借此興戎，以顯其海陸軍能力耳。戰事既開幕，予之愛國心油然而生，乃連發兩書，寄予友蔡錫勇君，蔡君前在公使館為予之通譯兼參贊者也。每書皆有條陳，規劃戰事，可使中國與日本繼續戰爭，直至無窮期而力不竟竭。

　　第一策，勸中國速向英倫商借一千五百萬圓，以購已成鐵甲三、四艘，僱用外兵五千人，由太平洋抄襲日本之後，使之首尾不能相顧。則日本在朝鮮之兵力，必以分而弱。中國乃可乘此暇隙，急練新軍，海陸並進，以敵日本。第二策與第一策同時並行，一面由中政府派員將台灣全島，抵押於歐西無論何強國，借款四萬萬美金，以為全國海陸軍繼續戰爭之軍費。時蔡為湖廣總督張文襄（之洞）幕府，得書後以予策譯為漢文，上之張督。此 1894 年冬間事也。予初不意張督竟贊成予之第一策，立電來美，派予速赴倫敦借款一千五百萬圓。此時駐倫敦之中國公使，為李文忠屬下之人。彼已先知予來英倫所任之事，故予亦無需另備特別公文，有事即可逕往謁公使。予抵倫敦不及一月，籌商借款已就緒，惟擔保品尚未指定。予乃托公使轉電政府，請以關稅為抵押。不意總稅務司赫德及直督李文忠不允所請，以為日本此時方要求一極大賠款，此關稅指為日本賠款之抵押品，尤且虞其不足云。實則此亦遁辭耳。蓋李文忠素與張文襄意見不合，戰事起後張、李二人尤時有爭議。張對於李所提議之和約，極端反對。然李方得慈禧太后寵，內有大援，故竭力主張和議。赫德之依附中央政府，又為必然之趨勢。於是張督擬借款一千五百萬之議，乃置諸不聞不問之列，此大借款遂以無成。而予之為經手人者，乃處於進退維谷之地位。倫敦承商借款之銀行團，幾欲以此事控予於法庭也。

予以借款無成歸紐約，乃電致張督，請其指示此後進行方針。張復電亦無他語，但速予立歸中國。予之去中國，十三年於茲矣。當 1883 年歸美時，自分此身與中國政府，已永遠脫離關係。詎知事竟不然，至今日而猶有欲招予歸國也。但此次招予之人，乃與予素未謀面。其人之學問、品行、政見若何，予除一、二得之傳聞者外，實毫無所知，而彼轉似能深知予者。蓋張已上奏清廷，召予歸國，奏中褒譽，至無以復加。余因思歸中國一探真相，果有機會能容予再作一番事業與否？惟予前在中國時，本屬於李文忠門下，今茲則將入文襄幕府，適處於與李反對地位矣。未首途之前，予所不能不注意者，即對於予之二子，必先為佈置妥貼，使得受良好教育。因托予妻兄開洛克博士 (Dr. Kellogg) 為二子之保護人。長子觀彤，此時已入耶路大學雪費爾專門學院 (Shefield Scientific School)，年齒較長，力足自顧。幼子觀槐，尚在哈特福德中學 (Hartford High School) 預備。予深慮其廢學，乃商之予友吐依曲爾夫婦 (Rev. and Mrs. Twitchwell)，令觀槐寄宿其家。吐依曲爾故一國之善士，學行俱優。彼視余子猶子，而余子得親炙其家庭教育，亦幸事也。屏當既竟，即航海歸國。

1895 年初夏抵上海，購中國官場禮服，耗費不貲。時文襄已由湖廣調署兩江，故予逕至南京，往總督署謁之。憶予於 1863 年，第一次見曾文正於安慶，覺文正之為人，具有一種無形之磁力，能吸引吾人，使心悅誠服。今見張督，則殊無此種吸力。張之為人，目空一世，而又有傲惰不振之態。談次，於一千五百萬借款之決裂，偶一及之即輕輕略過，亦不告予政府不允之故。但予於此中真象，早已了然。蓋張、李既冰炭，而李在北京政府中之勢力，遠勝於張。故張所主張借款之策，政府竟不採納。張自不樂自言其失敗，故僅以官話了事。次乃及李文忠，張斥其為貪鄙庸懦之匹夫，謂李水陸兩戰皆大失敗，坐是革職，幾不能自保其首領。中國因李一人，乃受此最可恥辱之挫敗，言次若有餘恨者。旋詢予中國新敗，當用何策補救？予謂中國不欲富強則已，苟其欲之，則非行一完全之新政策，決不能恢復其原有之榮譽。所謂新政策，政府至少須聘外人四員，以為外交、財政、海軍、陸軍四部之顧問，與之訂立十年合同。十年後若有成效，則更繼續聘請。惟所聘之顧問，必須有真確之經驗、高深之學識、純潔之品行而後可。既聘之後，其所陳之嘉言良策，政府當誠意採納，見諸實行。此外更派青年有才學之中國學生，處於各顧問之下，以資練習。如是行之數年，則中國行政各機關，不難依歐西之成規，從新組織也。以上所言，乃予對張督所發表之意見。顧張聞予言，始終未置可否，亦不發表其意見，默然靜坐，有如已乾之海綿，只能吸水入內而不復外吐也者。故此次之談話，較前與曾文正之晤談，乃大異其趣。曾文正之招予，將任予以何職，胸中已有成竹。其見予也，不過示予以進行之方針耳。張則對於中國全局，既無一定之宗旨，亦無方針之可言。而於予所獻之計劃，則又嫌其太新太激烈。不知予此次之回國，因恨中國之敗，慨然作積極進行之想，故所言如此。且捨此計劃，實無救亡之良策，不能以激烈為予咎也。張而果如曾文正之磊落光明，則一時縱不能實行予言，正不妨略以數語為鼓勵，使予知其人有舉行新政之決心。予之計劃，目前雖不能實施，而對於將來，尚有一線之希望也。乃張則不獨無此言語，且無如是之思想。於是予與張之交際，以此處為起點，亦即以此處為終點，此後更無機會再見其人。張之電招予歸國，僅於其未歸武昌之前，派予一江南交涉委員差使，聊以敷衍予遠來之意。迨後劉忠誠（坤一）實授兩江總督抵任後，張仍回武昌原任，去時亦未招予同行。可知張之意見，與予不合，故不欲予之臂助。雖不明言，而其心已昭然若揭矣。在予方面，此次歸國，既非謀升官發財而來，則亦何樂與之周旋，以仰其鼻息。予居劉坤一屬下，任交涉委員，亦不過三月之久，旋即自行辭職。在中國官場中，必謂予此舉為不敬上官，予則不暇計及矣。此三月內，每月領薪百五十圓，而無一事可為，不啻一掛名差使。此即予居張、劉兩督屬下之短期經驗也。

　　1896 年，予與江南政界斷絕關係，遂至上海。於時脫然無累，頗得自由。已而予又得一策，擬遊説中央政府，於北京設立一國家銀行。因欲為此條陳之預備，乃先將國家銀行律及其他有關係之法律，由 1875 年美國訂正之法律中譯為漢文。並聘一中國文士，助予合譯。而當時助予者有黃君開甲。黃曾出洋留學，曾為政府任以聖魯易 (St. Louis) 博覽會之副監督者也。予之譯事既畢，乃懷譯本入京，並攜一中國書記同行。至京，遇予之舊友張蔭桓君。其人即於 1884 至 1888 年，在華盛頓任中國公使者。張因邀予寓其家，寄榻於此凡數月。此時張蔭桓身兼二職，一為總理衙門（即外交部）大臣，一為戶部（後改度支部）左侍郎。而戶部尚書則為翁同龢，光緒帝之師傅也。張見予之國家銀行計劃，極為注意。將予譯本詳細參閱，加以評斷。謂其中有若干條，不合於中國國情，難期實行，但擇其最緊要而切實可行者，列入足矣。予如其教，斟酌損益後，乃上之戶部尚書翁同龢。翁與張意見相同，亦甚以為然，遂以遍示部中同僚，徵求意見。數星期後，部中重要之數大員，咸來予寓，對於予之條陳，讚賞不置，謂此事即當奏之清廷云。不數日，遂以予之國家銀行計劃，擬成奏折，由張蔭桓署名，翁同龢則從中贊助焉。

今試述予之計劃：予以為欲立國家銀行之基礎，必由政府預籌一千萬兩之資本，以為開辦費。中以二百萬兩購置各種機器，以鼓鑄銀幣、印刷國債券及一切鈔票，以二百萬兩為購地建屋之用。所餘六百萬兩存貯庫中，以備購金、銀、銅三者，將來鑄成各泉幣，以流通全國。此一千萬兩，祇足供國家銀行第一年之開辦費。將來中國商業發達，則國家銀行亦當隨商業發達之比例，而逐年增加其資本。此其大略也。

此事既有端緒，旋即着手進行，派委員，購地址。予則受戶部之委任，將赴美國，向美國財政部商酌此事，並調查設立國家銀行最良之方法。戶部奏折，亦邀清廷批准。部署粗定，乃忽橫生枝節，有為張蔭桓及發起諸人意料所不及者。先是有中國電報局總辦兼上海招商局總辦盛宣懷[1]其人者，與翁同龢交頗深。此時忽由上海來電，囑翁同龢暫緩此舉，俟兩星期彼抵京

1　編者按，名字據英文版補入。

後，再為區處。翁得電，遽允其請，而垂成之局，乃從此破壞矣。蓋盛道台之名，中國無人不知其為鉅富，家資累萬。無論何種大實業，盛必染指。盛雖身居上海，而北京為之耳目者極多，京中一舉一動，無不知之。北京有勢力之王公大臣，亦無不與結納。即慈禧太后最寵幸之太監李蓮英，盛亦交結其人。以故盛之勢力，在政界中卓卓有聲。此次銀行計劃，遂亦為盛之賄賂所破壞。有人謂盛宣懷此次來京，輦金三十萬兩，賄買二、三親貴及政府中重大人物，以阻撓其事。於是籌備設立國家銀行之一千萬兩現銀，遂為盛一人攫去，以營其私業云。

究國家銀行計劃失敗之原因，亦不外夫中國行政機關之腐敗而已。尊自太后，賤及吏胥，自上至下，無一不以賄賂造成。賄賂之為物，予直欲目之為螺釘，一經鑽入，即無堅不破也。簡言之，吾人之在中國，只需有神通廣大之金錢，即無事不可達其目的。事事物物，無非拍賣品，孰以重價購者孰得之。自中日、日俄兩次戰爭之後，東方空氣，乃略為之掃蕩清潔。中國人對於國家腐敗之情形，始稍稍有所覺悟也。

予之國家銀行計劃，既為盛宣懷所破壞，乃另改方針，擬向政府請求一築造鐵路之特權。予心中所欲造之鐵路，為由天津直達鎮江。天津居北，鎮江居南，在揚子江口。兩地相距，以直線計，不過五百英里。若繞山東，過黃河，經安徽，以達湖南，則此路須延長至七百英里。予所規劃之路線，則擬取其近者。惟德國政府抗議，不允有他線經過山東。謂山東造路之權，為德人所專有，無論何人，不能在山東另造鐵路云。此種理由，殊為奇特。任翻遍中國法律或國際法律，皆不能得其根據之所在。但彼時中國國勢屢弱，不能提出此問題，以爭回固有之主權。而外交部中，亦無人能引證條文，駁斥德國要求之無理，深恐惹起國際交涉，一惟外人之命是聽。以故政府只許予造一曲折之鐵路，即上所云山東過黃河者。予以極力欲成此事，遂擬以此鐵路讓與外國公司承造。乃政府又命予必招中國資本，不許外人入股，且僅限予六月之期。六月之內，若不能招齊路股者，則將特許狀取消。當彼時中國資本家，欲其出資任股以興造鐵路，殆難如登天。予既明知此事勢有所不能，遂不得已，復將此鐵路計劃捨去。予之種種政策，既皆無效。於是予救助中國之心，遂亦至此而止矣。

　　一年前予在北京時，常遇康有為、梁啟超二人。當予籌劃銀行、鐵路等策時，絕不意康、梁等亦正在籌劃維新事業也。康、梁等計劃進行之極點，即為後來之戊戌政變。其詳俟下章言之。

第二十二章
戊戌政變

　　1898 年 9 月之政變，乃清史中一極可紀念之事。因此事光緒帝幾被廢，所有皇帝之權力，盡為慈禧太后所奪，而己則幾成一國事犯，慈禧直以奸細目之。溯光緒即位之初，年才五齡，雖名為繼承大位，實則執航者仍慈禧耳。直至光緒婚禮後，乃將朝政交還。顧光緒雖親政，而慈禧如電之眼光，仍無時不鑒臨，以為監督。皇帝之一舉一動，莫不特別留意。總之慈禧之對於光緒，始終不懷善念。蓋慈禧當同治在位時（1864 年）曾垂簾聽政，故引起其好攬大權之野心。此念一起，不復能制。自是以後，遂無時不思竊取威權，絕不願安居深宮，百不聞問也。光緒當親政後，頗思革新庶政，其一種勵精圖治之決心，足使京內外人士注意，如北斗之見於天空，人人咸為引領。惟慈禧之眼光，則為嫉妒心所蔽，乃視光緒之舉動，大不以為然。甚且目之為癡人或狂夫，謂宜幽之冷宮，加以嚴酷之約束。平心論之，光緒實非癡，尤非狂。後人之讀清史者，必將許其為愛國之君，且為愛國之維新黨。其聰明睿智、洞悉治理，實為中國自古迄今未有之賢主也。天之誕生光緒於中國，殆特命之為中國革新之先導，故其舉措迥異常人，洵偉人也。

　　中國政治上當存亡危急之秋，適維新潮流澎湃而來，侵入北京。光緒帝受此奇異勢力之激動，遂奮起提倡維新之事業。全世界人見此，莫不驚奇，以為得未曾有。予覯此狀，乃決意留居北京，以覘其究竟。予之寓所，一時幾變為維新黨領袖之會議場。迨 1898 年秋，遂有政變之事。因此變局，光緒被廢，多數維新黨之領袖，皆被清廷捕殺。予以素表同情於維新黨，寓所以有會議場之目，故亦犯隱匿黨人之嫌，不得不遷徙以逃生。乃出北京，赴上海，託跡租界中，即在上海組織一會，名曰「中國強學會」，以討論關於維新事業及一切重要問題為宗旨，予竟被選為第一任會長。1899年，有人勸予，謂上海租界亦非樂土，不如遷地為良。予乃再遷至香港，請英人保護。居香港者二年，後遂歸美國。歸時幼子覲槐正畢業於耶路大學，予適見其行畢業禮也。

1901年春，予至台灣遊歷，謁見台灣總督兒玉子爵。子爵蓋於日俄戰爭時，曾為大山大將之參謀長者也。予晤子爵時，因子爵不諳英語，而予又未習日文，乃倩舌人以翻譯。子爵曰：「久仰大名，以數聞時人盛道君之事業，深以不得把晤為憾。今日識荊，異常欣幸。第惜初次晤面，即有一極惡之消息報君，茲抱歉也。」予聞而大異，急欲知彼所謂惡消息，究為何事。子爵答曰：「中國閩浙總督方有公文來，囑予留意，謂君設來此者，即倩予捕君送之中政府也。」子爵言時，意頗鎮定，無倉皇狀，面且有笑容。此惡消息雖出予意料之外，然予初不以是之故驚惶失措，亦以從容鎮定之態，答子爵曰：「予今在閣下完全治權之下，故無論何時，閣下可從心所欲，捕予送之中政府。予亦甚願為中國而死，死固得其所也。」子爵聞言，莊重而對曰：「容先生幸毋以予為中國警吏。君今請安居於此，慎無過慮。予決不能聽君往中國就戮也。第尚有他事，欲求教於君，不識君肯指示否？」予詢以何事，子爵即出一中國報紙，指示予曰：「此條陳果為何人所獻者？」予見此亦不假思索，立應曰：「是予所為也。」且語且以右拍胸，自示承認之堅。在旁諸人，睹予此狀，咸極注意。並有日本軍官數人在側，頗為予言所動。予又續言曰：「報紙所載，尚略有錯誤。君若見允者，予請得為更正之：報紙所云之數目為八萬萬，予當日所提議則四萬萬也。（按四萬萬美金，約合墨銀八萬萬圓。報紙所載之數，或照墨銀計處耳。）」子爵見予慷慨自承，且更正數目之誤，轉笑容可掬，異常愉快。蓋子爵示予報中所載，乃1894、1895兩年間，予所上於張之洞之條陳，請張轉奏清廷者也。時在李文忠於對馬島簽和約之前半年，予上此條陳，請政府將台灣全島為抵押品，向歐洲與中國通商之國，借款四萬萬金圓，以九十九年為期。用此借款，中國仍可招練海陸新軍，以與日人繼續爭戰。此議雖未實行，而一經報紙揭載，幾於舉國皆知，子爵亦不知於何處得此報紙。予甫至台灣，即遇此質問，亦可異也。予以有道德上威武不屈之氣，故敢於子爵前直承不諱，並更正報紙誤點，更告之曰：「設將來中國再有類似於此之事實發生，予仍當抱定此宗旨，上類似於此之條陳於中政府，以與日本抵抗也。」

此次予與日本台灣總督之談話，實為予一生最可紀念之事。予初聞子爵告予惡消息，以為此日本台灣總督者，必將予交付中政府，予之生命，且喪於其手。迨見其滿面笑容，予已知此身所處之地位，安如泰山。於是膽乃益壯，即對日人而談日本之事，亦毫無顧忌。以予之心地光明，胸無宿物，乃極荷子爵之激賞。子爵自謂不久將升遷歸日，欲邀予偕行，謂將介紹予以覲明治天皇，並結識彼國中重要人物。予此時適患氣喘之疾甚劇，不宜於旅行，因掬誠謝之。謂得此寵招，深為榮幸，惜病軀不堪旅行之苦，致力於願違，辜負盛意也。言畢，遂興辭而出。出時子爵復告予曰：「君之身命，今甚危險。惟若居台灣，在予治權之下，予必極力保護，當派護兵為君防衞，不致有意外之變云。」明日果有護兵四人來，夜間在予寓之四圍巡邏。日間逢予外出，無論何時，此四護兵必隨行。二居予前，二居予後，加意防護。予居台灣數日，承日人如是待遇，意良可感。迨後予自台灣首途赴香港，乃親往子爵處，而謝其隆情焉。

MY LIFE IN CHINA AND AMERICA

BY

YUNG WING

PREFACE

The first five chapters of this book give an account of my early education, previous to going to America, where it was continued, first at Monson Academy, in Monson, Massachusetts, and later, at Yale College.

The sixth chapter begins with my reëntrance into the Chinese world, after an absence of eight years. Would it not be strange, if an Occidental education, continually exemplified by an Occidental civilization, had not wrought upon an Oriental such a metamorphosis in his inward nature as to make him feel and act as though he were a being coming from a different world, when he confronted one so diametrically different? This was precisely my case, and yet neither my patriotism nor the love of my fellow-countrymen had been weakened. On the contrary, they had increased in strength from sympathy. Hence, the succeeding chapters of my book will be found to be devoted to the working out of my educational scheme, as an expression of my undying love for China, and as the most feasible method to my mind, of reformation and regeneration for her.

With the sudden ending of the Educational Commission, and the recall of the one hundred and twenty students who formed the vanguard of the pioneers of modern education in China, my educational work was brought to a close.

Of the survivors of these students of 1872, a few by dint of hard, persistent industry, have at last come forth to stand in the front ranks of the leading statesmen of China, and it is through them that the original Chinese Educational Commission has been revived, though in a modified form, so that now, Chinese students are seen flocking to America and Europe from even the distant shores of Sinim for a scientific education.

November,1909
16 Atwood St., Hartford, Conn.

CONTENTS

Chapter 1
Boyhood

I was born on the 17th of November, 1828, in the village of Nam Ping (South Screen) which is about four miles southwest of the Portuguese Colony of Macao, and is situated on Pedro Island lying west of Macao, from which it is separated by a channel of half a mile wide.

I was one of a family of four children. A brother was the eldest, a sister came next, I was the third, and another brother was the fourth and the youngest of the group. I am the only survivor of them all.

As early as 1834, an English lady, Mrs. Gutzlaff, wife of the Rev. Charles Gutzlaff, a missionary to China, came to Macao and, under the auspices of the Ladies' Association in London for the promotion of female education in India and the East, immediately took up the work of her mission by starting a girls' school for Chinese girls, which was soon followed by the opening of a school for boys also.

Mrs. Gutzlaff's comprador or factotum happened to come from the village I did and was, in fact, my father's friend and neighbor. It was through him that my parents heard about Mrs. Gutzlaff's school and it was doubtless through his influence and means that my father got me admitted into the school. It has always been a mystery to me why my parents should take it into their heads to put me into a foreign school, instead of a regular orthodox Confucian school, where my brother much older than myself was placed. Most assuredly such a step would have been more in play with Chinese public sentiment, taste, and the wants of the country at large, than to allow me to attend an English school; moreover, a Chinese cult is the only avenue in China that leads to political preferment, influence, power and wealth. I can only account for the departure thus taken on the theory that as foreign intercourse with China was just beginning to grow, my parents, anticipating that it might soon assume the proportions of a tidal wave, thought it worth while to take time by the forelock and put one of their sons to learning English that he might become one of the advanced interpreters and have a more advantageous position from which to make his way into the business and diplomatic world. This

I take to be the chief aim that influenced my parents to put me into Mrs. Gutzlaff's Mission School. As to what other results or sequences it has eventually brought about in my subsequent life, they were entirely left to Him who has control of all our devising and planning, as they are governed by a complete system of divine laws of antecedents and consequents, or of cause and effect.

In 1835, when I was barely seven years of age, my father took me to Macao. Upon reaching the school, I was brought before Mrs. Gutzlaff. She was the first English lady I had ever seen. On my untutored and unsophisticated mind she made a deep impression. If my memory serves me right, she was somewhat tall and well-built. She had prominent features which were strong and assertive; her eyes were of clear blue lustre, somewhat deep set. She had thin lips, supported by a square chin, —— both indicative of firmness and authority. She had flaxen hair and eyebrows somewhat heavy. Her features taken collectively indicated great determination and will power.

As she came forward to welcome me in her long and full flowing white dress (the interview took place in the summer), surmounted by two large globe sleeves which were fashionable at the time and which lent her an exaggerated appearance, I remember most vividly I was no less puzzled than stunned. I actually trembled all over with fear at her imposing proportions —— having never in my life seen such a peculiar and odd fashion. I clung to my father in fear. Her kindly expression and sympathetic smiles found little appreciative response at the outset, as I stood half dazed at her personality and my new environment. For really, a new world had dawned on me. After a time, when my homesickness was over and the novelty of my surroundings began gradually to wear away, she completely won me over through her kindness and sympathy. I began to look upon her more like a mother. She seemed to take a special interest in me; I suppose, because I was young and helpless, and away from my parents, besides being the youngest pupil in the school. She kept me among her girl pupils and did not allow me to mingle with what few boys there were at the time.

There is one escapade that I can never forget! It happened during the first year in the school, and was an attempt on my part to run away. I was shut up in the third story of the house, which had a wide open terrace on the top, —— the only place where the girls and myself played and found recreation. We were not allowed to go out of doors to play in the streets. The boy pupils had their quarters on the ground floor and had full liberty to go out for exercise. I used to envy them their freedom and smuggled down stairs to mingle with them in their sports after school hours. I felt ill at ease to be shut up with the girls all alone way up in the third story. I wanted to see something of the outside world. I occasionally stole down stairs and ventured out to the wharves around which were clustered a number of small ferry boats which had a peculiar fascination to my young fancy. To gain my freedom, I planned to run away. The girls were all much older than I was, and a few sympathized with me in my wild scheme; doubtless, from the same restlessness of being too closely cooped up. I told them of my plan. Six of the older ones fell in with me in the idea. I was to slip out of the house alone, go down to the wharf and engage a covered boat to take us all in.

The next morning after our morning meal, and while Mrs. Gutzlaff was off taking her breakfast, we stole out unbeknown to any one and crowded into the boat and started off in hot haste for the opposite shore of Pedro Island. I was to take the whole party to my home and from there the girls were to disperse to their respective villages. We were half way across the channel when, to my great consternation, I saw a boat chasing us, making fast time and gaining on us all the while. No promise of additional pay was of any avail, because our two oars against their four made it impossible for us to win out; so our boatmen gave up the race at the waving of handkerchiefs in the other boat and the whole party was captured. Then came the punishment. We were marched through the whole school and placed in a row, standing on a long narrow school table placed at one end of the school room facing all the pupils in front of us. I was placed in the center of the row, with a tall foolscap mounted on my head, having three girls on the right and three on the left. I had pinned on my breast a large square placard bearing the inscription, "Head of the Runaways;" there we stood for a whole hour till school was dismissed. I never felt so humiliated in my life as I did when I was undergoing that ordeal. I felt completely crestfallen. Some of the mischievous fellows would extract a little fun out of this display by taking furtive glances and making wry faces at us. Mrs. Gutzlaff, in order to aggravate our punishment, had ordered ginger snaps and oranges to be distributed among the other pupils right before us.

Mrs. Gutzlaff's school, started in September, 1835, was originally for girls only. Pending the organization and opening of the so-called "Morrison Education Society School," in the interval between 1835 and 1839, a department for boys was temporarily incorporated into her school, and part of the subscription fund belonging to the M.E.S. School was devoted to the maintenance of this one.

This accounts for my entrance into Mrs. Gutzlaff's School, as one of only two boys first admitted. Her school being thus enlarged and modified temporarily, Mrs.

Gutzlaff's two nieces —— the Misses Parkes, sisters to Mr. Harry Parkes who was afterwards knighted, by reason of the conspicuous part he played in the second Opium War, in 1864[1], of which he was in fact the originator —— came out to China as assistants in the school. I was fortunately placed under their instruction for a short time.

Afterwards the boys' school under Mrs. Gutzlaff and her two nieces, the Misses Parkes, was broken up; that event parted our ways in life in divergent directions. Mrs. Gutzlaff went over to the United States with three blind girls, —— Laura, Lucy and Jessie. The Misses Parkes were married to missionaries, one to Dr. William Lockhart, a medical missionary; the other to a Rev. Mr. MacClatchy, also a missionary. They labored long in China, under the auspices of the London Missionary Society. The three blind girls whom Mrs. Gutzlaff took with her were taught by me to read on raised letters till they could read from the Bible and *Pilgrim's Progress*.

On my return to my home village I resumed my Chinese studies.

In the fall of 1840, while the Opium War was still going on, my father died, leaving four children on my mother's hands without means of support.

Fortunately, three of us were old enough to lend a helping hand. My brother was engaged in fishing, my sister helped in housework, and I took to hawking candy through my own village and the neighboring one. I took hold of the business in good earnest, rising at three o'clock every morning, and I did not come home until six o'clock in the evening. My daily earnings netted twenty-five cents, which I turned over to my mother, and with the help given by my brother, who was the main stay of the family, we managed to keep the wolf away from our door. I was engaged in hawking candy for about five months, and when winter was over, when no candy was made, I changed my occupation and went into the rice fields to glean rice after the reapers. My sister usually accompanied me in such excursions. But unlike Ruth of old, I had no Boaz to help me out when I was short in my gleaning. But my knowledge of English came to my rescue. My sister told the head reaper that I could speak, read and write English. This awakened the curiosity of the reaper. He beckoned me to him and asked me whether I wouldn't talk some "Red Hair Men" talk to him. He said he never heard of such talk in his life. I felt bashful and diffident at first, but my sister encouraged me and said "the reaper may give you a large bundle of rice sheaf to take home." This was said as a kind of prompter.

---

1   Incorrect year.

The reaper was shrewd enough to take it up, and told me that if I would talk, he would give me a bundle heavier than I could carry. So I began and repeated the alphabet to him. All the reapers as well as the gleaners stood in vacant silence, with mouths wide open, grinning with evident delight. A few minutes after my maiden speech was delivered in the paddy field with water and mud almost knee deep, I was rewarded with several sheaves, and I had to hurry away in order to get two other boys to carry what my sister and I could not lug. Thus I came home loaded with joy and sheaves of golden rice to my mother, little dreaming that my smattering knowledge of English would serve me such a turn so early in my career. I was then about twelve years old. Even Ruth with her six measures of corn did not fare any better than I did.

Soon after the gleaning days, all too few, were over, a neighbor of mine who was a printer in the printing office of a Roman Catholic priest happened to be home from Macao on a vacation. He spoke to my mother about the priest wanting to hire a boy in his office who knew enough English to read the numerals correctly, so as to be able to fold and prepare the papers for the binders. My mother said I could do the work. So I was introduced to the priest and a bargain was struck. I returned home to report myself, and a few days later I was in Macao and entered upon my duty as a folder on a salary of $4.50 a month. My board and lodging came to $1.50 —— the balance of $3.00 was punctually sent to my mother every month. I did not get rich quickly in this employment, for I had been there but four months when a call for me to quit work came from a quarter I least expected. It had more the sound of heaven in it. It came from a Dr. Benjamin Hobson, a medical missionary in Macao whose hospital was not more than a mile from the printer's office. He sent word that he wanted to see me; that he had been hunting for me for months. I knew Dr. Hobson well, for I saw him a number of times at Mrs. Gutzlaff's. So I called on him. At the outset, I thought he was going to take me in to make a doctor of me, but no, he said he had a promise to fulfill. Mrs. Gutzlaff's last message to him, before she embarked for America with the three blind girls, was to be sure to find out where I was and to put me into the Morrison Education Society School as soon as it was opened for pupils.

"This is what I wanted to see you for," said Dr. Hobson. "Before you leave your employment and after you get the consent of your mother to let you go to the Morrison School, I would like to have you come to the hospital and stay with me for a short time so that I may become better acquainted with you, before I take you to the Morrison School, which is already opened for pupils, and introduce you to the teacher."

At the end of the interview, I went home to see my mother who, after some reluctance, gave her consent. I returned to Macao, bade farewell to the priest who, though reticent and reserved, not having said a word to me during all the four months I was in his employ, yet did not find fault with me in my work. I went over to the hospital. Dr. Hobson immediately set me to work with the mortar and pestle, preparing materials for ointments and pills. I used to carry a tray and accompany him in his rounds to visit the patients, in the benevolent work of alleviating their pains and sufferings. I was with him about a couple of months in the hospital work, at the end of which time he took me one day and introduced me to the Rev. Samuel Robins Brown, the teacher of the Morrison Education Society School.

Chapter 2
School Days

The Morrison School was opened on the 1st of November, 1839, under the charge of the Rev. S. R. Brown who, with his wife, Mrs. Brown, landed at Macao on the 19th of February, 1839. Brown, who was afterwards made a D.D., was a graduate of Yale of the class of 1832. From his antecedents, he was eminently fitted to pioneer the first English school in China. I entered the school in 1841. I found that five other boys had entered ahead of me by one year. They were all studying primary arithmetic, geography, and reading. I had the start of them only in reading and pronouncing English well. We studied English in the forenoon, and Chinese in the afternoon. The names of the five boys were: 1. Wong Shing; 2. Li Kan; 3. Chow Wan; 4. Tong Chik; 5. Wong Foon. I made the sixth one and was the youngest of all. We formed the first class of the school, and became Brown's oldest pupils throughout, from first to last, till he left China in December, 1846, on account of poor health. Half of our original number accompanied him to this country, on his return.

The Morrison Education Society School came about in this way: Not long after the death of Dr. Robert Morrison, which occurred on the 1st of August, 1834, a circular was issued among the foreign residents on the 26th of January, 1835, calling for the formation of an Association to be named the "Morrison Education Society." Its object was to "improve and promote English education in China by schools and other means." It was called "Morrison" to commemorate the labors and works of that distinguished man who was sent out by the London Missionary Society as the first missionary to China in 1807. He crossed the Atlantic from London to New York where he embarked for China in the sailing vessel "Trident" on the 31st of January, 1807. He tried to land in Macao, but the jealousy of the Jesuits thwarted his purpose. He was obliged to go up to Canton. Finally, on account of the unsettled relations between the Chinese government and the foreign merchants there, he repaired to Malacca, and made that place the basis of his labors. He was the author of the first Anglo-Chinese dictionary, of three quarto volumes. He translated the Bible into Chinese; Leang Afah was his first Chinese convert and trained by him to preach. Leang afterwards became a powerful preacher. The importance and bearing of his dictionary and the translation of the Bible into Chinese, on subsequent missionary work in China, were fundamental and paramount. The preaching of his convert, Leang Afah, likewise contributed in no small degree towards opening up a new era in the religious life of China. His memory, therefore, is worthy of being kept alive by the establishment of a school named after him. Indeed, a university ought to have been permanently founded for that purpose instead of a school, whose existence was solely dependent upon the precarious and ephemeral subscriptions of transient foreign merchants in China.

At the close of the Opium War in 1840, and after the Island of Hong Kong had been ceded to the British government, the Morrison school was removed to Hong Kong in 1842. The site chosen for it was on the top of a hill about six hundred feet above the level of the sea. The hill is situated on the eastern end of Victoria Colony and was called "Morrison Hill" after the name of the school. It commands a fine view of the harbor, as that stretches from east to west. The harbor alone made Hong Kong the most coveted concession in Southern China. It is spacious and deep enough to hold the Navy of Great Britain, and it is that distinguishing feature and its strategic location that have made it what it is.

On the 12th of March, 1845, Mr. Wm. Allen Macy arrived in Hong Kong as an assistant teacher in the school. His arrival was timely, because the school, since its removal from Macao to Hong Kong, had been much enlarged. Three more classes of new pupils had been formed and the total number of pupils all told was more than forty. This was more than one man could manage. The assistant teacher was much needed. Brown continued his work in the school till the fall of 1846. Macy had a whole year in which to be broken into the work.

Between Brown and Macy there was a marked difference in temperament and character. Brown, on the one hand, showed evidences of a self-made man. He was cool in temperament, versatile in the adaptation of means to ends, gentlemanly and agreeable, and somewhat optimistic. He found no difficulty in endearing himself to his pupils, because he sympathized with them in their efforts to master their studies, and entered heart and soul into his work. He had an innate faculty of making things clear to the pupils and conveying to them his understanding of a subject without circumlocution, and with great directness and facility. This was owing in a great measure to his experience as a pedagogue, before coming out to China, and even before he entered college. He knew how to manage boys, because he knew boys' nature well, whether Chinese, Japanese or American. He impressed his pupils as being a fine teacher and one eminently fitted from inborn tact and temperament to be a successful school master, as he proved himself to be in his subsequent career in Auburn, N. Y., and in Japan.

Macy, the assistant teacher, was likewise a Yale man. He had never taught school before in his life, and had no occasion to do so. He possessed no previous experience to guide him in his new work of pedagogy in China. He was evidently well brought up and was a man of sensitive nature, and of fine moral sensibilities, —— a soul full of earnestness and lofty ideals.

After the Morrison School was broken up in 1850, he returned to this country with his mother and took up theology in the Yale Theological Seminary. In 1854, he went back to China as a missionary under the American Board. I had graduated from Yale College then and was returning to China with him. We were the only passengers in that long, wearisome and most trying passage of 154 days from Sandy Hook to Hong Kong.

Brown left China in the winter of 1846. Four months before he left, he one day sprang a surprise upon the whole school. He told of his contemplated return to America on account of his health and the health of his family. Before closing his remarks by telling us of his deep interest in the school, he said he would like to take a few of his old pupils home with him to finish their education in the United States, and that those who wished to accompany him would signify it by rising. This announcement, together with his decision to return to America, cast a deep gloom over the whole school. A dead silence came over all of us. And then for several days afterwards the burden of our conversation was about Brown's leaving the school for good. The only cheerful ones among us were those who had decided to accompany him home. These were Wong Shing, Wong Foon and myself. When he requested those who wished to accompany him to the States to signify it by rising, I was the first one on my feet. Wong Foon was the second, followed by Wong Shing. But before regarding our cases as permanently settled, we were told to go home and ask the consent of our respective parents. My mother gave her consent with great reluctance, but after my earnest persuasion she yielded, though not without tears and sorrow. I consoled her with the fact that she had two more sons besides myself, and a daughter to look after her comfort. Besides, she was going to have a daughter-in-law to take care of her, as my elder brother was engaged to be married.

It may not be out of place to say that if it had depended on our own resources, we never could have come to America to finish our education, for we were all poor. Doubtless Brown must have had the project well discussed among the trustees of the school months before he broached the subject to his pupils.

It was also through his influence that due provision was made for the support of our parents for at least two years, during our absence in America. Our patrons who bore all our expenses did not intend that we should stay in this country longer than two years. They treated us nobly. They did a great work for us. Among those who bore a conspicuous part in defraying our expenses while in America, besides providing for the support of our aged parents, I can recall the names of Andrew Shortrede, proprietor and editor of the *Hong Kong China Mail* (he was a Scotchman, an old bachelor, and a noble and handsome specimen of humanity), A. A. Ritchie, an American merchant, and A. A. Campbell, another Scotchman. There were others unknown to me. The Olyphant Sons, David, Talbot and Robert, three brothers, leading merchants of New York, gave us a free passage from Hong Kong to New York in their sailing vessel, the "Huntress," which brought a cargo of tea at the same time. Though late in the day for me to mention the names of these benefactors who from pure motives of Christian philanthropy aided me in my education, yet it may be a source of satisfaction to their descendants, if there are any living in different parts of the world, to know that their sires took a prominent part in the education of the three Chinese youths, —— Wong Shing, Wong Foon and myself.

Chapter 3
Journey to America and First Experiences There

Being thus generously provided for, we embarked at Whampoa on the 4th of January, 1847, in the good ship "Huntress" under Captain Gillespie. As stated above, she belonged to the Olyphant Brothers and was loaded with a full cargo of tea. We had the northeast trade wind in our favor, which blew strong and steady all the way from Whampoa to St. Helena. There was no accident of any kind, excepting a gale as we doubled the Cape of Good Hope. The tops of the masts and ends of the yards were tipped with balls of electricity. The strong wind was howling and whistling behind us like a host of invisible Furies. The night was pitch dark and the electric balls dancing on the tips of the yards and tops of the masts, back and forth and from side to side like so many infernal lanterns in the black night, presented a spectacle never to be forgotten by me. I realized no danger, although the ship pitched and groaned, but enjoyed the wild and weird scene hugely. After the Cape was doubled, our vessel ploughed through the comparatively smooth waters of the Atlantic until we reached the Island of St. Helena where we were obliged to stop for fresh water and provisions. Most sailing vessels that were bound from the East for the Atlantic board were accustomed to make St. Helena their stopping place. St. Helena, as viewed from the shipboard, presented an outward appearance of a barren volcanic rock, as though freshly emerged from the baptism of fire and brimstone. Not a blade of grass could be seen on its burnt and charred surface. We landed at Jamestown, which is a small village in the valley of the Island. In this valley there was rich and beautiful vegetation. We found among the sparse inhabitants a few Chinese who were brought there by the East India Company's ships. They were middle-aged people, and had their families there. While there, we went over to Longwood where was Napoleon's empty tomb. A large weeping willow hung and swept over it. We cut a few twigs, and kept them alive till we reached this country and they were brought to Auburn, N. Y., by Mr. Brown, who planted them near his residence when he was teaching in the Auburn Academy for several years before his departure for Japan. These willows proved to be fine, handsome trees when I visited Auburn in 1854.

From St. Helena we took a northwesterly course and struck the Gulf Stream, which, with the wind still fair and favorable, carried us to New York in a short time. We landed in New York on the 12th of April, 1847, after a passage of ninety-eight days of unprecedented fair weather. The New York of 1847 was altogether a different city from the New York of 1909. It was a city of only 250,000 or 300,000 inhabitants; now it is a metropolis rivaling London in population, wealth and commerce. The whole of Manhattan Island is turned into a city of skyscrapers, churches and palatial residences.

Little did I realize when in 1845 I wrote, while in the Morrison School, a composition on "An Imaginary Voyage to New York and up the Hudson", that I was to see New York in reality. This incident leads me to the reflection that sometimes our imagination foreshadows what lies uppermost in our minds and brings possibilities within the sphere of realities. The Chinese Education Scheme is another example of the realities that came out of my day dreams a year before I graduated. So was my marrying an American wife. Still there are other day dreams yet to be realized; whether or no they will ever come to pass the future will determine.

Our stay in New York was brief. The first friends we had the good fortune to make in the new world, were Prof. David E. Bartlett and his wife. He was a professor in the New York Asylum for the Deaf and Dumb, and was afterwards connected with a like institution in Hartford. The Professor died in 1879. His wife, Mrs. Fanny P. Bartlett, survived him for nearly thirty years and passed away in the spring of 1907. She was a woman highly respected and beloved for her high Christian character and unceasing activities for good in the community in which she lived. Her influence was even extended to China by the few students who happened to enjoy her care and instruction. I count her as one of my most valued friends in America.

From New York we proceeded by boat to New Haven where we had an opportunity to see Yale College and were introduced to President Day. I had not then the remotest idea of becoming a graduate of one of the finest colleges of the country, as I did a few years afterwards. We went by rail from New Haven to Warehouse Point and from there to East Windsor, the home of Mrs. Elizabeth Brown, wife of Dr. Brown. Her parents were then living. Her father, the Rev. Shubael Bartlett, was the pastor of the East Windsor Congregational Church. I well remember the first Sabbath we attended his church. We three Chinese boys sat in the pastor's pew which was on the left of the pulpit, having a side view of the minister, but in full view of the whole congregation. We were the cynosure of the whole church. I doubt whether much attention was paid to the sermon that day.

The Rev. Shubael Bartlett was a genuine type of the old New England Puritan. He was exact and precise in all his manners and ways. He spoke in a deliberate and solemn tone, but full of sincerity and earnestness. He conducted himself as though he was treading on thin ice, cautiously and circumspectly. One would suppose from his appearance that he was austere and exacting, but he was gentle and thoughtful. He would have his family Bible and hymn book placed one on top of the other, squared and in straight lines, on the same spot on the table every morning for morning prayers. He always sat in the same spot for morning prayers. In other words, you always knew where to find him. His habits and daily life were as regular as clock work. I never heard him crack a joke or burst out in open laughter.

Mrs. Bartlett, Mrs. Brown's mother, was of a different makeup. She was always cheerful. A smile lighted up her features nearly all the time and for everyone she had a kind and cheerful word, while the sweet tone of her voice always carried with it cheerfulness and good will. Her genial temperament and her hospitality made the parsonage a favorite resort to all the friends and relatives of the family, who were quite numerous. It was always a puzzle to me how the old lady managed to make ends meet when her husband's salary was not over $400 a year. To be sure, the farm annually realized something, but Daniel, the youngest son, who was the staff of the old couple, had to work hard to keep up the prestige of the parsonage. It was in this parsonage that I found a temporary home while at school in Monson, and also in Yale.

Chapter 4
At Monson Academy

We were in East Windsor for about a week; then we went up to Monson, Mass., to enter the Academy there. Monson Academy was, at one time, quite a noted preparatory school in New England, before high schools sprang into existence. Young men from all parts of the country were found here, undergoing preparation for colleges. It was its fortune, at different periods of its history, to have had men of character and experience for its principals. The Rev. Charles Hammond was one of them. He was in every sense a self-made man. He was a graduate of Yale; he was enthusiastically fond of the classics, and a great admirer of English literature. He was a man of liberal views and broad sympathies. He was well-known in New England as an educator and a champion of temperance and New England virtues. His high character gave the Academy a wide reputation and the school was never in a more prosperous condition than when he was principal. He took a special interest in us, the three Chinese students —— Wong Shing, Wong Foon and myself —— not so much from the novelty of having Chinese in the school as from his interest in China, and the possible good that might come out of our education.

In our first year in the Academy, we were placed in the English department. Greenleaf's Arithmetic, English Grammar, Physiology, and *Upham's Mental Philosophy* were our studies. In the last two studies we recited to the new preceptress, Miss Rebekah Brown, a graduate of Mt. Holyoke, the valedictorian of her class. She afterwards became the wife of Doctor A. S. McClean, of Springfield, Mass. She was a fine teacher and a woman of exceptional Christian virtues. She had an even and sweet temper, and was full of good will and good works. She and her husband, the good Doctor, took a genuine interest in me; they gave me a home during some of my college vacations, and helped me in various ways in my struggle through Yale. I kept up my correspondence with them after my return to China, and upon my coming back to this country, I was always cordially invited to their home in Springfield. It was on account of such a genuine friendship that I made Springfield my headquarters in 1872, when I brought the first installment of government students to this country.

Brown placed us under the care of his mother, Mrs. Phoebe H. Brown. We boarded with her, but had a separate room assigned us in a dwelling right across the road, opposite to her cottage. Her widowed daughter with her three boys had taken up all the spare rooms in the cottage, which accounts for the want of accommodation for us.

In those primitive days, board and lodging in the country were very reasonable. Indigent students had a fair chance to work their way for an education. I remember we paid for board and lodging, including fuel, light and washing, only $1.25 a week for each, but we had to take care of our own rooms and, in the winter, saw and split our own wood, which we found to be capital exercise.

Our lodging was about half a mile from the academy. We had to walk three times a day to school and back, in the dead of winter when the snow was three feet deep; that gave us plenty of exercise, keen appetites and kept us in fine condition.

I look back upon my acquaintance with Mrs. Phoebe H. Brown with a mingled feeling of respect and admiration. She certainly was a remarkable New England woman —— a woman of surpassing strength of moral and religious character. Those who have had the rare privilege of reading her stirring biography, will, I am sure, bear me out in this statement. She went through the crucible of unprecedented adversities and trials of life and came out one of the rare shining lights that beautify the New England sky. She is the authoress of the well-known hymn, "I love to steal awhile away from every cumbering care," etc., which breathes the calm spirit of contentment and resignation wherever sung.

The Rev. Charles Hammond, the principal of the academy when we joined it, was a graduate of Yale, as I stated before, and a man of a fine cultivated taste. He was an enthusiastic admirer of Shakespeare, who was his favorite poet; among orators, he was partial to Daniel Webster. He had the faculty of inspiring his pupils with the love of the beautiful, both in ancient and modern literature. In our daily recitations, he laid a greater stress on pointing out the beauties of a sentence and its construction, than he did on grammatical rules, moods and tenses. He was a fine writer. His addresses and sermons were pointed and full of life. Like Dr. Arnold of Rugby, he aimed to build character in his pupils and not to convert them into walking encyclopedias, or intelligent parrots. It was through him that I was introduced to Addison, Goldsmith, Dickens, Sir Walter Scott, *the Edinburgh Reviews*, Macaulay and Shakespeare, which formed the bulk of my reading while in Monson.

During my first year in the Monson Academy, I had no idea of taking a collegiate course. It was well understood that I was to return to China at the end of 1849, and the appropriation was made to suit such a plan. In the fall of 1848, after Wong Shing —— the eldest of the three of us —— had returned to China on account of his poor health, Wong Foon and myself, who were left behind to continue our studies for another year, frequently met to talk over future plans for the end of the prescribed time. We both decided finally to stay in this country to continue our studies, but the question arose, who was going to back us financially after 1849? This was the Gordian Knot. We concluded to consult Mr. Hammond and Mr. Brown on the subject. They both decided to have the matter referred to our patrons in Hong Kong. Reply came that if we wished to prosecute our studies after 1849, they would be willing to continue their support through a professional course, if we were willing to go over to Scotland to go through the University of Edinburgh. This was a generous and noble-hearted proposal.

Wong Foon, on his part, after much deliberation, decided to accept the offer and go over to Scotland at the end of 1849, while, on my part, I preferred to remain in this country to continue my studies here with the view of going to Yale. Wong Foon's decision had relieved him of all financial anxieties, while the problem of how I was to pay my education bills after 1849, still remained to be solved. But I did not allow the perplexities of the future to disturb my peace of mind. I threw all my anxieties to the wind, trusting to a wise providence to care for my future, as it had done for my past.

Wong Foon and I, having taken our decisive steps, dropped our English studies at the close of the school year of 1849, and in the fall of the same year we began the A B C's of our classical course. In the summer of 1850, we graduated from the academy. Wong Foon, by previous arrangements, went over to Scotland and entered the University of Edinburgh. I remained in this country and finally entered Yale. It was fully a decade since we had met for the first time in the Morrison School in Macao, in 1840, to become school-mates as well as class-mates. Now that link was broken.

Wong was in the University seven years. After completing his professional studies as a doctor, he returned to China in 1857. He was a fine scholar. He graduated the third man in his medical class. He also distinguished himself in his profession. His ability and skill secured for him an enviable reputation as one of the ablest surgeons east of the Cape of Good Hope at that time. He had a fine practice in Canton, where the foreign residents retained him as their physician in preference to European doctors. He was very successful and made quite a fortune before his death, which took place in 1879. Both the native and foreign communities felt his loss. He was highly respected and honored by Chinese and foreigners for his Christian character and the purity of his life.

Chapter 5
My College Days

Before entering Yale, I had not solved the problem of how I was to be carried through the collegiate course without financial backing of a definite and well-assured character. It was an easy matter to talk about getting an education by working for it, and there is a kind of romance in it that captivates the imagination, but it is altogether a different thing to face it in a business and practical way. So it proved to me, after I had put my foot into it. I had no one except Brown, who had already done so much for me in bringing me to this country, and Hammond, who fitted me for college. To them I appealed for advice and counsel. I was advised to avail myself of the contingent fund provided for indigent students. It was in the hands of the trustees of the academy and so well guarded that it could not be appropriated without the recipient's signing a written pledge that he would study for the ministry and afterwards become a missionary. Such being the case, I made up my mind that it would be utterly useless for me to apply for the fund. However, a day was appointed for me to meet the trustees in the parsonage, to talk over the subject. They said they would be too glad to have me avail myself of the fund, provided I was willing to sign a pledge that after graduation I should go back to China as a missionary. I gave the trustees to understand that I would never give such a pledge for the following reasons: First, it would handicap and circumscribe my usefulness. I wanted the utmost freedom of action to avail myself of every opportunity to do the greatest good in China. If necessary, I might be obliged to create new conditions, if I found old ones were not favorable to any plan I might have for promoting her highest welfare.

In the second place, the calling of a missionary is not the only sphere in life where one can do the most good in China or elsewhere. In such a vast empire, there can be hardly any limit put upon one's ambition to do good, if one is possessed of the Christ-spirit; on the other hand, if one has not such a spirit, no pledge in the world could melt his ice-bound soul.

In the third place, a pledge of that character would prevent me from taking advantage of any circumstance or event that might arise in the life of a nation like China, to do her a great service.

"For these reasons," I said, "I must decline to give the pledge and at the same time decline to accept your kind offer to help me. I thank you, gentlemen, very much, for your good wishes."

Both Brown and Hammond afterwards agreed that I took the right view on the subject and sustained me in my position. To be sure, I was poor, but I would not allow my poverty to gain the upper hand and compel me to barter away my inward convictions of duty for a temporary mess of pottage.

During the summer of 1850, it seems that Brown who had been making a visit in the South to see his sister, while there had occasion to call on some of the members of "The Ladies' Association" in Savannah, Ga., to whom he mentioned my case. He returned home in the nick of time, just after I had the interview with the board of trustees of the academy. I told him of the outcome, when, as stated above, he approved of my position, and told me what he had done. He said that the members of the association agreed to help me in college. On the strength of that I gathered fresh courage, and went down to New Haven to pass my examination for entrance. How I got in, I do not know, as I had had only fifteen months of Latin and twelve months of Greek, and ten months of mathematics. My preparation had been interrupted because the academy had been broken up by the Palmer & New London R.R. that was being built close by. As compared with the college preparations of nine-tenths of my class-mates, I was far behind. However, I passed without condition. But I was convinced I was not sufficiently prepared, as my recitations in the class-room clearly proved. Between the struggle of how to make ends meet financially and how to keep up with the class in my studies, I had a pretty tough time of it. I used to sweat over my studies till twelve o'clock every night the whole Freshman year. I took little or no exercise and my health and strength began to fail and I was obliged to ask for a leave of absence of a week. I went to East Windsor to get rested and came back refreshed.

In the Sophomore year, from my utter aversion to mathematics, especially to differential and integral calculus, which I abhorred and detested, and which did me little or no good in the way of mental discipline, I used to fizzle and flunk so often that I really thought I was going to be dropped from the class, or dismissed from college. But for some unexplained reasons I was saved from such a catastrophe, and I squeezed through the second year in college with so low a mark that I was afraid to ask my division tutor, who happened to be Tutor Blodget, who had me in Greek, about it. The only redeeming feature that saved me as a student in the class of 1854, was the fortunate circumstance that I happened to be a successful competitor on two occasions in English composition in my division. I was awarded the first prize in the second term, and the first prize in the third term of the year. These prizes gave me quite an éclat in the college as well as in the outside world, but I was not at all elated over them on account of my poor scholarship which I felt keenly through the whole college course.

Before the close of my second year, I succeeded in securing the stewardship of a boarding club consisting of sophomores and juniors. There were altogether twenty members. I did all the marketing and served at the table. In this way, I earned my board through the latter half of my college course. In money matters, I was supplied with remittances from "The Ladies' Association" in Savannah, and also contributions from the Olyphant Brothers of New York. In addition to these sources of supply, I was paid for being an assistant librarian to the "Brothers in Unity," which was one of the two college debating societies that owned a library, and of which I was a member.

In my senior year I was again elected librarian to the same Society and got $30. These combined sums were large enough to meet all my cash bills, since my wants had to be finely trimmed to suit the cloth. If most of the country parsons of that period could get along with a salary of $200 or $300 a year (supplemented, of course, with an annual donation party, which sometimes carried away more than it donated), having as a general thing a large family to look after, I certainly ought to have been able to get through college with gifts of nearly a like amount, supplemented with donations of shirts and stockings from ladies who took an interest in my education.

The class of 1854, to which I had the honor and the good fortune to belong, graduated ninety-eight all told. Being the first Chinaman who had ever been known to go through a first-class American college, I naturally attracted considerable attention; and from the fact that I was librarian for one of the college debating societies (Linonia was the other) for two years, I was known by members of the three classes above, and members of the three classes below me. This fact had contributed toward familiarizing me with the college world at large, and my nationality, of course, added piquancy to my popularity.

As an undergraduate, I had already acquired a factitious reputation within the walls of Yale. But that was ephemeral and soon passed out of existence after graduation.

All through my college course, especially in the closing year, the lamentable condition of China was before my mind constantly and weighed on my spirits. In my despondency, I often wished I had never been educated, as education had unmistakably enlarged my mental and moral horizon, and revealed to me responsibilities which the sealed eye of ignorance can never see, and sufferings and wrongs of humanity to which an uncultivated and callous nature can never be made sensitive. The more one knows, the more he suffers and is consequently less happy; the less one knows, the less he suffers, and hence is more happy. But this is a low view of life, a cowardly feeling and unworthy of a being bearing the impress of divinity. I had started out to get an education. By dint of hard work and self-denial I had finally secured the coveted prize and although it might not be so complete and symmetrical a thing as could be desired, yet I had come right up to the conventional standard and idea of a liberal education. I could, therefore, call myself an educated man and, as such, it behooved me to ask, "What am I going to do with my education?" Before the close of my last year in college I had already sketched out what I should do. I was determined that the rising generation of China should enjoy the same educational advantages that I had enjoyed; that through western education China might be regenerated, become enlightened and powerful. To accomplish that object became the guiding star of my ambition. Towards such a goal, I directed all my mental resources and energy. Through thick and thin, and the vicissitudes of a checkered life from 1854 to 1872, I labored and waited for its consummation.

Chapter 6
Return to China

.

In entering upon my life's work which to me was so full of meaning and earnestness, the first episode was a voyage back to the old country, which I had not seen for nearly ten years, but which had never escaped my mind's eye nor my heart's yearning for her welfare. I wanted very much to stay a few years longer in order to take a scientific course. I had taken up surveying in the Sheffield Scientific School just as that department was starting into existence under Professor Norton. Had I had the means to prosecute a practical profession, that might have helped to shorten and facilitate the way to the goal I had in view; but as I was poor and my friends thought that a longer stay in this country might keep me here for good, and China would lose me altogether, I was for this and other reasons induced to return. The scientific course was accordingly abandoned. The persons who were most interested in my return to China were Pelatiah Perit of Messrs. Goodhue & Co., merchants in the China trade, and the Olyphant Brothers, who had taken such a lively interest eight years before in helping me to come over in their ship, the "Huntress." These gentlemen had no other motive in desiring me to return to China than that of hoping to see me useful in Christianizing the Chinese, which was in harmony with their well-known broad and benevolent characters.

On the 13th of November, 1854, the Rev. William Allen Macy, who went out to Hong Kong to take the place of the Rev. Dr. Brown, as teacher in the Morrison Education Society School in 1845, went back to China as a missionary under the American Board, and we were fellow-passengers on board the sailing clipper ship "Eureka," under Captain Whipple, of Messrs. Chamber, Heisser & Co., of New York.

Winter is the worst season of the year to go on an eastern voyage in a sailing vessel, via the Cape of Good Hope. The northeast trade winds prevail then and one is sure to have head winds all the way. The "Eureka," in which Macy and myself were the only passengers, took that route to Hong Kong. We embarked on board of her as she rode in midstream of the East River. The day was bleak and bitingly cold. No handkerchiefs were fluttering in the air, waving a good voyage; no sound from the shore cheered us as the anchor was weighed, and as the tug towed us out as far as Sandy Hook. There we were left to our own resources. The sails were not furled to their full extent, but were reefed for tacking, as the wind was nearly dead ahead and quite strong. We found the "Eureka" to be empty of cargo, and empty even of ballast of any kind; for that reason she acted like a sailor who had just had his nip before he went out to sea. She tossed up and down and twisted from right to left, just as though she had a little too much to keep her balance. It was in such a fashion that she reeled her way from Sandy Hook to Hong Kong —— a distance of nearly 13,000 nautical miles, which took her 154 days to accomplish. It was decidedly the most uninteresting and wearisome voyage I ever took in my life. The skipper was a Philadelphian. He had the unfortunate habit of stuttering badly, which tended to irritate a temper naturally quick and fiery. He was certainly a ludicrous object to look at. It was particularly in the morning that he might be seen pacing the quarter deck, scanning the sky. This, by the spectator, was deemed necessary for the skipper to work himself up to the right pitch, preliminary to his pantomimic performances in his battle with the head wind. All at once, he halted, stared at the quarter of the sky from whence the malicious head wind came. With a face all bloated and reddened by intense excitement, his eyes almost standing out of their sockets, and all ablaze with uncontrollable rage, with arms uplifted, he would clutch his hair as if plucking it out by the roots, gnash his teeth, and simultaneously he would jump up and down, stamping on the deck, and swear at the Almighty for sending him head winds. The air for the moment was split with his revolting imprecations and blasphemous oaths that were ejaculated through the laborious process of stammering and stuttering, which made him a most pitiable object to behold. In the early part of the voyage it was a painful sight to see him working himself up to that pitch of contortion and paroxysm of rage which made him appear more like an insane than a sane man, but as these exhibitions were of daily occurrence for the greater part of the voyage, we came to regard him as no longer deserving of sympathy and pity, but rather with contempt. After his passion had spent its force, and he subsided into his calmer and normal mood, he would drop limply into a cane chair, where he would sit for hours all by himself. For the sake of diversion, he would rub his hands together, and soliloquize quietly to himself, an occasional smile breaking over his face, which made him look like an innocent idiot. Before the voyage was half through, the skipper had made such a fool of himself through his silly and insane conduct about the wind, that he became the laughing stock of the whole crew, who, of course, did not dare to show any outward signs of insubordination. The sailing of the vessel was entirely in the hands of the first mate, who was literally a sea-tyrant. The crew was composed of Swedes and Norwegians. If it had been made up of Americans, the inhuman treatment by the officers might have driven them to desperate extremities, because the men were over-worked night and day in incessant tacking. The only time that they found a resting spell was when the ship was becalmed in the tropics when not a breath of wind was to be had for several days at a time. Referring to my diary kept in that memorable voyage, —— it took us nearly two weeks to beat up the Macassar straits. This event tried our patience sorely. After it was passed, the skipper made the remark within the hearing of the Rev. Macy that the reason he had bad luck was because he had a Jonah on board. My friend Macy took the remark in a good-natured way and gave me a significant smile. We were just then discussing the feat of going through the Macassar straits and I remarked in a tone just loud enough to be heard by the old skipper that if I had charge of the vessel, I could take her through in less than ten days. This was meant as a direct reflection on the poor seamanship of the old fellow (for he really was a miserable sailor), as well as to serve as a retaliation for what he said a few minutes before, that there was a Jonah on board.

In the dead of winter, the passage to the East should have been taken around Cape Horn instead of the Cape of Good Hope, in which case we would no doubt have had strong and fair wind all the way from New York to Hong Kong, which would not only have shortened the voyage but also saved the captain a world of swearing and an incalculable amount of wear and tear on his nervous system. But as a passenger only, I had no idea of the financial motive back of the move to send the ship off perfectly empty and unballasted, right in the teeth of the northeast monsoon. I would have been glad to go around Cape Horn, as that would have added a new route to my journeying around the world, and furnished me with new incidents as well.

As we approached Hong Kong, a Chinese pilot boarded us. The captain wanted me to ask him whether there were any dangerous rocks and shoals nearby. I could not for the life of me recall my Chinese in order to interpret for him; the pilot himself understood English, and he was the first Chinese teacher to give me the terms in Chinese for dangerous rocks and shoals. So the skipper and Macy, and a few other persons who were present at the time, had the laugh on me, who, being a Chinese, yet was not able to speak the language.

My first thought upon landing was to walk up to the office of the *China Mail* to pay my respects to Andrew Shortrede, the proprietor and editor of the paper, and the friend who supported me for over a year, while I was in Monson Academy. After seeing him and accepting his hospitality by way of an invitation to take up my quarters in his house, I lost no time in hastening over to Macao to see my aged and beloved mother, who, I knew, yearned to see her long-absent boy. Our meeting was arranged a day beforehand. I was in citizen's dress and could not conveniently change the same for my Chinese costume. I had also allowed a pair of mustaches to grow, which, according to Chinese custom, was not becoming for an unmarried young man to do. We met with tears of joy, gratitude and thanksgiving. Our hearts were too full even to speak at first. We gave way to our emotions. As soon as we were fairly composed, she began to stroke me all over, as expressive of her maternal endearment which had been held in patient suspense for at least ten years. As we sat close to each other, I gave her a brief recital of my life in America, for I knew she would be deeply interested in the account. I told her that I had just finished a long and wearisome voyage of five months' duration, but had met with no danger of any kind; that during my eight years of sojourn in the United States, I was very kindly treated by the good people everywhere; that I had had good health and never been seriously sick, and that my chief object during the eight years was to study and prepare myself for my life work in China. I explained to her that I had to go through a preparatory school before entering college; that the college I entered was Yale —— one of the leading colleges of the United States, and that the course was four years, which accounted for my long stay and delayed my return to China. I told her that at the end of four years I had graduated with the degree of A.B., —— analogous to the Chinese title of Siu Tsai, which is interpreted "Elegant Talent;" that it was inscribed on a parchment of sheep skin and that to graduate from Yale College was considered a great honor, even to a native American, and much more so to a Chinese. She asked me näively how much money it conferred. I said it did not confer any money at once, but it enabled one to make money quicker and easier than one can who has not been educated; that it gave one greater influence and power among men and if he built on his college education, he would be more likely to become the leader of men, especially if he had a well-established character. I told her my college education was worth more to me than money, and that I was confident of making plenty of money.

"Knowledge," I said, "is power, and power is greater than riches. I am the first Chinese to graduate from Yale College, and that being the case, you have the honor of being the first and only mother out of the countless millions of mothers in China at this time, who can claim the honor of having a son who is the first Chinese graduate of a first-class American college. Such an honor is a rare thing to possess." I also assured her that as long as I lived all her comforts and wants would be scrupulously and sedulously looked after, and that nothing would be neglected to make her contented and happy. This interview seemed to give her great comfort and satisfaction. She seemed very happy over it. After it was ended, she looked at me with a significant smile and said, "I see you have already raised your mustaches. You know you have a brother who is much older than you are; he hasn't grown his mustaches yet. You must have yours off." I promptly obeyed her mandate, and as I entered the room with a clean face, she smiled with intense satisfaction, evidently thinking that with all my foreign education, I had not lost my early training of being obedient to my mother. And if she could only have read my heart, she would have found how every throb palpitated with the most tender love for her. During the remaining years of her life, I had the rare privilege of seeing her often and ministered to her every comfort that it was in my power to bestow. She passed away in 1858, at the age of sixty-four, twenty-four years[1] after the death of my father. I was in Shanghai at the time of her death. I returned to my native village in time to attend her funeral.

In the summer of 1855, I took up my residence in Canton, with the Rev. Mr. Vrooman, a missionary under the American Board. His headquarters were in Ham Ha Lan, in the vicinity of the government execution ground, which is in the southwestern outskirts of the city, close to the bank of the Pearl River. While there, I began my Chinese studies and commenced to regain the dialect of Canton, which I had forgotten during my stay in the United States. In less than six months, the language came back to me readily, although I was still a little rusty in it. I was also making slow progress in recovering the written language, in which I was not well-grounded before leaving China, in 1846. I had studied it only four years, which was considered a short time in which to master the written language. There is a greater difference between the written and the spoken language of China than there is between the written and spoken English language. The Chinese written language is stilted and full of conventional forms. It is understood throughout the whole empire, but differently pronounced in different provinces and localities. The spoken language is cut up into endless dialects and in certain provinces like

---

1   Should be eighteen years. Yung Wing's father died in 1840.

Fuhkien, Anhui and Kiangsu, the people are as foreigners to each other in the matter of dialects. Such are the peculiar characteristics of the ideographic and spoken languages of China.

During the six months of my residence in Canton, while trying to recover both the written and spoken languages, Kwang Tung province was thrown into a somewhat disorganized condition. The people of Canton attempted to raise a provincial insurrection or rebellion entirely distinct from the Taiping rebellion which was being carried on in the interior of China with marked success. To suppress and nip it in the bud, drastic measures were resorted to by Viceroy Yeh Ming Hsin, who, in the summer of 1855, decapitated seventy-five thousand people, most of whom, I was told, were innocent. My residence was within half a mile of the execution ground, as stated above, and one day, out of curiosity, I ventured to walk over to the place. But, oh! what a sight. The ground was perfectly drenched with human blood. On both sides of the driveway were to be seen headless human trunks, piled up in heaps, waiting to be taken away for burial. But no provision had been made to facilitate their removal.

The execution was carried on on a larger scale than had been expected, and no provision had been made to find a place large enough to bury all the bodies. There they were, left exposed to a burning sun. The temperature stood from morning to night in midsummer steadily at 90° Fahrenheit, and sometimes higher. The atmosphere within a radius of two thousand yards of the execution ground was heavily charged with the poisonous and pestilential vapor that was reeking from the ground already over-saturated with blood and from the heaps of corpses which had been left behind for at least two days, and which showed signs of rapid decomposition. It was a wonder to me that no virulent epidemic had sprung up from such an infectious spot to decimate the compact population of the city of Canton. It was a fortunate circumstance that at last a deep and extensive ravine, located in the far-off outskirts of the western part of the city, was found, which was at once converted into a sepulchral receptacle into which this vast human hecatomb was dumped. It was said that no earth was needed to be thrown over these corpses to cover them up; the work was accomplished by countless swarms of worms of a reddish hue and of an appearance that was perfectly hideous and revolting.

I was told that during the months of June, July and August, of 1855, seventy-five thousand people had been decapitated; that more than half of that number were declared to be innocent of the charge of rebellion, but that the accusation was made as a pretext to exact money from them. This wholesale slaughter, unparalleled in the annals of modern civilization, eclipsing even the enormities and blood-thirstiness of Caligula and Nero, or even the French Revolution, was perpetrated by Yeh Ming Hsin, who was appointed viceroy of Kwang Tung and Kwangsi in 1854.

Yeh Ming Hsin was a native of Han-Yang. Han-Yang is a part of the port of Hankau, and was destroyed with it when the Taiping rebels took possession of it. It was said that Yeh Ming Hsin had immense estates in Han-Yang, which were completely destroyed by fire. This circumstance embittered him towards the Taiping rebels and as the Taiping leaders hailed from Kwang Tung and Kwangsi, he naturally transferred his hatred to the people of those two provinces. It was in the lofty position of a viceroy that he found his opportunity to wreak his private and personal vengeance upon the Canton people. This accounts for his indiscriminate slaughter of them, and for the fact that he did not deign to give them even the semblance of a trial, but hurried them from life to death like packs of cattle to the shambles.

But this human monster did not dream that his day of reckoning was fast approaching. Several years after this appalling sacrifice of human life, in 1855, he got into trouble with the British government. He was captured by the British forces and banished to some obscure and remote corner in India where he led a most ignominious life, hated by the whole Chinese nation, and despised by the world at large.

On my return to headquarters, after my visit to the execution ground, I felt faint-hearted and depressed in spirit. I had no appetite for food, and when night came, I was too nervous for sleep. The scene I had looked upon during the day had stirred me up. I thought then that the Taiping rebels had ample grounds to justify their attempt to overthrow the Manchu régime. My sympathies were thoroughly enlisted in their favor and I thought seriously of making preparations to join the Taiping rebels, but upon a calmer reflection, I fell back on the original plan of doing my best to recover the Chinese language as fast as I possibly could and of following the logical course of things, in order to accomplish the object I had at heart.

Chapter 7
Effort to Find a Position

Having at last succeeded in mastering the spoken language sufficiently to speak it quite fluently, I at once set to work to find a position in which I could not only support myself and mother, but also form a plan for working out my ideas of reform in China.

Doctor Peter Parker, who had been a medical missionary under the American Board for many years in Canton, was at that time made United States Commissioner as a temporary expedient, to take the place of an accredited minister plenipotentiary —— a diplomatic appointment not yet come into existence, because the question of a foreign minister resident in Peking was still under negotiation, and had not been fully settled as a permanent diplomatic arrangement between the Peking government and the Treaty Powers. Dr. Parker was given the appointment of commissioner on account of his long residence in China and his ability to speak the Chinese language, but not on account of any special training as a diplomat, nor for legal knowledge. It was through Mr. M. N. Hitchcock, an American merchant of the firm of Messrs. King & Co., and a mutual friend of Dr. Parker and myself, that I became the Doctor's private secretary. I knew Dr. Parker while I was at Mrs. Gutzlaff's School, and he doubtless knew I had recently graduated from Yale, which was his Alma Mater also. His headquarters were in Canton, but he spent his summers in Macao. I was with him only three months. My salary was $15 a month (not large enough to spoil me at any rate). He had very little for me to do, but I thought that by being identified with him, I might possibly come in contact with Chinese officials. However, this was far from being the case. Seeing that I could neither learn anything from him, nor enlarge my acquaintance with the Chinese officials, I gave up my position as his secretary and went over to Hong Kong to try to study law. Through my old friend, Andrew Shortrede, who generously extended to me the hospitality of his house, I succeeded in securing the position of the interpretership in the Hong Kong Supreme Court. The situation paid me $75 a month. Having this to fall back upon, I felt encouraged to go ahead in my effort to study law. Accordingly, I was advised to apprentice myself to an attorney or solicitor-at-law. In the English court of practice, it seems that there are two distinct classes of lawyers —— attorneys or solicitors, and barristers. The first prepares in writing all evidences, facts, and proofs of a case, hands them to the barrister or counsel, who argues the case in court according to law.

I apprenticed myself to an attorney, who was recommended to me by my old patron and friend, Shortrede. I was not aware that by going into the British Colony in Hong Kong to become an attorney, I was stepping on the toes of the British legal fraternity, nor that by apprenticing myself to an attorney instead of to the new attorney-general of the Colony, who, without my knowledge, wanted me himself, I had committed another mistake, which eventually necessitated my leaving Hong Kong altogether.

First of all, all the attorneys banded themselves together against me, because, as they openly stated in all the local papers except the *China Mail*, if I were allowed to practice my profession, they might as well pack up and go back to England, for as I had a complete knowledge of both English and Chinese I would eventually monopolize all the Chinese legal business. So they made it too hot for me to continue in my studies.

In the next place, I was not aware that the attorney-general wanted me to apprentice myself to him, for he did all he could in his capacity as attorney-general of the Colony to use his influence to open the way for me to become an attorney, by draughting a special colonial ordinance to admit Chinese to practice in the Hong Kong Colony as soon as I could pass my examinations. This ordinance was sent to the British government to be sanctioned by Parliament before it became valid and a colonial law. It was sanctioned and thus became a colonial ordinance.

In the meanwhile, Anstey, the attorney-general, found out that I had already apprenticed myself to Parson, the attorney. From that time forth I had no peace. I was between two fires —— the batteries operated by the attorneys opened on me with redoubled energy, and the new battery, operated by the attorney-general, opened its fire. He found fault with my interpreting, which he had never done previously. Mr. Parson saw how things stood. He himself was also under a hot fire from both sides. So in order to save himself, he told me plainly and candidly that he had to give me up and made the article of apprenticeship between us null and void. I, on my part, had to give up my position as interpreter in the Supreme Court. Parson, himself, not long after I had abandoned my apprenticeship and my position as interpreter, for reasons satisfactory to himself, gave up his business in

Hong Kong and returned to England. So master and pupil left their posts at pretty nearly the same time.

A retrospective view of my short experience in Hong Kong convinced me that it was after all the best thing that I did not succeed in becoming a lawyer in Hong Kong, as the theatre of action there would have been too restricted and circumscribed. I could not have come in touch with the leading minds of China, had I been bound up in that rocky and barren Colony. Doubtless I might have made a fortune if I had succeeded in my legal profession, but as circumstances forced me to leave the Colony, my mind was directed northward to Shanghai, and in August, 1856, I left Hong Kong in the tea clipper, "Florence," under Captain Dumaresque, of Boston. He was altogether a different type of man from the captain of the "Eureka" which brought me out in 1855. He was kind, intelligent and gentlemanly. When he found out who I was, he offered me a free passage from Hong Kong to Shanghai. He was, in fact, the sole owner of the vessel, which was named after his daughter, Florence. The passage was a short one —— lasting only seven days —— but before it was over, we became great friends.

Not long after my arrival in Shanghai, I found a situation in the Imperial Customs Translating Department, at a salary of Tls. 75 a month, equivalent to $100 Mexican. For want of a Chinese silver currency the Mexican dollar was adopted. This was one point better than the interpretership in the Hong Kong Supreme Court. The duties were not arduous and trying. In fact, they were too simple and easy to suit my taste and ambition. I had plenty of time to read. Before three months of trial in my new situation, I found that things were not as they should be, and if I wished to keep a clean and clear record and an untarnished character, I could not remain long in the service. Between the interpreters who had been in the service many years and the Chinese shippers there existed a regular system of graft. After learning this, and not wishing to be implicated with the others in the division of the spoils in any way or shape, I made up my mind to resign. So one day I called upon the Chief Commissioner of Customs, ostensibly to find out what my future prospects were in connection with the Customs Service —— whether or not there were any prospects of my being promoted to the position of a commissioner. I was told that no such prospects were held out to me or to any other Chinese interpreter. I, therefore, at once decided to throw up my position. So I sent in my resignation, which was at first not accepted. A few days after my first interview, Lay, the chief commissioner, strenuously tried to persuade me to change my mind, and offered as an inducement to raise my salary to Tls. 200 a month, evidently thinking that

I was only bluffing in order to get higher wages. It did not occur to him that there was at least one Chinaman who valued a clean reputation and an honest character more than money; that being an educated man, I saw no reason why I should not be given the same chances to rise in the service of the Chinese government as an Englishman, nor why my individuality should not be recognized and respected in every walk of life. He little thought that I had aspirations even higher than his, and that I did not care to associate myself with a pack of Custom-house interpreters and inspectors, who were known to take bribes; that a man who expects others to respect him, must first respect himself. Such were my promptings. I did not state the real cause of my quitting the service, but at the end of four months' trial I left the service in order to try my fortune in new fields more congenial.

My friends at the time looked upon me as a crank in throwing up a position yielding me Tls. 200 a month for something uncertain and untried. This in their estimation was the height of folly. They little realized what I was driving at. I had a clean record and I meant to keep it clean. I was perfectly aware that in less than a year since my return to China, I had made three shifts. I myself began to think I was too mercurial to accomplish anything substantial, or that I was too dreamy to be practical or too proud to succeed in life. But in a strenuous life one needs to be a dreamer in order to accomplish possibilities. We are not called into being simply to drudge for an animal existence. I had had to work hard for my education, and I felt that I ought to make the most of what little I had, not so much to benefit myself individually as to make it a blessing common to my race. By these shifts and changes I was only trying to find my true bearing, and how I could make myself a blessing to China.

Chapter 8
Experiences in Business

The next turn I took, after leaving the Imperial Customs, was clerk in an English house —— tea and silk merchants. During the few months that I was with them, I gained quite an insight into mercantile business, and the methods of conducting it, which proved to be profitable knowledge and experience to me later on. Six months after I had entered upon my new sphere as a make-shift, the firm dissolved partnership, which once more threw me out of a position, and I was again cast upon the sea of uncertainty. But during my connection with the firm, two little incidents occurred which I must not fail to relate.

One Thursday evening, as I was returning home from a prayer meeting held in the Union Chapel in Shanghai, I saw ahead of me on Szechuen Road in front of the Episcopal church, a string of men; each had a Chinese lantern swinging in the air over his head, and they were singing and shouting as they zigzagged along the road, evidently having a jolly, good time, while Chinese on both sides of the road were seen dodging and scampering about in great fright in all directions, and acting as though they were chased by the Old Nick himself. I was at a distance of about one hundred yards from the scene. I took in the situation at once. My servant, who held a lantern ahead of me, to light the way, was so frightened that he began to come back towards me. I told him not to be afraid, but walk right straight ahead. Pretty soon we confronted three or four of the fellows, half tipsy. One of them snatched the lantern from my servant and another, staggering about, tried to give me a kick. I walked along coolly and unconcerned till I reached the last batch of two or three fellows. I found these quite sober and in their senses and they were lingering behind evidently to enjoy the fun and watch the crowd in their hilarious antics. I stopped and parleyed with them, and told them who I was. I asked them for the names of the fellows who snatched my boy's lantern and of the fellow who tried to kick me. They declined at first, but finally with the promise that I would not give them any trouble, they gave me the name of one of the fellows, his position on the vessel, and the name of the vessel he belonged to. It turned out that the man was the first mate of the ship "Eureka," the very vessel that brought me out to China, in 1855, and which happened to be consigned to the firm I was working for. The next morning, I wrote a note to the captain, asking him to hand the note to his first officer. The captain, on receiving the note, was quite excited, and handed it to the first mate, who immediately came ashore and apologized. I made it very pleasant for him and told him that Americans in China were held in high esteem by the people, and every American landing in China should be jealous of the high estimation in which they were held and not do anything to compromise it. My motive in writing the note was merely to get him on shore and give him this advice. He was evidently pleased with my friendly attitude and extended his hand for a shake to thank me for the advice. He invited me to go on board with him to take a glass of wine and be good friends. I thanked him for his offer, but declined it, and we parted in an amicable way.

My second incident, which happened a couple of months after the first, did not have such a peaceful ending.

After the partnership of the firm, in whose employ I was, dissolved, an auction sale of the furniture of the firm took place. In the room where the auction was proceeding, I happened to be standing in a mixed crowd of Chinese and foreigners. A stalwart six-footer of a Scotchman happened to be standing behind me. He was not altogether a stranger to me, for I had met him in the streets several times. He began to tie a bunch of cotton balls to my queue, simply for a lark. But I caught him at it and in a pleasant way held it up and asked him to untie it. He folded up his arms and drew himself straight up with a look of the utmost disdain and scorn. I at once took in the situation, and as my countenance sobered, I reiterated my demand to have the appendage taken off. All of a sudden, he thrust his fist against my mouth, without drawing any blood, however. Although he stood head and shoulders above me in height, yet I was not at all abashed or intimidated by his burly and contemptuous appearance. My dander was up and oblivious to all thoughts of our comparative size and strength, I struck him back in the identical place where he punched me, but my blow was a stinger and it went with lightning rapidity to the spot, without giving him time to think. It drew blood in great profusion from lip and nose. He caught me by the wrist with both his hands. As he held my right wrist in his powerful grasp, for he was an athlete and a sportsman, I was just on the point of raising my right foot for a kick, which was aimed at a vital point, when the head partner of the firm, who happened to be near, suddenly stepped in between and separated us. I then stood off to one side, facing my antagonist, who was moving off into the crowd. As I moved away, I was asked by a voice from the crowd:

"Do you want to fight?"

I said, "No, I was only defending myself. Your friend insulted me and added injury to insult. I took him for a gentleman, but he has proved himself a blackguard."

With this stinging remark, which was heard all over the room, I retired from the scene into an adjoining room, leaving the crowd to comment on the incident. The British Consul, who happened to be present on the occasion, made a casual remark on the merits of the case and said, as I was told afterwards by a friend, that "The young man was a little too fiery; if he had not taken the law into his own hands, he could have brought suit for assault and battery in the consular court, but since he has already retaliated and his last remark before the crowd has inflicted a deeper cut to his antagonist than the blow itself, he has lost the advantage of a suit."

The Scotchman, after the incident, did not appear in public for a whole week. I was told he had shut himself up in his room to give his wound time to heal, but the reason he did not care to show himself was more on account of being whipped by a little Chinaman in a public manner; for the affair, unpleasant and unfortunate as it was, created quite a sensation in the settlement. It was the chief topic of conversation for a short time among foreigners, while among the Chinese I was looked upon with great respect, for since the foreign settlement on the extraterritorial basis was established close to the city of Shanghai, no Chinese within its jurisdiction had ever been known to have the courage and pluck to defend his rights, point blank, when they had been violated or trampled upon by a foreigner. Their meek and mild disposition had allowed personal insults and affronts to pass unresented and unchallenged, which naturally had the tendency to encourage arrogance and insolence on the part of ignorant foreigners. The time will soon come, however, when the people of China will be so educated and enlightened as to know what their rights are, public and private, and to have the moral courage to assert and defend them whenever they are invaded. The triumph of Japan over Russia in the recent war has opened the eyes of the Chinese world. It will never tolerate injustice in any way or shape, much less will it put up with foreign aggression and aggrandizement any longer. They see now in what plight their national ignorance, conceit and conservatism, in which they had been fossilized, had placed them. They were on the verge of being partitioned by the European

Powers and were saved from that catastrophe only by the timely intervention of the United States government. What the future will bring forth, since the Emperor Kwangsu and Dowager Empress Chi Hsi have both passed away, no one can predict.

The breaking up of the firm by which I was employed, once more, as stated before, and for the fourth time, threw me out of a regular business. But I was not at all disconcerted or discouraged, for I had no idea of following a mercantile life as a permanent calling. Within the past two years, my knowledge of the Chinese language had decidedly improved. I was not in hot haste to seek for a new position. I immediately took to translating as a means of bridging over the breaks of a desultory life. This independent avocation, though not a lucrative one, nevertheless led the way to a wider acquaintance with the educated and mercantile classes of the Chinese; to widen my acquaintance was my chief concern. My translating business brought me in contact with the comprador of one of the leading houses in Shanghai. The senior partner of this house died in 1857. He was well-known and thought much of by both the Chinese and the foreign mercantile body. To attest their high regard for his memory, the prominent Chinese merchants drew up an elaborate and eulogistic epitaph on the occasion of his death. The surviving members of the firm selected two translators to translate the epitaph. One was the interpreter in the British Consulate General, a brother to the author of *The Chinese and their Rebellions* and the other was (through the influence of the comprador) myself. To my great surprise, my translation was given the preference and accepted by the manager of the firm. The Chinese committee were quite elated that one of their countrymen knew enough English to bring out the inner sense of their epitaph. It was adopted and engraved on the monument. My name began to be known among the Chinese, not as a fighter this time, but as a Chinese student educated in America.

Soon after this performance, another event unexpectedly came up in which I was again called upon to act; that was the inundation of the Yellow River, which had converted the northern part of Kiangsu province into a sea, and made homeless and destitute thousands of people of that locality. A large body of refugees had wandered to and flocked near Shanghai. A Chinese deputation, consisting of the leading merchants and gentry, who knew or had heard of me, called and asked me to draw up a circular appealing to the foreign community for aid and contributions to relieve the widespread suffering among the refugees. Several copies were immediately put into circulation and in less than a week, no less than $20,000 were subscribed and paid. The Chinese Committee were greatly elated over their success and their joy was unbounded. To give a finishing touch to this stroke of business, I wrote in the name of the committee a letter of acknowledgment and thanks to the foreign community for the prompt and generous contribution it had made. This was published in the Shanghai local papers —— *The Shanghai Mail* and *Friend of China* —— so that inside of three months after I had started my translating business, I had become widely known among the Chinese as the Chinese student educated in America. I was indebted to Tsang Kee Foo, the comprador, for being in this line of business, and for the fact that I was becoming known in Shanghai. He was a well-educated Chinese —— a man highly respected and trusted for his probity and intelligence. His long connection with the firm and his literary taste had gathered around him some of the finest Chinese scholars from all parts of China, while his business transactions brought him in touch with the leading Chinese capitalists and business men in Shanghai and elsewhere. It was through him that both the epitaph and the circular mentioned above were written;and it was Tsang Kee Foo who introduced me to the celebrated Chinese mathematician, Li Jen Shu, who years afterwards brought me to the notice of Viceroy Tsang Kwoh Fan —— the distinguished general and statesman, who, as will be seen hereafter, took up and promoted the Chinese Education Scheme. In the great web of human affairs, it is almost impossible to know who among our friends and acquaintances may prove to be the right clue to unravel the skein of our destiny. Tsang Kee Foo introduced me to Li Jen Shu, the latter introduced me to Tsang Kwoh Fan, who finally through the Chinese Education Scheme grafted Western education to the Oriental culture, a union destined to weld together the different races of the world into one brotherhood.

My friend Tsang Kee Foo afterwards introduced me to the head or manager of Messrs. Dent & Co., who kindly offered me a position in his firm as comprador in Nagasaki, Japan, soon after that country was opened to foreign trade. I declined the situation, frankly and plainly stating my reason, which was that the compradorship, though lucrative, is associated with all that is menial, and that as a graduate of Yale, one of the leading colleges in America, I could not think of bringing discredit to my Alma Mater, for which I entertained the most profound respect and reverence, and was jealous of her proud fame. What would the college and my class-mates think of me, if they should hear that I was a comprador —— the head servant of servants in an English establishment? I said there were cases when a man from stress of circumstances may be compelled to play the part of a menial for a shift, but I was not yet reduced to that strait, though I was poor financially. I told him I would prefer to travel for the firm as its agent in the interior and correspond directly with the head of the firm. In that case, I would not sacrifice my manhood for the sake of making money in a position which is commonly held to be servile. I would much prefer to pack tea and buy silk as an agent —— either on a salary or on commission. Such was my ground for declining. I, however, thanked him for the offer. This interview took place in the presence of my friend, Tsang Kee Foo, who without knowing the details of the conversation, knew enough of the English language to follow the general tenor of the talk. I then retired and left the manager and my friend to talk over the result. Tsang afterwards told me that Webb said, "Yung Wing is poor but proud. Poverty and pride usually go together, hand in hand." A few days afterwards Tsang informed me that Webb had decided to send me to the tea districts to see and learn the business of packing tea.

Chapter 9
My First Trip to the Tea Districts

On the 11th of March, 1859, I found myself on board of a Woo-Sik-Kwei, a Chinese boat built in Woo-Sik, a city situated on the borders of the Grand Canal, within a short distance of the famous city of Suchau —— a rival of the city of Hangchau, for wealth, population, silk manufacture, and luxury. The word "Kwei" means "fast." Therefore, Woo-Sik-Kwei means fast boats of Woo-Sik. These passenger boats which plied between the principal cities and marts situated near the waters of the canal and lake system in southern Kianksu, were usually built of various sizes and nicely fitted up for the comfort and convenience of the public. Those intended for officials, and the wealthy classes, were built on a larger scale and fitted up in a more pretentious style. They were all flat-bottom boats. They sailed fairly well before the wind, but against it, they were either tracked by lines from the mast to the trackers on shore, or by sculling, at which the Chinese are adepts. They can give a boat a great speed by a pair of sculls resting on steel pivots that are fastened at the stern, one on each side, about the middle of the scull, with four men on each scull; the blades are made to play in the water astern, right and left, which pushes and sends the boat forward at a surprisingly rapid rate. But in recent years, steam has made its way into China and steam launches have superseded these native craft which are fast disappearing from the smooth waters of Kiangsu province —— very much as the fast sailing ships, known as Baltimore Clippers, that in the fifties and sixties were engaged in the East India and China trade, have been gradually swept from the ocean by steam.

At the end of three days, I was landed in the historic city of Hangchau, which is the capital of Chêhkiang. It is situated on a plain of uneven ground, with hills in the southwest and west, and northeast. It covers an area of about three or four square miles. It is of a rectangular shape. Its length is from north to south; its breadth, from east to west. On the west, lies the Si-Hoo or West Lake, a beautiful sheet of limpid water with a gravelly or sandy bottom, stretching from the foot of the city wall to the foot of the mountains which appear in the distance in the rear, rising into the clouds like lofty bulwarks guarding the city on the north.

The Tsientang River, about two miles distant, flanks the city on the east. It takes its rise from the high mountain range of Hwui Chow in the southeast and follows a somewhat irregular course to the bay of the same name, and rushes down the rocky declivities like a foaming steed and empties itself into the bay about forty miles east of the city. This is one of the rivers that have periodical bores in which the tidal waters in their entrance to the bay create a noise like thunder, and the waves rise to the height of eight or ten feet.

Hangchau, aside from her historic fame as having been the seat of the government of the Sung Dynasty of the 12th and 13th centuries, has always maintained a wide reputation for fine buildings, public and private, such as temples, pagodas, mosques and bridges, which go to lend enchantment to the magnificent natural scenery with which she is singularly endowed. But latterly, age and the degeneration of the times have done their work of mischief. Her past glory is fast sinking into obscurity; she will never recover her former prestige, unless a new power arises to make her once more the capital of a regenerated government.

On the 15th of March, I left Hangchau to ascend the Tsientang River, at a station called Kang Kow, or mouth of the river, about two miles east of the city, where boats were waiting for us. Several hundreds of these boats of a peculiar and unique type were riding near the estuary of the river. These boats are called Urh Woo, named after the district where they were built. They vary from fifty to one hundred feet in length, from stem to stern, and are ten or fifteen feet broad, and draw not more than two or three feet of water when fully loaded. They are all flat-bottom boats, built of the most limber and flexible material that can be found, as they are expected to meet strong currents and run against rocks, both in their ascent and descent, on account of the irregularity and rocky bottom of the river. These boats, when completely equipped and covered with bamboo matting, look like huge cylinders, and are shaped like cigars. The interior from stem to stern is divided into separate compartments, or rooms, in which bunks are built to accommodate passengers. These compartments and bunks are removed when room is needed for cargoes. These boats ply between Hangchau and Sheong Shan and do all the interior transportation by water between these entrepôts in Chêhkiang and Kiangsi. Sheong Shan is the important station of Chêhkiang, and Yuh-Shan is that of Kiangsi. The distance between the two entrepôts is about fifty lis, or about sixteen English miles, connected by one of the finest macadamized roads in China. The road is about thirty feet wide, paved with slabs of granite and flanked with greenish-colored cobbles. A fine stone arch which was erected as a land-mark of the boundary line separating Chêhkiang and Kiangsi provinces, spans the whole width of the road. On both sides of the key-stone of the arch are carved four fine Chinese characters, painted in bright blue, viz., Leang Hsing Tung Chu. (兩省通衢)

This is one of the most notable arch-ways through which the inter-provincial trade has been carried on for ages past. At the time when I crossed from Sheong Shan to Yuh-Shan, the river ports of Hankau, Kiukiang, Wuhu and Chinkiang were not opened to foreign trade and steam-boats had not come in to play their part in the carrying trade of the interior of China. This magnificent thoroughfare was crowded with thousands of porters bearing merchandise of all kinds to and fro —— exports and imports for distribution. It certainly presented an interesting sight to the traveller, as well as a profound topic of contemplation to a Chinese patriot.

The opening of the Yangtze River, which is navigable as far as Kingchau, on the borders of Szechwan province, commanding the trade of at least six or seven provinces along its whole course of nearly three thousand miles to the ocean, presents a spectacle of unbounded possibilities for the amelioration of nearly a third of the human race, if only the grasping ambition of the West will let the territorial integrity and the independent sovereignty of China remain intact. Give the people of China a fair chance to work out the problems of their own salvation, as for instance the solution of the labor question, which has been so radically disorganized and broken up by steam, electricity and machinery. This has virtually taken the breath and bread away from nine-tenths of the people of China, and therefore this immovable mass of population should be given ample time to recover from its demoralization.

To go back to my starting point at Kang Kow, the entrance to the river, two miles east of Hangchau, we set sail, with a fair wind, at five o'clock in the morning of the 15th of March, and in the evening at ten o'clock we anchored at a place named the "Seven Dragons," after having made about one hundred miles during the day. The eastern shore in this part of the Tsientang River is evidently of red sandstone formation, for we could see part of the strata submerged in the water, and excavations of the stone may be seen strewn about on the shore. In fact, red sandstone buildings may be seen scattered about here and there. But the mountain about the Seven Dragons is picturesque and romantic.

Early the next day, we again started, but the rain poured down in torrents. We kept on till we reached the town of Lan Chi and came to anchor in the evening, after having made about forty miles. This is the favorite entrepôt where the Hupeh and Hunan congou teas were brought all the way from the tea districts of these provinces, to be housed and transhipped to Shanghai via Hangchau. Lan Chi is an entrepôt of only one street, but its entire length is six miles. It is famous for its nice hams, which are known all over China. On account of the incessant rain, we stopped half a day at Lan Chi. In the afternoon the sky began to clear and at twelve o'clock in the night we again started and reached the walled city of Ku Chow, which was besieged by the Taiping rebels in March, 1858, just a year before; after four months' duration the siege was raised and no great damage was done. We put up in an inn for the night. Ku Chow is a departmental city of Chêhkiang and is about thirty miles distant from Sheong Shan, already mentioned in connection with Yuh-Shan. We were delayed by the Custom House officials, as well as on account of the scarcity of porters and chair-bearers to take us over to Sheong Shan. We arrived at Yuh-Shan from Sheong Shan by chair in the evening. We put up in an inn for the night, having first engaged fishing boats to take us to the city of Kwangshun, thirty miles from Yuh-Shan, the next morning. After reaching Yuh-Shan, we were in Kiangsi territory, and our route now lay in a west by north direction, down stream towards the Po Yang Lake, whose southern margin we passed, and reached Nan Cheong, the capital of Kiangsi province. The city presented a fine outward appearance. We did not stop long enough to go through the city and see its actual condition since its evacuation by the rebels.

Our route from Nan Cheong was changed in a west by south direction, making the great entrepôt of Siang Tan our final goal. In this route, we passed quite a number of large cities that had nothing of special importance, either commercially or historically, to relate. We passed Cheong Sha, the capital of Hunan, in the night. We arrived at Siang Tan on the morning of the 15th of April. Siang Tan is one of the noted entrepôts in the interior of China and used to be the great distributing center of imports when foreign trade was confined to the single port of Canton. It was also the emporium where the tea and silk goods of China were centered and housed, to be carried down to Canton for exportation to foreign countries. The overland transport trade between Siang Tan and Canton was immense. It gave employment to at least one hundred thousand porters, carrying merchandise over the Nan Fung pass, between the two cities, and supported a large population along both sides of the thoroughfare. Steam, wars and treaties of very recent dates have not only broken up this system of labor and changed the complexion of the whole labor question throughout China, but will also alter the economical, industrial and political conditions of the Chinese Empire during the coming years of her history.

At Siang Tan, our whole party, composed of tea-men, was broken up and each batch began its journey to the district assigned it, to begin the work of purchasing raw tea and preparing it to be packed for shipment in Shanghai.

I stayed in Siang Tan about ten days and then made preparations for a trip up to the department of Kingchau in Hupeh province, to look into the yellow silk produced in a district called Ho-Yung.

We left Siang Tan on the 26th of April, and proceeded northward to our place of destination. Next morning at eight o'clock we reached Cheong Sha, the capital of Hunan province. As the day was wet and gloomy, we stopped and tried to make the best of it by going inside of the city to see whether there was anything worth seeing, but like all Chinese cities, it presented the same monotonous appearance of age and filth, the same unchangeable style of architecture and narrow streets. Early next morning, we resumed our boat journey, crossed the Tung Ting Lake and the great river Yangtze till we entered the mouth of the King Ho which carried us to Ho Yung. On this trip to hunt after the yellow silk —— not the golden fleece —— we were thirteen days from Siang Tan. The country on both banks of the King Ho seemed quiet and peaceful and people were engaged in agricultural pursuits. We saw many buffaloes and donkeys, and large patches of wheat, interspersed with beans. A novel sight presented itself which I have never met with elsewhere in China. A couple of country lassies were riding on a donkey, and were evidently in a happy mood, laughing and talking as they rode by. Arriving in Ho Yung, we had some difficulty in finding an inn, but finally succeeded in securing quarters in a silk hong. No sooner were we safely quartered, than a couple of native constables called to know who we were; our names and business were taken down. Our host, the proprietor of the hong, who knew the reason of our coming, explained things to the satisfaction of the men, who went away perfectly satisfied that we were honest traders and no rebel spies. We were left to transact our business unmolested. As soon as our object was known, numerous samples of yellow silk were brought for our inspection. We selected quite a number of samples, which altogether weighed about sixty-five pounds, and had them packed to be taken to Shanghai.

At the end of a fortnight, we concluded to take our journey back. Accordingly, on the 26th of May we bade Ho Yung farewell, and started for the tea district of Nih Kia Shi, in the department of Cheong Sha, via Hankau. We arrived at Hankau on the 5th of June, and put up in a native inn. The weather was hot and muggy, and our quarters were narrow and cut off from fresh air. Three days after our arrival, three deputies visited us to find out who we were. It did not take long to convince them that we were not rebel spies. We showed them the package of yellow silk, which bore marks of a war-tax which we had to pay on it, all along the route from Ho Yung to Hankau. We were left unmolested.

The port of Hankau had not been opened for foreign trade, though it was well understood that it was to be opened very soon. Before its capture by the Taiping rebels, or rather before the Taiping rebels had made their appearance on the stage of action, Hankau was the most important entrepôt in China. When the Taiping rebels captured Woochang in 1856, Hankau and Han Yang fell at the same time, and the port was destroyed by fire and was reduced to ashes. At the time of my visit, the whole place was rebuilt and trade began to revive. But the buildings were temporary shifts. Now the character of the place is completely changed and the foreign residences and warehouses along the water's edge have given it altogether a European aspect, so that the Hankau of today may be regarded as the Chicago or St. Louis of China, and in no distant day she is destined to surpass both in trade, population and wealth. I was in Hankau a few days before I crossed the Yangtze-Kiang to the black tea district of Nih Kia Shi.

We left Hankau on the 30th of June and went over to the tea packing houses in Nih Kia Shi and Yang Liu Tung on the 4th of July. I was in those two places over a month and gained a complete knowledge of the whole process of preparing the black tea for the foreign market. The process is very simple and can be easily learned. I do not know through what preparations the Indian and Assam teas have to go, where machinery is used, but they cannot be very elaborate. Undoubtedly, since the fifties, manual labor, the old standby in preparing teas for foreign consumption, has been much improved with a view of retaining a large percentage of the tea trade in China. The reason why a large percentage of the tea business has passed away from China to India is not because machinery is used in the one case and manual labor is retained in the other, but chiefly on account of the quality of the tea that is raised in the different soil of the two countries. The Indian or Assam tea is much stronger (in proportion to the same quantity) than the Chinese tea. The Indian tea is 2-1 to Chinese tea, in point of strength, whereas the Chinese tea is 2-1 to the Indian tea in point of delicacy and flavor. The Indian is rank and strong, but the Chinese tea is superior in the quality of its fine aroma. The higher class of tea-drinkers in America, Europe and Russia prefer China tea to Indian, whereas the laboring and common class in those countries take to Indian and Assam, from the fact that they are stronger and cheaper.

In the latter part of August I decided to return to Shanghai, not by way of Siang Tan, but via Hankau, down the Yangtze River to Kiu Kang and across the Poh Yang Lake. I arrived at Hankau again the second time on the 29th of August, having left there two months previous, in July. This time I came in a Hunan junk loaded with tea for Shanghai. At Ho Kow, the southern shore of the Poh Yang Lake, I had to follow the same route I took in March, and on the 21st of September I landed at Hangchau and from there I took a Woo-Sik-Kwei for Shanghai, where I arrived in the night of the 30th of September, the time consumed on this journey having been seven months —— from March to October. It was my first journey into the interior of China, and it gave me a chance to gain an insight into the actual condition of the people, while a drastic rebellion was going on in their midst. The zone of the country through which I had passed had been visited by the rebels and the imperialists, but was, to all outward appearance, peaceful and quiet. To what extent the people had suffered both from rebel and imperialist devastations in those sections of the country, no one can tell. But there was one significant fact that struck me forcibly and that was the sparseness of population, which was at variance with my preconceived notions regarding the density of population in China which I had gathered from books and accounts of travelers. This was particularly noticeable through that section of Chêhkiang, Kiangsi, Hunan and Hupeh, which I visited. The time of the year, when crops of all kinds needed to be planted, should have brought out the peasantry into the open fields with oxen, mules, donkeys, buffaloes and horses, as indispensable accessories to farm life. But comparatively few farmers were met with.

Shortly after my arrival from the interior, in October, an English friend of mine requested me to go to Shau Hing to buy raw silk for him. Shau Hing is a city located in a silk district about twenty miles southwest of Hangchau, and noted for its fine quality of silk. I was about two months in this business, when I was taken down with fever and ague and was compelled to give it up. Shau Hing, like most Chinese cities, was filthy and unhealthy and the water that flowed through it was as black as ink. The city was built in the lowest depression of a valley, and the outlet of the river was so blocked that there was hardly any current to carry off the filth that had been accumulating for ages. Hence the city was literally located in a cesspool —— a breeding place for fever and ague, and epidemics of all kinds. But I soon recovered from the attack of the fever and ague and as soon as I could stand on my legs again, I immediately left the malarial atmosphere, and was, in a short time, breathing fresher and purer air.

Chapter 10
My Visit to the Taipings

In the fall of 1859 a small party of two missionaries, accompanied by Tsang Laisun, planned a trip to visit the Taiping rebels in Nanking. I was asked to join them, and I decided to do so. My object in going was to find out for my own satisfaction the character of the Taipings; whether or not they were the men fitted to set up a new government in the place of the Manchu Dynasty. Accordingly, on the 6th of November, 1859, we left Shanghai in a Woo-Sik-Kwei boat, with a stiff northeast breeze in our favor, though we had to stem an ebb tide for an hour. The weather was fine and the whole party was in fine spirits. We happened to have an American flag on board, and on the spur of the moment, it was flung to the breeze, but on a sober second thought, we had it hauled down so as not to attract undue attention and have it become the means of thwarting the purpose of our journey. Instead of taking the Sung-Kiang route which was the highway to Suchau, we turned off into another one in order to avoid the possibility of being hauled up by the imperialists and sent back to Shanghai, as we were told that an imperial fleet of Chinese gun-boats was at anchor at Sung Kiang. We found the surrounding country within a radius of thirty miles of Shanghai to be very quiet and saw no signs of political disturbance. The farmers were busily engaged in gathering in their rice crops.

It might be well to mention here that during my sojourn in the interior, the Taiping rebels had captured the city of Suchau, and there was some apprehension on the part of foreigners in the settlement that they might swoop down to take possession of the city of Shanghai, as well as the foreign settlement. That was the reason the Sung Kiang River was picketed by Chinese gun-boats, and the foreign pickets were extended miles beyond the boundary line of the foreign concession.

We reached Suchau on the morning of the 9th of November without meeting with any difficulty or obstacles all the way, nor were we challenged either by the imperialists or rebels, which went to show how loosely and negligently even in time of war, things were conducted in China. On arriving at the Lau Gate of the city, we had to wait at the station where tickets were issued to those who went into the city and taken from those who left, for Suchau was then under martial law. As we wished to go into the city to see the commandant, in order to get letters of introduction from him to the chiefs of other cities along our route to Nanking, we had to send two of our party to headquarters to find out whether we were permitted to enter. At the station, close to the Lau Gate, we waited over an hour. Finally our party appeared accompanied by the same messenger who had been deputed by the head of the police to accompany them to the commandant's office. Permission was given us, and all four went in. The civil officer was absent, but we were introduced to the military commandant, Liu. He was a tall man, dressed in red. His affected hauteur at the start was too thin to disguise his want of a solid character. He became very inquisitive and asked the object of our journey to Nanking. He treated us very kindly, however, and gave us a letter of introduction to the commandant in Tan Yang, and furnished us with passports all the way through the cities of Woo Sik and Cheong Chow. In the audience hall of Commandant Liu, we were introduced to four foreigners —— two Americans, one Englishman, and a French noble. One of the Americans said he was a doctor, the Englishman was supposed to be a military officer, and the Frenchman, as stated above, claimed to be a nobleman. Doubtless they were all adventurers. Each had his own ax to grind. One of the Americans had a rifle and cartridges for sale. He asked quite an exorbitant price for them and they were summarily rejected. The Frenchman said he had lost a fortune and had come out to China to make it up. Our missionary companions were much pleased after being entertained by Liu in hearing him recite the doxology, which he did glibly. Towards evening, when we returned to our boat, he sent us a number of chickens and a goat to boot. We were thus amply provisioned to prosecute our journey to Tan Yang. We left Suchau on the morning of the 11th of November. On our arrival at Woo Sik, our passports were examined and we were very courteously treated by the rebels. We were invited to dinner by the chief in command. After that he sent us fruits and nuts, and came on board himself to see us off. We held quite a long conversation with him, which ended in his repeating the doxology.

On November 12th we left Woo Sik and started for Cheong Chow. From Suchau onward we were on the Grand Canal. The road on the bank of the canal was in good condition. Most of the people we saw and met were rebels, traveling between Tan Yang and Suchau, and but few boats were seen passing each other. All the country surrounding the canal between those cities seemed to have been abandoned by the peasantry and the cultivated fields were covered with rank grass and weeds, instead of flourishing crops. A traveler, not knowing the circumstances, would naturally lay the blame wholly upon the Taiping rebels, but the imperialists in their conflicts with the rebels, were as culpable as their enemies. The rebels whom we met on the public road were generally very civil and tried in every way to protect the people in order to gain their confidence. Incendiarism, pillage, robbery and ill-treatment of the people by the rebels, were punished by death. We reached Cheong Chow in the night. We found nearly all the houses along the road between Woo Sik and Cheong Chow to be completely deserted and emptied of all their inmates. There were occasionally a few of the inhabitants to be seen standing on the bank with small baskets, peddling eggs, oranges and cakes, vegetables and pork. They were principally old people, with countenances showing their suffering and despair. On November 13th, at six o'clock in the morning, we resumed our journey to Tan Yang. As we drew near Tan Yang, the people seemed to have regained their confidence and the fields seemed to be cultivated. The conduct of the rebels towards them was considerate and commendable. During the morning we saw a force of one thousand men marching towards Tan Yang. We did not quite reach Tan Yang and came to anchor for the night in plain sight of it.

Early next morning, we went into the city to see the Commandant Liu, to present to him the letter we received in Suchau, but he was absent from the city. The man next to Liu, a civilian, came out to meet us. He was very affable and treated us kindly and with great civility. One of our party referred to the religious character of the Taipings.

Chin then gave us his views of Christianity, as taught by Hung Siu Chune —— he leader of the rebellion. He said:

"We worship God the Heavenly Father, with whom Jesus and the Holy Spirit constitute the true God; that Shang Ti is the True Spirit."

He then repeated the doxology. He said the rebels had two doxologies —— the old and the new; they had discarded the new and adopted the old. He said, the Tien Wong —— the Celestial Emperor —— was taken up to Heaven and received orders from the Heavenly Father to come and exterminate all evil and rectify all wrong; to destroy idolatry and evil spirits, and finally to teach the people the knowledge of God. He did not know whether the Tien Wong was translated to Heaven bodily or in spirit, or both. He said the Tien Wong himself explained that he could not hold the same footing with God himself; that the homage paid to God was an act of religious worship, but that rendered to the Tien Wong was merely an act of court etiquette, which ministers and officers always paid to their sovereigns in every dynasty, and could not be construed as acts of worship. He also said that Tien Wong was a younger brother of Christ, but that it did not follow that he was born of the same mother. Tien Wong, he claimed, was a younger brother of Christ in the sense that he was especially appointed by God to instruct the people. Christ was also appointed by God to reform and redeem the world. With regard to the three cups of tea, —— he said that they were intended as a thank-offering, and were not propitiatory in their character.

"Whenever we drink a cup of tea, we offer thanksgiving to the Heavenly Father. The three cups of tea have no reference to the Trinity whatever. One cup answers the same purpose. The number three was purposely chosen, because it is the favorite number with the Chinese, —— it is even mentioned in the Chinese classics."

As for redemption, he said, —— "No sacrificial offering can take away our sins; the power of redemption is in Christ; he redeems us and it is our duty to repent of our sins. Even the Tien Wong is very circumspect and is afraid to sin against God."

In the matter of the soldiery keeping aloof from the people in time of war, he said, —— "It has been an immemorial custom, adopted by almost every dynasty, that the people should go to the country, and the soldiers be quartered in the city. When a city is captured or taken, it is easy to subjugate the surrounding country."

The places we saw in ruins, both at Suchau and all the way up the canal, were partly destroyed by Cheong Yuh Leang's troops in their retreat, partly by local predatory parties for the sake of plunder, and partly by the Taipings themselves. When Chung Wong was in Suchau, he did all he could to suppress incendiarism by offering rewards of both money and rank to those who took an active part in suppressing it. He issued three orders: 1. That soldiers were not allowed to kill or slaughter the inhabitants. 2. They were prohibited from slaughtering cattle. 3. They were prohibited from setting fire to houses. A violation of any of these orders was attended with capital punishment. When he came down to Woo Sik, he had a country elder decapitated for allowing local bandits to burn down the houses of the people. This was the information we gathered from our conversation with Chin. He also said that Ying Wong and Chung Wong were both talented men —— not only in military but also in civil affairs.

He gave us a long account of the capture of different places by the rebels, and how they had been defeated before Nanking, when that city was laid siege to by the imperialists in the early part of 1860. He also showed us a letter by a chief at Hwui Chow regarding the utter defeat and rout of Tsang Kwoh Fan, who was hemmed in by an immense force of the rebels. Tsang was supposed to have been killed in the great battle. He said that Cheong Yuh Leang, the imperialist general, who laid siege to Nanking, after his defeat went to Hangchau for medical treatment for hemorrhage of the lungs; that all the country along the canal, north of the Yangtze, was in the hands of the rebels, and that Princes Chung and Ying were marching up the river to take possession of Hupeh, and that Shih Ta Kai, another chief, was assigned the conquest of Yun Nan, Kwai Chow and Sze Chune provinces. At that time Chin Kiang was being besieged by the rebels, and Chi Wong was in command of an army of observation in Kiang Nan. Such was the rambling statement given us by Chin regarding the disposition of the rebel forces under different chiefs or princes.

After dining with him in the evening, we repaired to our boat for the night. The next morning, November 15th, we again went into the city and called upon Liu, but, failing to see him, we again called upon Chin to arrange for the conveyance of our luggage and ourselves from Tan Yang to Nanking. The aide told us to send all our things to Chin's office and that our boat, if left in Tan Yang until our return, would be well cared for and protected during our absence. So next morning, the 16th of November, we started on foot and walked fifteen miles from Tan Yang to a village called Po Ying, about six miles from the city of Ku Yung, where we halted to pass the night. We had some difficulty in securing a resting place. The people were poor and had no confidence in strangers. We, however, after some coaxing, were supplied with straws spread out on the ground, and the next morning we gave the old women a dollar. We had boiled rice gruel, cold chicken and crackers for our breakfast. When we reached Ku Yung about nine o'clock on the 17th of November, we found that every gate of the city was closed against us, as well as all others, because a rumor was afloat that the rebels before Chin Kiang were defeated, and that they were flocking towards Ku Yung for shelter. So we concluded to continue on our journey towards Nanking, though our missionary friends came near deciding to return to Tan Yang and wend our way back to Shanghai. We proceeded not far from Ku Yung, when we finally succeeded in getting chairs and mules to prosecute our journey.

On the 18th of November, after a trying and wearisome journey, we reached Nanking. I was the first one to reach the South Gate, waiting for the rest of the party to come up before entering. We were reported inside of the gate and messengers accompanied us to the headquarters of the Rev. Mr. Roberts, close by the headquarters of Hung Jin, styled Prince Kan.

After our preliminary introduction to the Rev. Mr. Roberts, I excused myself, and leaving the rest of the party to continue their conversation with him, retired to my quarters to clean up and get rested from the long and tedious journey. In fact, I had little or nothing to say while in Mr. Roberts' presence, nor did I attempt to make myself known to him. I had seen him often in Macao when in Mrs. Gutzlaff's school, twenty or more years before, and I had recognized him at once as soon as I set my eyes on him. He certainly appeared old to me, being dressed in his yellow satin robe of state and moving leisurely in his clumsy Chinese shoes. Exactly in what capacity he was acting in Nanking, I was at a loss to know; whether still as a religious adviser to Hung Siu Chune, or playing the part of secretary of state for the Taiping Dynasty, no one seemed able to tell.

The next day (the 19th of November) I was invited to call on Kan Wong. He was a nephew of Hung Siu Chune, the rebel chief who was styled Tien Wong or the Celestial Sovereign. Before Hung Jin came to Nanking, I had made his acquaintance, in 1856, at Hong Kong. He was then connected with the London Mission Association as a native preacher and was under Dr. James Legge, the distinguished translator of the Chinese classics. I saw considerable of him while in Hong Kong and even then he had expressed a wish that he might see me some day in Nanking. He was then called Hung Jin, but since he had joined his uncle in Nanking, he was raised to the position of a prince. Kan means "Protecting," and Kan Wong signifies "Protecting Prince." He greeted me very cordially and evidently was glad to see me. After the usual exchange of conventionalities, he wanted to know what I thought of the Taipings; whether I thought well enough of their cause to identify myself with it. In reply, I said I had no intention of casting my lot with them, but came simply to see him and pay my respects. At the same time, I wanted to find out for my own satisfaction the actual condition of things in Nanking. I said the journey from Suchau to Nanking had suggested several things to me, which I thought might be of interest to him. They were as follows:

1. To organize an army on scientific principles.

2. To establish a military school for the training of competent military officers.

3. To establish a naval school for a navy.

4. To organize a civil government with able and experienced men to act as advisers in the different departments of administration.

5. To establish a banking system, and to determine on a standard of weight

and measure.

6. To establish an educational system of graded schools for the people, making the Bible one of the text books.

7. To organize a system of industrial schools.

These were the topics that suggested themselves to me during the journey. If the Taiping government would be willing, I said, to adopt these measures and set to work to make suitable appropriations for them, I would be perfectly willing to offer my services to help carry them out. It was in that capacity that I felt I could be of the most service to the Taiping cause. In any other, I would simply be an encumbrance and a hindrance to them.

Such was the outcome of my first interview. Two days later, I was again invited to call. In the second interview, we discussed the merits and the importance of the seven proposals stated in our first interview. Kan Wong, who had seen more of the outside world than the other princes or leaders, and even more than Hung Siu Chune himself, knew wherein lay the secret of the strength and power of the British government and other European powers, and fully appreciated the paramount importance and bearing of these proposals. But he was alone and had no one to back him in advocating them. The other princes, or leaders, were absent from the city, carrying on their campaign against the imperialists. He said he was well aware of the importance of these measures, but nothing could be done until they returned, as it required the consent of the majority to any measure before it could be carried out.

A few days after this a small parcel was presented to me as coming from Kan Wong. On opening it, I found to my great surprise a wooden seal about four inches long and an inch wide, having my name carved with the title of "E" (義), which means "Righteousness," and designates the fourth official rank under that of a prince, which is the first. My title was written out on a piece of yellow satin stamped with the official seal of the Kan Wong. I was placed in a quandary and was at a loss to know its purport, —— whether it was intended to detain me in Nanking for good or to commit me irretrievably to the Taiping cause, nolens volens. At all events, I had not been consulted in the matter and Kan Wong had evidently acted on his own responsibility and taken it for granted that by conferring on me such a high rank as the fourth in the official scale of the Taipings, I might be induced to accept and thus identify myself with the Taiping cause —— of the final success of which I had strong doubts, judging from the conduct, character and policy of the leading men connected with it. I talked the matter over with my associates, and came to the decision that I must forthwith return the seal and decline the tempting bauble. I went in person to thank Kan Wong for this distinguished mark of his high consideration, and told him that at any time when the leaders of the Taipings decided to carry out either one or all of my suggestions, made in my first interview with him, I should be most happy to serve them, if my services were needed to help in the matter. I then asked him as a special favor for a passport that would guarantee me a safe conduct in traveling through the territory under the jurisdiction of the Taipings, whether on business or pleasure. The passport was issued to me the next day, on the 24th of December, and we were furnished with proper conveyances and provisions to take us back to the city of Tan Yang, where our boat lay under the protection of Chin, second in command of the city, waiting our return from Nanking. We started on our return trip for Shanghai on the 27th of December by the same route as we came, and arrived safely in Tan Yang in the early part of January, 1861.

On my way back to Shanghai, I had ample time to form an estimate of the Taiping Rebellion —— its origin, character and significance.

Chapter 11
Reflections on the Taiping Rebellion

Rebellions and revolutions in China are not new and rare historic occurrences. There have been at least twenty-four dynasties and as many attendant rebellions or revolutions. But with the exception of the Feudatory period, revolutions in China (since the consolidation of the three Kingdoms into one Empire under the Emperor Chin) meant only a change of hands in the government, without a change either of its form, or principles. Hence the history of China for at least two thousand years, like her civilization, bears the national impress of a monotonous dead level —— jejune in character, wanting in versatility of genius, and almost devoid of historic inspiration.

The Taiping Rebellion differs from its predecessors in that in its embryo stage it had taken onto itself the religious element, which became the vital force that carried it from the defiles and wilds of Kwangsi province in the southwest to the city of Nanking in the northeast, and made it for a period of fifteen years a constantly impending danger to the Manchu Dynasty, whose corruption, weakness and maladministration were the main causes that evoked the existence of this great rebellion.

The religious element that gave it life and character was a foreign product, introduced into China by the early Protestant missionaries, of whom Dr. Robert Morrison was the first English pioneer sent out by the London Mission, followed a decade later by the Rev. Icabod J. Roberts, an American missionary. These two missionaries may properly claim the credit, if there is any, of having contributed (each in his particular sphere) in imparting to Hung Siu Chune a knowledge of Christianity. Dr. Morrison, on his part, had translated the Bible into Chinese, and the Emperor Khang Hsi's dictionary into English; both these achievements gave the missionary work in China a basis to go upon in prosecuting the work of revising and of bringing the Bible to the Chinese standard of literary taste, so as to commend it to the literary classes, and in making further improvements in perfecting the Chinese-English dictionary, which was subsequently done by such men as Dr. Medhurst, Bishop Boone, Dr. Legge, E. C. Bridgeman, and S. Wells Williams.

Besides these works of translation, which undoubtedly called for further revision and improvement, Dr. Morrison also gave China a native convert —— Leang Ahfah —— who became afterwards a noted preacher and the author of some religious tracts.

Hung Siu Chune, in his quest after religious knowledge and truths, got hold of a copy of Dr. Morrison's Bible and the tracts of Leang Ahfah. He read and studied them, but he stood in need of a teacher to explain to him many points in the Bible, which appeared to him mysterious and obscure. He finally made the acquaintance of the Rev. Mr. Icabod J.Roberts, an American missionary from Missouri, who happened to make his headquarters in Canton. Hung Siu Chune called upon him often, till their acquaintance ripened into a close and lasting friendship, which was kept up till Hung Siu Chune succeeded in taking Nanking, when Mr. Roberts was invited to reside there in the double capacity of a religious teacher and a state adviser. This was undoubtedly done in recognition of Mr. Roberts' services as Hung's teacher and friend while in Canton. No one knew what had become of Mr. Roberts when Nanking fell and reverted to the imperialists in 1864.

It was about this time, when he was sedulously seeking Mr. Roberts' religious instructions at Canton, that Hung failed to pass his first competitive examination as a candidate to compete for official appointment, and he decided to devote himself exclusively to the work of preaching the Gospel to his own people, the Hakkas of Kwang Tung and Kwangsi. But as a colporter and native preacher, Hung had not reached the climax of his religious experience before taking up his stand as the leader of his people in open rebellion against the Manchu Dynasty.

We must go back to the time when, as a candidate for the literary competitive examinations, he was disappointed. This threw him into a fever, and when he was tossing about in delirium, he was supposed to have been translated to Heaven, where he was commanded by the Almighty to fill and execute the divine mission of his life, which was to destroy idolatry, to rectify all wrong, to teach the people a knowledge of the true God, and to preach redemption through Christ. In view of such a mission, and being called to the presence of God, he at once assumed himself to be the son of God, co-equal with Christ, whom he called his elder brother.

It was in such a state of mental hallucination that Hung Siu Chune appeared before his little congregation of Hakkas—migrating strangers—in the defiles and wilds of Kwangsi. Their novel and strange conduct as worshippers of Shangti—the Supreme Ruler—their daily religious exercises, their prayers, and their chanting of the doxology as taught and enjoined by him, had attracted a widespread attention throughout all the surrounding region of Kwangsi. Every day fresh accessions of new comers flocked to their fold and swelled their ranks, till their numerical force grew so that the local mandarins were baffled and at their wits' end to know what to do with these believers of Christianity. Such, in brief, was the origin, growth and character of the Christian element working among the simple and rustic mountaineers of Kwangsi and Kwang Tung.

It is true that their knowledge of Christianity, as sifted through the medium of the early missionaries from the West, and the native converts and colporters, was at best crude and elementary, but still they were truths of great power, potential enough to turn simple men and religiously-inclined women into heroes and heroines who faced dangers and death with the utmost indifference, as was seen subsequently, when the government had decided to take the bull by the horns and resorted to persecution as the final means to break up this religious, fanatical community. In their conflicts with the imperial forces, they had neither guns nor ammunition, but fought with broomsticks, flails and pitchforks. With these rustic and farming implements they drove the imperialist hordes before them as chaff and stubble before a hurricane. Such was their pent-up religious enthusiasm and burning ardor.

Now this religious persecution was the side issue that had changed the resistance of Hung Siu Chune and his followers, in their religious capacity, into the character of a political rebellion. It is difficult to say whether or not, if persecution had not been resorted to, Hung Siu Chune and his followers would have remained peaceably in the heart of China and developed a religious community. We are inclined to think, however, that even if there had been no persecution, a rebellion would have taken place, from the very nature of the political situation.

Neither Christianity nor religious persecution was the immediate and logical cause of the rebellion of 1850. They might be taken as incidents or occasions that brought it about, but they were not the real causes of its existence. These may be found deeply seated in the vitals of the political constitution of the government. Foremost among them was the corruption of the administrative government. The whole official organization, from head to foot, was honeycombed and tainted by a system of bribery, which passed under the polite and generic term of "presents," similar in character to what is now known as "graft." Next comes the exploitation of the people by the officials, who found an inexhaustible field to build up their fortunes. Finally comes the inevitable and logical corollary to official bribery and exploitation, namely, that the whole administrative government was founded on a gigantic system of fraud and falsehood.

This rebellion rose in the arena of China with an enigmatic character like that of the Sphinx, somewhat puzzling at the start. The Christian world throughout the whole West, on learning of its Christian tendencies, such as the worship of the true and living God; Christ the Savior of the world; the Holy Spirit, the purifier of the soul; the destruction of temples and idols that was found wherever their victorious arms carried them; the uncompromising prohibition of the opium habit; the observance of a Sabbath; the offering of prayers before and after meals; the invocation of divine aid before a battle —— all these cardinal points of a Christian faith created a world-wide impression that China, through the instrumentality of the Taipings, was to be evangelized; that the Manchu Dynasty was to be swept out of existence, and a "Celestial Empire of Universal Peace," as it was named by Hung Siu Chune, was going to be established, and thus China, by this wonderful intervention of a wise Providence, would be brought within the pale of Christian nations. But Christendom was a little too credulous and impulsive in the belief. It did not stop to have the Christianity of the Taipings pass through the crucible of a searching analysis.

Their first victory over their persecutors undoubtedly gave Hung Siu Chune and his associates the first intimation of a possible overturning of the Manchu Dynasty and the establishment of a new one, which he named in his religious ecstasy "The Celestial Empire of Universal Peace." To the accomplishment of this great object, they bent the full force of their iconoclastic enthusiasm and religious zeal.

En route from Kwang Si, their starting point, to Nanking, victory had perched on their standard all the way. They had despatched a division of their army to Peking, and, on its way to the northern capitol, it had met with a repulse and defeat at Tientsin from whence they had turned back to Nanking. In their victorious march through Hunan, Hupeh, Kiang Si and part of An Hwui, their depleted forces were replenished and reinforced by fresh and new accessions gathered from the people of those provinces. They were the riffraff and scum of their populations. This rabble element added no new strength to their fighting force, but proved to be an encumbrance and caused decided weakness. They knew no discipline, and had no restraining religious power to keep them from pillage, plunder and indiscriminate destruction. It was through such new accessions that the Taiping cause lost its prestige, and was defeated before Tientsin and forced to retreat to Nanking. After their defeat in the North, they began to decline in their religious character and their bravery. Their degeneracy was accelerated by the capture of Yang Chow, Suchau, and Hangchau, cities noted in Chinese history for their great wealth as well as for their beautiful women. The capture of these centers of a materialistic civilization poured into their laps untold wealth and luxury which tended to hasten their downfall.

The Taiping Rebellion, after fifteen years of incessant and desultory fighting, collapsed and passed into oblivion, without leaving any traces of its career worthy of historical commemoration beyond the fact that it was the outburst of a religious fanaticism which held the Christian world in doubt and bewilderment, by reason of its Christian origin. It left no trace of its Christian element behind either in Nanking, where it sojourned for nearly ten years, or in Kwang Si, where it had its birth. In China, neither new political ideas nor political theories or principles were discovered which would have constituted the basal facts of a new form of government. So that neither in the religious nor yet in the political world was mankind in China or out of China benefited by that movement. The only good that resulted from the Taiping Rebellion was that God made use of it as a dynamic power to break up the stagnancy of a great nation and wake up its consciousness for a new national life, as subsequent events in 1894, 1895, 1898, 1900, 1901, and 1904-5 fully demonstrated.

Chapter 12
Expedition to the Taiping Tea District

My Nanking visit was utterly barren of any substantial hope of promoting any scheme of educational or political reform for the general welfare of China or for the advancement of my personal interest. When I was thoroughly convinced that neither the reformation nor the regeneration of China was to come from the Taipings, I at once turned my thoughts to the idea of making a big fortune as my first duty, and as the first element in the successful carrying out of other plans for the future.

One day, while sauntering about in the tea garden inside the city of Shanghai, I came across a few tea-merchants regaling themselves with that beverage in a booth by themselves, evidently having a very social time. They beckoned to me to join their party. In the course of the conversation, we happened to touch on my late journey through the tea districts of Hunan, Hupeh and Kiang Si and also my trip to Nanking. Passing from one topic of conversation to another, we lighted upon the subject of the green tea district of Taiping in An Hwui province. It was stated that an immense quantity of green tea could be found there, all packed and boxed ready for shipment, and that the rebels were in possession of the goods, and that whoever had the hardihood and courage to risk his life to gain possession of it would become a millionaire. I listened to the account with deep and absorbing interest, taking in everything that was said on the subject. It was stated that there were over 1,000,000 chests of tea there. Finally the party broke up, and I wended my way to my quarters completely absorbed in deep thought. I reasoned with myself that this was a chance for me to make a fortune, but wondered who would be foolhardy enough to furnish the capital, thinking that no business man of practical experience would risk his money in such a wild goose adventure, surrounded as it was with more than ordinary dangers and difficulties, in a country where highway robbery, lawlessness and murder were of daily occurrence. But with the glamor of a big fortune confronting me, all privations, dangers and risks of life seemed small and faded into airy nothing.

My friend, Tsang Mew, who had been instrumental in having me sent traveling into the interior a year before, was a man of great business experience. He had a long head and a large circle of business acquaintances, besides being my warm friend, so I concluded to go to him and talk over the whole matter, as I knew he would not hesitate to give me his best advice. I laid the whole subject before him. He said he would consider the matter fully and in a few days let me know what he had decided to do about it. After a few days, he told me that he had had several consultations with the head of the firm, of which he was comprador, and between them the company had decided to take up my project.

The plan of operation as mapped out by me was as follows: I was to go to the district of Taiping by the shortest and safest route possible, to find out whether the quantity of tea did exist; whether it was safe to have treasure taken up there to pay the rebels for the tea; and whether it was possible to have the tea supply taken down by native boats to be transhipped by steamer to Shanghai. This might be called the preliminary expedition. Then, I was to determine which of the two routes would be the more feasible, —— there being two, one by way of Wuhu, a treaty port, and another by way of Ta Tung, not a treaty port, a hundred miles above Wuhu. Wuhu and the whole country leading to Taiping, including the district itself, was under the jurisdiction of the rebels, whereas Ta Tung was still in possession of the imperialists. From Wuhu to Taiping by river the distance was about two hundred and fifty miles, whereas, by way of Ta Tung, the way, though shorter, was mostly overland, which made transportation more difficult and expensive, besides having to pay the imperialists a heavy war-tax at Ta Tung, while duty and war-tax were entirely free at Wuhu.

In this expedition of inspection, I chose Wuhu as the basis of my operation. I started with four Chinese tea-men, natives of Taiping who had fled to Shanghai as refugees when the whole district was changed into a theatre of bloody conflicts between the imperialist and rebel forces for two years. On the way up the Wuhu River, we passed three cities mostly deserted by their inhabitants, but occupied by rebels. Paddy fields on both sides of the river were mostly left uncultivated and deserted, overrun with rank weeds and tall grass. As we ascended towards Taiping, the whole region presented a heartrending and depressing scene of wild waste and devastation. Whole villages were depopulated and left in a dilapidated condition. Out of a population of 500,000 only a few dozen people were seen wandering about in a listless, hopeless condition, very much emaciated and looking like walking skeletons.

After a week's journey we reached the village of San Kow, where we were met and welcomed by three tea-men who had been in Shanghai about four years previous. It seemed that they had succeeded in weathering the storm which had swept away the bulk of the population and left them among the surviving few. They were mighty glad to see us, and our appearance in the village seemed to be a God-send. Among the houses that were left intact, I selected the best of them to be my headquarters for the transaction of the tea business. The old tea-men were brought in to co-operate in the business and they showed us where the tea was stored. I was told that in San Kow there were at least five hundred thousand boxes, but in the whole district of Taiping there were at least a million and a half boxes, about sixty pounds of tea to a box.

At the end of another week, I returned to Wuhu and reported all particulars. I had found that the way up from Wuhu by river to Taiping was perfectly safe and I did not anticipate any danger to life or treasure. I had seen a large quantity of the green tea myself and found out that all that was needed was to ship as much treasure as it was safe to have housed in Wuhu, and from there to have it transferred in country tea-boats, well escorted by men in case of any emergency. I also sent samples of the different kinds of green tea to Shanghai to be inspected and listed. These proved to be satisfactory, and the order came back to buy as much of the stock as could be bought.

I was appointed the head of all succeeding expeditions to escort treasure up the river to San Kow and cargoes of tea from there to Wuhu. In one of these expeditions, I had a staff of six Europeans and an equal number of Chinese tea-men. We had eight boxes of treasure containing altogether Tls. 40,000. A tael, in the sixties, according to the exchange of that period, was equal to $1.33, making the total amount in Mexican dollars to be a little over $53,000. We had a fleet of eight tea-boats, four large ones and four smaller ones. The treasure was divided into two equal parts and was placed in the two largest and staunchest boats. The men were also divided into two squads, three Europeans and three Chinese in one large boat and an equal number in the other. We were well provided with firearms, revolvers and cutlasses. Besides the six Europeans, we had about forty men including the boatmen, but neither the six tea-men nor the boatmen could be relied upon to show fight in case of emergency. The only reliable men I had to fall back upon, in case of emergency, were the Europeans; even in these I was not sure I could place implicit confidence, for they were principally runaway sailors of an adventurous character picked up in Shanghai by the company and sent up to

Wuhu to escort the treasure up to the interior. Among them was an Englishman who professed to be a veterinary doctor. He was over six feet tall in his stocking feet, a man of fine personal appearance, but he did not prove himself to be of very stout heart, as may be seen presently. Thus prepared and equipped, we left Wuhu in fine spirits. We proceeded on our journey a little beyond the city of King Yuen, which is about half the way to San Kow. We could have gone a little beyond King Yuen, but thinking it might be safer to be near the city, where the rebel chief had seen my passport, obtained in Nanking, and knew that I had influential people in Nanking, we concluded to pass the night in a safe secluded little cove in the bend of the river just large enough for our little boats to moor close to each other, taking due precaution to place the two largest ones in the center, flanked by the other boats on the right and left of them; the smaller boats occupied the extreme ends of the line.

Before retiring, I had ordered all our firearms to be examined and loaded and properly distributed. Watchmen were stationed in each boat to keep watch all night, for which they were to be paid extra. The precautionary steps having thus been taken, we all retired for the night. An old tea-man and myself were the only ones who lay wide awake while the rest gave unmistakable signs of deep sleep. I felt somewhat nervous and could not sleep. The new moon had peeked in upon us occasionally with her cold smile, as heavy and dark clouds were scudding across her path. Soon she was shut in and disappeared, and all was shrouded in pitch darkness. The night was nearly half spent, when my ears caught the distant sound of whooping and yelling which seemed to increase in volume. I immediately started up to dress myself and quietly woke up the Europeans and Chinese in both boats. As the yelling and whooping drew nearer and nearer it seemed to come from a thousand throats, filling the midnight air with unearthly sounds. In another instant countless torch lights were seen dancing and whirling in the dismal darkness right on the opposite bank. Fortunately the river was between this marauding band and us, while pitch darkness concealed our boats from their sight. In view of such impending danger, we held a council of war. None of us were disposed to fight and endanger our lives in a conflict in which the odds were fearfully against us, there being about a thousand to one. But the English veterinary doctor was the foremost and most strenuous of the Europeans to advocate passive surrender. His countenance actually turned pale and he trembled all over, whether from fear or the chilly atmosphere of the night I could not tell. Having heard from each one what he had to say, I could do nothing but step forward and speak to them, which I did in this wise: "Well, boys, you have all decided not to fight in case we are attacked, but to surrender our treasure. The ground for taking such a step is that we are sure to be outnumbered by a rebel host. So that in such a dilemma discretion is the better part of valor, and Tls. 40,000 are not worth sacrificing our lives for. But by surrendering our trust without making an effort of some kind to save it, we would be branded as unmitigated cowards, and we could never expect to be trusted with any responsible commission again. Now, I will tell you what I propose to do. If the rebel horde should come over and attempt to seize our treasure, I will spring forward with my yellow silk passport, and demand to see their chief, while you fellows with your guns and arms must stand by the treasure. Do not fire and start the fight. By parleying with them, it will for the moment check their determination to plunder, and they will have a chance to find out who we are, and where I obtained the passport; and, even if they should carry off the treasure, I shall tell their chief that I will surely report the whole proceeding in Nanking and recover every cent of our loss."

These remarks seemed to revive the spirit and courage of the men, after which we all sat on the forward decks of our boats anxiously waiting for what the next moment would bring forth. While in this state of expectancy, our hearts palpitating in an audible fashion, our eyes were watching intently the opposite shore. All the shouting and yelling seemed to have died away, and nothing could be seen but torches moving about slowly and leisurely in regular detachments, each detachment stopping occasionally and then moving on again. This was kept up for over two hours, while they constantly receded from us. I asked an old boatman the meaning of such movements and was told that the marauding horde was embarking in boats along the whole line of the opposite shore and was moving down stream. It was three o'clock in the morning, and it began to rain. A few of the advance boats had passed us without discovering where we were. They were loaded with men and floated by us in silence. By four o'clock the last boats followed the rest and soon disappeared from sight. Evidently, from the stillness that characterized the long line of boats as they floated down stream, the buccaneering horde was completely used up by their looting expedition, and at once abandoned themselves to sound sleep when they got on board the boats. We thanked our stars for such a narrow escape from such an unlooked-for danger. We owed our safety to the darkness of the night, the rain and to the fact that we were on the opposite shore in a retired cove. By five o'clock all our anxieties and fears were laid aside and turned into joy and thankfulness. We resumed our journey with light hearts and reached San Kow two days later in peace and safety. In less than two weeks we sent down to Wuhu, escorted by Europeans and tea-men, the first installment, consisting of fifteen boatloads of tea to be transhipped by steamer to Shanghai. The next installment consisted of twelve boatloads. I escorted that down the river in person. The river, in some places, especially in the summer, was quite shallow and a way had to be dug to float the boats down. In one or two instances the boatmen were very reluctant to jump into the water to do the work of deepening the river, and on one occasion I had to jump in, with the water up to my waist, in order to set them an example. When they caught the idea and saw me in the water, every man followed my example and vied with each other in clearing a way for the boats, for they saw I meant business and there was no fooling about it either.

I was engaged in this Taiping tea business for about six months, and took away about sixty-five thousand boxes of tea, which was hardly a tenth part of the entire stock found in the district. Then I was taken down with the fever and ague of the worst type. As I could get no medical relief at Wuhu, I was obliged to return to Shanghai, where I was laid up sick for nearly two months. Those two months of sickness had knocked all ideas of making a big fortune out of my head. I gave up the Taiping tea enterprise, because it called for a greater sacrifice of health and wear upon my nervous system than I was able to stand. The King Yuen midnight incident, which came near proving a disastrous one for me, with the marauding horde of unscrupulous cut-throats, had been quite a shock on my nervous system at the time and may have been the primal cause of my two months' sickness; it served as a sufficient warning to me not to tax my nervous system by further encounters and disputes with the rebel chiefs, whose price on the tea we bought of them was being increased every day. A dispassionate and calm view of the enterprise convinced me that I would have to preserve my life, strength and energy for a higher and worthier object than any fortune I might make out of this Taiping tea, which, after all, was plundered property. I am sure that no fortune in the world could be brought in the balance to weigh against my life, which is of inestimable value to me.

Although I had made nothing out of the Taiping teas, yet the fearless spirit, the determination to succeed, and the pluck to be able to do what few would undertake in face of exceptional difficulties and hazards, that I had exhibited in the enterprise, were in themselves assets worth more to me than a fortune. I was well-known, both among foreign merchants and native business men, so that as soon as it was known that I had given up the Taiping tea enterprise on account of health,

I was offered a tea agency in the port of Kew Keang for packing teas for another foreign firm. I accepted it as a temporary shift, but gave it up in less than six months and started a commission business on my own account. I continued this business for nearly three years and was doing as well as I had expected to do. It was at this time while in Kew Keang that I caught the first ray of hope of materializing the educational scheme I had been weaving during the last year of my college life.

Chapter 13
My Interviews with Tsang Kwoh Fan

In 1863, I was apparently prospering in my business, when, to my great surprise, an unexpected letter from the city of Ngan Khing, capital of An Whui province, was received. The writer was an old friend whose acquaintance I had made in Shanghai in 1857. He was a native of Ningpo, and was in charge of the first Chinese gunboat owned by the local Shanghai guild. He had apparently risen in official rank and had become one of Tsang Kwoh Fan's secretaries. His name was Chang Shi Kwei. In this letter, Chang said he was authorized by Viceroy Tsang Kwoh Fan to invite me to come down to Ngan Khing to call, as he (the Viceroy) had heard of me and wished very much to see me. On the receipt of the letter I was in a quandary and asked myself many questions: What could such a distinguished man want of me? Had he got wind of my late visit to Nanking and of my late enterprise to the district of Taiping for the green tea that was held there by the rebels? Tsang Kwoh Fan himself had been in the department of Hwui Chow fighting the rebels a year before and had been defeated, and he was reported to have been killed in battle. Could he have been told that I had been near the scene of his battle and had been in communication with the rebels, and did he want, under a polite invitation, to trap me and have my head off? But Chang, his secretary, was an old friend of many years' standing. I knew his character well; he wouldn't be likely to play the cat's paw to have me captured. Thus deliberating from one surmise to another, I concluded not to accept the invitation until I had learned more of the great man's purpose in sending for me.

In reply to the letter, I wrote and said I thanked His Excellency for his great condescension and considered it a great privilege and honor to be thus invited, but on account of the tea season having set in (which was in February), I was obliged to attend to the orders for packing tea that were fast coming in; but that as soon as they were off my hands, I would manage to go and pay my respects to His Excellency.

Two months after receiving the first letter, a second one came urging me to come to Ngan Khing as early as possible. This second letter enclosed a letter written by Li Sien Lan, the distinguished Chinese mathematician, whose acquaintance I had also made while in Shanghai. He was the man who assisted a Mr. Wiley, a missionary of the London Board of Missions, in the translation of several mathematical works into Chinese, among which was the Integral and Differential Calculus over which I well remember to have "flunked and fizzled" in my sophomore year in college; and, in this connection, I might as well frankly own that in my make-up mathematics was left out. Mr. Li Sien Lan was also an astronomer. In his letter, he said he had told Viceroy Tsang Kwoh Fan who I was and that I had had a foreign education; how I had raised a handsome subscription to help the famine refugees in 1857; that I had a strong desire to help China to become prosperous, powerful and strong. He said the viceroy had some important business for me to do, and that Chu and Wa, who were interested in machinery of all kinds, were also in Ngan Khing, having been invited there by the Viceroy. Mr. Li's letter completely dispelled all doubts and misgivings on my part as to the viceroy's design in wishing to see me, and gave me an insight as to his purpose for sending for me.

As an answer to these letters, I wrote saying that in a couple of months I should be more at liberty to take the journey. But my second reply did not seem to satisfy the strong desire on the part of Tsang Kwoh Fan to see me. So in July, 1863, I received a third letter from Chang and a second one from Li. In these letters the object of the viceroy was clearly and frankly stated. He wanted me to give up my mercantile business altogether and identify myself under him in the service of the state government, and asked whether or not I could come down to Ngan Khing at once. In view of this unexpected offer, which demanded prompt and explicit decision, I was not slow to see what possibility there was of carrying out my educational scheme, having such a powerful man as Tsang Kwoh Fan to back it. I immediately replied that upon learning the wishes of His Excellency, I had taken the whole situation into consideration, and had concluded to go to his headquarters at Ngan Khing, just as soon as I had wound up my business, which would take me a complete month, and that I would start by August at the latest. Thus ended the correspondence which was really the initiatory step of my official career.

Tsang Kwoh Fan was a most remarkable character in Chinese history. He was regarded by his contemporaries as a great scholar and a learned man. Soon after the Taiping Rebellion broke out and began to assume vast proportions, carrying before it province after province, Tsang began to drill an army of his own compatriots of Hunan who had always had the reputation of being brave and hardy fighters. In his work of raising a disciplined army, he secured the co-operation of other Hunan men, who afterwards took a prominent part in building up a flotilla of river gun-boats. This played a great and efficient part as an auxiliary force on the Yangtze River, and contributed in no small measure to check the rapid and ready concentration of the rebel forces, which had spread over a vast area on both banks of the great Yangtze River. In the space of a few years the lost provinces were gradually recovered, till the rebellion was narrowed down within the single province of Kiang Su, of which Nanking, the capital of the rebellion, was the only stronghold left. This finally succumbed to the forces of Tsang Kwoh Fan in 1864.

To crush and end a rebellion of such dimensions as that of the Taipings was no small task. Tsang Kwoh Fan was made the generalissimo of the imperialists. To enable him to cope successfully with the Taipings, Tsang was invested with almost regal power. The revenue of seven or eight provinces was laid at his feet for disposal, also official ranks and territorial appointments were at his command. So Tsang Kwoh Fan was literally and practically the supreme power of China at the time. But true to his innate greatness, he was never known to abuse the almost unlimited power that was placed in his hands, nor did he take advantage of the vast resources that were at his disposal to enrich himself or his family, relatives or friends. Unlike Li Hung Chang, his protégé and successor, who bequeathed Tls. 40,000,000 to his descendants after his death, Tsang died comparatively poor, and kept the escutcheon of his official career untarnished and left a name and character honored and revered for probity, patriotism and purity. He had great talents, but he was modest. He had a liberal mind, but he was conservative. He was a perfect gentleman and a nobleman of the highest type. It was such a man that I had the great fortune to come in contact with in the fall of 1863.

After winding up my business in New Keang, I took passage in a native boat and landed at Ngan Khing in September. There, in the military headquarters of Viceroy Tsang Kwoh Fan, I was met by my friends, Chang Si Kwei, Li Sien Lan, Wha Yuh Ting and Chu Siuh Chune, all old friends from Shanghai. They were glad to see me, and told me that the viceroy for the past six months, after hearing them tell that as a boy I had gone to America to get a Western education, had manifested the utmost curiosity and interest to see me, which accounted for the three letters which Chang and Li had written urging me to come. Now, since I had arrived, their efforts to get me there had not been fruitless, and they certainly claimed some credit for praising me up to the viceroy. I asked them if they knew what His Excellency wanted me for, aside from the curiosity of seeing a native of China made into a veritable Occidental. They all smiled significantly and told me that I would find out after one or two interviews. From this, I judged that they knew the object for which I was wanted by the Viceroy, and perhaps, they were at the bottom of the whole secret.

The next day I was to make my début, and called. My card was sent in, and without a moment's delay or waiting in the ante-room, I was ushered into the presence of the great man of China. After the usual ceremonies of greeting, I was pointed to a seat right in front of him. For a few minutes he sat in silence, smiling all the while as though he were much pleased to see me, but at the same time his keen eyes scanned me over from head to foot to see if he could discover anything strange in my outward appearance. Finally, he took a steady look into my eyes which seemed to attract his special attention. I must confess I felt quite uneasy all the while, though I was not abashed. Then came his first question.

"How long were you abroad?"

"I was absent from China eight years in pursuit of a Western education."

"Would you like to be a soldier in charge of a company?"

"I should be pleased to head one if I had been fitted for it. I have never studied military science."

"I should judge from your looks, you would make a fine soldier, for I can see from your eyes that you are brave and can command."

"I thank Your Excellency for the compliment. I may have the courage of a soldier, but I certainly lack military training and experience, and on that account I may not be able to meet Your Excellency's expectations."

When the question of being a soldier was suggested, I thought he really meant to have me enrolled as an officer in his army against the rebels; but in this I was mistaken, as my Shanghai friends told me afterwards. He simply put it forward to find out whether my mind was at all martially inclined. But when he found by my response that the bent of my thought was something else, he dropped the military subject and asked me my age and whether or not I was married. The last question closed my first introductory interview, which had lasted only about half an hour. He began to sip his tea and I did likewise, which according to Chinese official etiquette means that the interview is ended and the guest is at liberty to take his departure.

I returned to my room, and my Shanghai friends soon flocked around me to know what had passed between the viceroy and myself. I told them everything, and they were highly delighted.

Tsang Kwoh Fan, as he appeared in 1863, was over sixty years of age,[1] in the very prime of life. He was five feet, eight or nine inches tall, strongly built and well-knitted together and in fine proportion. He had a broad chest and square shoulders surmounted by a large symmetrical head. He had a broad and high forehead; his eyes were set on a straight line under triangular-shaped eyelids, free from that obliquity so characteristic of the Mongolian type of countenance usually accompanied by high cheek bones, which is another feature peculiar to the Chinese physiognomy. His face was straight and somewhat hairy. He allowed his side whiskers their full growth; they hung down with his full beard which swept across a broad chest and added dignity to a commanding appearance. His eyes though not large were keen and penetrating. They were of a clear hazel color. His mouth was large but well compressed with thin lips which showed a strong will and a high purpose. Such was Tsang Kwoh Fan's external appearance, when I first met him at Ngan Khing.

Regarding his character, he was undoubtedly one of the most remarkable men of his age and time. As a military general, he might be called a self-made man; by dint of his indomitable persistence and perseverance, he rose from his high scholarship as a Hanlin (Chinese LL.D.) to be a generalissimo of all the imperial forces that were levied against the Taiping rebels, and in less than a decade after he headed his Hunan raw recruits, he succeeded in reducing the wide devastations of the rebellion that covered a territorial area of three of the richest provinces of China to the single one of Kiang Nan, till finally, by the constriction of his forces, he succeeded in crushing the life out of the rebellion by the fall and capture of Nanking. The Taiping Rebellion was of fifteen years' duration, from 1850 to 1865. It was no small task to bring it to its extinction. Its rise and progress had cost the Empire untold treasures, while 25,000,000 human lives were immolated in that political hecatomb. The close of the great rebellion gave the people a breathing respite. The Dowager Empress had special reasons to be grateful to the genius of Tsang Kwoh Fan, who was instrumental in restoring peace and order to the Manchu Dynasty. She was not slow, however, to recognize Tsang Kwoh Fan's merits and moral worth and created him a duke. But Tsang's greatness was not to be measured by any degree of conventional nobility; it did not consist in his victories

---

1   Tsang was born in 1811.

over the rebels, much less in his re-capture of Nanking. It rose from his great virtues: his pure, unselfish patriotism, his deep and far-sighted statesmanship, and the purity of his official career. He is known in history as "the man of rectitude." This was his posthumous title conferred on him by imperial decree.

To resume the thread of my story, I was nearly two weeks in the viceroy's headquarters, occupying a suite of rooms in the same building assigned to my Shanghai friends —— Li, Chang, Wha and Chu. There were living in his military headquarters at least two hundred officials, gathered there from all parts of the Empire, for various objects and purposes. Besides his secretaries, who numbered no less than a hundred, there were expectant officials, learned scholars, lawyers, mathematicians, astronomers and machinists; in short, the picked and noted men of China were all drawn there by the magnetic force of his character and great name. He always had a great admiration for men of distinguished learning and talents, and loved to associate and mingle with them. During the two weeks of my sojourn there, I had ample opportunity to call upon my Shanghai friends, and in that way incidentally found out what the object of the Viceroy was in urging me to be enrolled in the government service. It seemed that my friends had had frequent interviews with the Viceroy in regard to having a foreign machine shop established in China, but it had not been determined what kind of a machine shop should be established. One evening they gave me a dinner, at which time the subject of the machine shop was brought up and it became the chief topic. After each man had expressed his views on the subject excepting myself, they wanted to know what my views were, intimating that in all likelihood in my next interview with the Viceroy he would bring up the subject. I said that as I was not an expert in the matter, my opinions or suggestions might not be worth much, but nevertheless from my personal observation in the United States and from a common-sense point of view, I would say that a machine shop in the present state of China should be of a general and fundamental character and not one for specific purposes. In other words, I told them they ought to have a machine shop that would be able to create or reproduce other machine shops of the same character as itself; each and all of these should be able to turn out specific machinery for the manufacture of specific things. In plain words, they would have to have general and fundamental machinery in order to turn out specific machinery. A machine shop consisting of lathes of different kinds and sizes, planers and drills would be able to turn out machinery for making guns, engines, agricultural implements, clocks, etc. In a large country like China, I told them, they would need many primary or fundamental machine shops, but that after they had one (and a first-class one at that) they could make it the mother shop for reproducing others —— perhaps better and more improved. If they had a number of them, it would enable them to have the shops co-operate with each other in case of need. It would be cheaper to have them reproduced and multiplied in China, I said, where labor and material were cheaper, than in Europe and America. Such was my crude idea of the subject. After I had finished, they were apparently much pleased and interested, and expressed the hope that I would state the same views to the Viceroy if he should ask me about the subject.

Several days after the dinner and conversation, the Viceroy did send for me. In this interview he asked me what in my opinion was the best thing to do for China at that time. The question came with such a force of meaning, that if I had not been forwarned by my friends a few evenings before, or if their hearts had not been set on the introduction of a machine shop, and they had not practically won the Viceroy over to their pet scheme, I might have been strongly tempted to launch forth upon my educational scheme as a reply to the question as to what was the best thing to do for China. But in such an event, being a stranger to the Viceroy, having been brought to his notice simply through the influence of my friends, I would have run a greater risk of jeopardizing my pet scheme of education than if I were left to act independently. My obligations to them were great, and I therefore decided that my constancy and fidelity to their friendship should be correspondingly great. So, instead of finding myself embarrassed in answering such a large and important question, I had a preconceived answer to give, which seemed to dove-tail into his views already crystallized into definite form, and which was ready to be carried out at once. So my educational scheme was put in the background, and the machine shop was allowed to take precedence. I repeated in substance what I had said to my friends previously in regard to establishing a mother machine shop, capable of reproducing other machine shops of like character, etc. I especially mentioned the manufacture of rifles, which, I said, required for the manufacture of their component parts separate machinery, but that the machine shop I would recommend was not one adapted for making the rifles, but adapted to turn out specific machinery for the making of rifles, cannons, cartridges, or anything else.

"Well," said he, "this is a subject quite beyond my knowledge. It would be well for you to discuss the matter with Wha and Chu, who are more familiar with it than I am and we will then decide what is best to be done."

This ended my interview with the Viceroy. After I left him, I met my friends, who were anxious to know the result of the interview. I told them of the outcome. They were highly elated over it. In our last conference it was decided that the matter of the character of the machine shop was to be left entirely to my discretion and judgment, after consulting a professional mechanical engineer. At the end of another two weeks, Wha was authorized to tell me that the Viceroy, after having seen all the four men, had decided to empower me to go abroad and make purchases of such machinery as in the opinion of a professional engineer would be the best and the right machinery for China to adopt. It was also left entirely to me to decide where the machinery should be purchased, —— either in England, France or the United States of America.

The location of the machine shop was to be at a place called Kow Chang Meu, about four miles northwest of the city of Shanghai. The Kow Chang Meu machine shop was afterwards known as the Kiang Nan Arsenal, an establishment that covers several acres of ground and embraces under its roof all the leading branches of mechanical work. Millions have been invested in it since I brought the first machinery from Fitchburg, Mass., in order to make it one of the greatest arsenals east of the Cape of Good Hope. It may properly be regarded as a lasting monument to commemorate Tsang Kwoh Fan's broadmindedness as well as far-sightedness in establishing Western machinery in China.

Chapter 14
My Mission to America to Buy Machinery

A week after my last interview with the Viceroy and after I had been told that I was to be entrusted with the execution of the order, my commission was made out and issued to me. In addition to the commission, the fifth official rank was conferred on me. It was a nominal civil rank, with the privilege of wearing the blue feather, as was customary only in war time and limited to those connected with the military service, but discarded in the civil service, where the peacock's feather is conferred only by imperial sanction. Two official despatches were also made out, directing me where to receive the Tls. 68,000, the entire amount for the purchase of the machinery. One-half of the amount was to be paid by the Taotai of Shanghai, and the other half by the Treasurer of Canton. After all the preliminary preparations had been completed, I bade farewell to the Viceroy and my Shanghai friends and started on my journey.

On my arrival in Shanghai in October, 1863, I had the good fortune to meet Mr. John Haskins, an American mechanical engineer, who came out to China with machinery for Messrs. Russell & Co. He had finished his business with that firm and was expecting soon to return to the States with his family —— a wife and a little daughter. He was just the man I wanted. It did not take us long to get acquainted and as the time was short, we soon came to an understanding. We took the overland route from Hong Kong to London, via the Isthmus of Suez. Haskins and his family took passage on the French Messagerie Imperial line, while I engaged mine on board of one of the Peninsular & Oriental steamers. In my route to London, I touched at Singapore, crossed the Indian Ocean, and landed at Ceylon, where I changed steamers for Bengal up the Red Sea and landed at Cairo, where I had to cross the Isthmus by rail. The Suez Canal was not finished; the work of excavating was still going on. Arriving at Alexandria, I took passage from there to Marseilles, the southern port of France, while Haskins and his family took a steamer direct for Southampton. From Marseilles I went to Paris by rail. I was there about ten days, long enough to give me a general idea of the city, its public buildings, churches, gardens, and of Parisian gaiety. I crossed the English channel from Calais to Dover and went thence by rail to London —— the first time in my life to touch English soil, and my first visit to the famous metropolis. While in London, I visited Whitworth's machine shop, and had the pleasure of renewing my acquaintance with Thomas Christy, whom I knew in China in the 50's. I was about a month in England, and then crossed the Atlantic in one of the Cunard steamers and landed in New York in the early spring of 1864, just ten years after my graduation from Yale and in ample time to be present at the decennial meeting of my class in July. Haskins and his family had preceded me in another steamer for New York, in order that he might get to work on the drawings and specifications of the shop and machinery and get them completed as soon as possible. In 1864, the last year of the great Civil War, nearly all the machine shops in the country, especially in New England, were preoccupied and busy in executing government orders, and it was very difficult to have my machinery taken up. Finally Haskins succeeded in getting the Putnam Machine Co., Fitchburg, Mass., to fill the order.

While Haskins was given sole charge of superintending the execution of the order, which required at least six months before the machinery could be completed for shipment to China, I took advantage of the interim to run down to New Haven and attend the decennial meeting of my class. It was to me a joyous event and I congratulated myself that I had the good luck to be present at our first reunion. Of course, the event that brought me back to the country was altogether unpretentious and had attracted little or no public attention at the time, because the whole country was completely engrossed in the last year of the great Civil War, yet I personally regarded my commission as an inevitable and preliminary step that would ultimately lead to the realization of my educational scheme, which had never for a moment escaped my mind. But at the meeting of my class, this subject of my life plan was not brought up. We had a most enjoyable time and parted with nearly the same fraternal feeling that characterized our parting at graduation. After the decennial meeting, I returned to Fitchburg and told Haskins that I was going down to Washington to offer my services to the government as a volunteer for the short period of six months, and that in case anything happened to me during the six months so that I could not come back to attend to the shipping of the machinery to Shanghai, he should attend to it. I left him all the papers —— the cost and description of the machinery, the bills of lading, insurance, and freight, and directed him to send everything to the Viceroy's agent in Shanghai. This precautionary step having been taken, I slipped down to Washington .

Brigadier-General Barnes of Springfield, Mass., happened to be the general in charge of the Volunteer Department. His headquarters were at Willard's Hotel. I called on him and made known to him my object, that I felt as a naturalized citizen of the United States, it was my bounden duty to offer my services as a volunteer courier to carry despatches between Washington and the nearest Federal camp for at least six months, simply to show my loyalty and patriotism to my adopted country, and that I would furnish my own equipments. He said that he remembered me well, having met me in the Yale Library in New Haven, in 1853, on a visit to his son, William Barnes, who was in the college at the time I was, and who afterwards became a prominent lawyer in San Francisco. General Barnes asked what business I was engaged in. I told him that since my graduation in 1854 I had been in China and had recently returned with an order to purchase machinery for a machine shop ordered by Viceroy and Generalissimo Tsang Kwoh Fan. I told him the machinery was being made to order in Fitchburg, Mass., under the supervision of an American mechanical engineer, and as it would take at least six months before the same could be completed, I was anxious to offer my services to the government in the meantime as an evidence of my loyalty and patriotism to my adopted country. He was quite interested and pleased with what I said.

"Well, my young friend," said he, "I thank you very much for your offer, but since you are charged with a responsible trust to execute for the Chinese government, you had better return to Fitchburg to attend to it. We have plenty of men to serve, both as couriers and as fighting men to go to the front." Against this peremptory decision, I could urge nothing further, but I felt that I had at least fulfilled my duty to my adopted country.

Chapter 15
My Second Return to China

The machinery was not finished till the early spring of 1865. It was shipped direct from New York to Shanghai, China; while it was doubling the Cape of Good Hope on its way to the East, I took passage in another direction, back to China. I wanted to encircle the globe once in my life, and this was my opportunity. I could say after that, that I had circumnavigated the globe. So I planned to go back by way of San Francisco. In order to do that, I had to take into consideration the fact that the Union Pacific from Chicago to San Francisco via Omaha was not completed, nor was any steamship line subsidized by the United States government to cross the Pacific from San Francisco to any seaport, either in Japan or China at the time. On that account I was obliged to take a circuitous route, by taking a coast steamer from New York to Panama, cross the Isthmus, and from there take passage in another coast steamer up the Mexican coast to San Francisco, Cal.

At San Francisco, I was detained two weeks where I had to wait for a vessel to bridge me over the broad Pacific, either to Yokohama or Shanghai. At that time, as there was no other vessel advertised to sail for the East, I was compelled to take passage on board the "Ida de Rogers," a Nantucket bark. There were six passengers, including myself. We had to pay $500 each for passage from San Francisco to Yokohama. The crew consisted of the captain, who had with him his wife, and a little boy six years old, a mate, three sailors and a cook, a Chinese boy. The "Ida de Rogers" was owned by Captain Norton who hailed from Nantucket. She was about one hundred and fifty feet long —— an old tub at that. She carried no cargo and little or no ballast, except bilge-water, which may have come from Nantucket, for aught I know. The skipper, true to the point of the country where they produce crops of seamen of microscopic ideas, was found to be not at all deficient in his close calculations of how to shave closely in every bargain and, in fact, in everything in life. In this instance, we had ample opportunity to find out under whom we were sailing. Before we were fairly out of the "Golden Gate," we were treated every day with salted mackerel, which I took to be the daily and fashionable dish of Nantucket. The cook we had made matters worse, as he did not seem to know his business and was no doubt picked up in San Francisco just to fill the vacancy. The mackerel was cooked and brought on the table without being freshened, and the Indian meal cakes that were served with it, were but half baked, so that day after day we practically all left the table disgusted and half starved. Not only was the food bad and unhealthy, but the skipper's family was of a very low type. The skipper himself was a most profane man, and although I never heard the wife swear, yet she seemed to enjoy her husband's oaths. Their little boy who was not more than six years old, seemed to have surpassed the father in profanity. It may be said that the young scamp had mastered his shorter and longer catechism of profanity completely, for he was not wanting in expressions of the most disgusting and repulsive kind, as taught him by his sire, yet his parents sat listening to him with evident satisfaction, glancing around at the passengers to catch their approval. One of the passengers, an Englishman, who stood near listening and smoking his pipe, only remarked ironically, "You have a smart boy there." At this the skipper nodded, while the mother seemed to gloat over her young hopeful. Such a scene was of daily occurrence, and one that we could not escape, since we were cooped up in such narrow quarters on account of the smallness of the vessel. There was not even a five-foot deck where one could stretch his legs. We were most of the time shut up in the dining room, as it was the coolest spot we could find. Before our voyage was half over, we had occasion to land at one of the most northerly islands of the Hawaiian group for fresh water and provisions. While the vessel was being victualed, all the passengers landed and went out to the country to take a stroll, which was a great relief. We were gone nearly all day. We all re-embarked early in the evening. It seemed that the captain had filled the forward hold with chickens and young turkeys. We congratulated ourselves that the skipper after all had swung round to show a generous streak, which had only needed an opportunity to show itself, and that for the rest of the voyage he was no doubt going to feed us on fresh chickens and turkeys to make up for the salted mackerel, which might have given us the scurvy had we continued on the same diet. For the first day or so, after we resumed our voyage, we had chicken and fish for our breakfast and dinners, but that was the last we saw of the fresh provisions. We saw no turkey on the table. On making inquiry, the cook told us that both the chickens and the turkeys were bought, not for our table, but for speculation, to be sold on arrival in Yokohama. Unfortunately for the skipper, the chickens and turkeys for want of proper food and fresh air, had died a few days before our arrival at the port.

Immediately upon reaching Yokohama, I took passage in a P. & O. steamer for Shanghai.

On my arrival there, I found the machinery had all arrived a month before; it had all been delivered in good condition and perfect working order. I had been absent from China a little over a year. During that time Viceroy Tsang Kwoh Fan, with the co-operation of his brother, Tsang Kwoh Chuen, succeeded in the capture of Nanking, which put an end to the great Taiping Rebellion of 1850.[1]

On my arrival in Shanghai, I found that the Viceroy had gone up to Chu Chow, the most northerly department of Kiangsu province, close to the border line of Shan Tung, and situated on the canal. He made that his headquarters in superintending the subjugation of the Nienfi or Anwhui rebels, against whom Li Hung Chang had been appointed as his lieutenant in the field. I was requested to go up to Chu Chow to make a report in person regarding the purchase of the machinery.

On my journey to Chu Chow, I was accompanied by my old friend Wha Yuh Ting part of the way. We went by the Grand Canal from Sinu-Mew at the Yangtze up as far as Yang Chow, the great entrepôt for the Government Salt Monopoly. There we took mule carts overland to Chu Chow. We were three days on our journey. Chu Chow is a departmental city and here, as stated before, Viceroy Tsang made his quarters. I was there three days. The Viceroy complimented me highly for what I had done. He made my late commission to the States to purchase machinery the subject of a special memorial to the government. Such a special memorial on any political event invariably gives it political prominence and weight, and in order to lift me at once from a position of no importance to a territorial civil appointment of the bona fide fifth rank, was a step seldom asked for or conceded. He made out my case to be an exceptional one, and the following is the language he used in his memorial:

> *"Yung Wing is a foreign educated Chinese. He has mastered the English language. In his journey over thousands of miles of ocean to the extreme ends of the earth to fulfill the commission I entrusted to him, he was utterly oblivious to difficulties and dangers that lay in his way. In this respect even the missions of the Ancients present no parallel equal to his. Therefore, I would recommend that he be*

---

1   Note: incorrect year.

promoted to the expectancy of one of the Kiangsu sub-prefects, and he is entitled to fill the first vacancy presenting itself, in recognition of his valuable services."

His secretary, who drew up the memorial at his dictation, gave me a copy of the memorial before I left Chu Chow for Shanghai, and congratulated me on the great honor the Viceroy had conferred on me. I thanked the Viceroy before bidding him good-bye, and expressed the hope that my actions in the future would justify his high opinion of me.

In less than two months after leaving him, an official document from the Viceroy reached me in Shanghai, and in October, 1865, I was a full-fledged mandarin of the fifth rank. While waiting as an expectant sub-prefect, I was retained by the provincial authorities as a government interpreter and translator. My salary was $250 per month. No other expectant official of the province —— not even an expectant Taotai (an official of the fourth rank) —— could command such a salary.

Ting Yih Chang was at the time Taotai of Shanghai. He and I became great friends. He rose rapidly in official rank and became successively salt commissioner, provincial treasurer and Taotai or governor of Kiang Nan. Through him, I also rose in official rank and was decorated with the peacock's feather. While Ting Yih Chang was salt commissioner, I accompanied him to Yang Chow and was engaged in translating *Colton's geography* into Chinese, for about six months. I then returned to Shanghai to resume my position as government interpreter and translator. I had plenty of time on my hands. I took to translating *Parsons on Contracts*, which I thought might be useful to the Chinese. In this work I was fortunate in securing the services of a Chinese scholar to help me. I found him well versed in mathematics and in all Chinese official business, besides being a fine Chinese scholar and writer. He finally persuaded me not to continue the translation, as there was some doubt as to whether such a work, even when finished, would be in demand, because the Chinese courts are seldom troubled with litigations on contracts, and in all cases of violation of contracts, the Chinese code is used.

In 1867, Viceroy Tsang Kwoh Fan, with Li Hung Chang's co-operation, succeeded in ending the Nienfi rebellion, and came to Nanking to fill his viceroyalty of the two Kiangs.

Before taking up his position as viceroy of the Kiangs permanently, he took a tour of inspection through his jurisdiction and one of the important places he visited was Shanghai and the Kiang Nan Arsenal —— an establishment of his own creation. He went through the arsenal with undisguised interest. I pointed out to him the machinery which I bought for him in America. He stood and watched its automatic movement with unabated delight, for this was the first time he had seen machinery, and how it worked. It was during this visit that I succeeded in persuading him to have a mechanical school annexed to the arsenal, in which Chinese youths might be taught the theory as well as the practice of mechanical engineering, and thus enable China in time to dispense with the employment of foreign mechanical engineers and machinists, and to be perfectly independent. This at once appealed to the practical turn of the Chinese mind, and the school was finally added to the arsenal. They are doubtless turning out at the present time both mechanical engineers and machinists of all descriptions.

Chapter 16
Proposal of My Educational Scheme

Having scored in a small way this educational victory, by inducing the Viceroy to establish a mechanical training school as a corollary to the arsenal, I felt quite worked up and encouraged concerning my educational scheme which had been lying dormant in my mind for the past fifteen years, awaiting an opportunity to be brought forward.

Besides Viceroy Tsang Kwoh Fan, whom I counted upon to back me in furthering the scheme, Ting Yih Chang, an old friend of mine, had become an important factor to be reckoned with in Chinese politics. He was a man of progressive tendencies and was alive to all practical measures of reform. He had been appointed governor of Kiangsu province, and after his accession to his new office, I had many interviews with him regarding my educational scheme, in which he was intensely interested. He told me that he was in correspondence with Wen Seang, the prime minister of China, who was a Manchu, and that if I were to put my scheme in writing, he would forward it to Peking, and ask Wen Seang to use his influence to memorialize the government for its adoption. Such an unexpected piece of information came like a clap of thunder and fairly lifted me off my feet. I immediately left Suchau for Shanghai. With the help of my Nanking friend, who had helped me in the work of translating *Parsons on Contracts*, I drew up four proposals to be presented to Governor Ting, to be forwarded by him to Minister Wen Seang, at Peking. They were as follows:

【First Proposal】 The first proposal contemplated the organization of a Steamship Company on a joint stock basis. No foreigner was to be allowed to be a stockholder in the company. It was to be a purely Chinese company, managed and worked by Chinese exclusively.

To insure its stability and success, an annual government subsidy was to be made in the shape of a certain percentage of the tribute rice carried to Peking from Shanghai and Chinkiang, and elsewhere, where tribute rice is paid over to the government in lieu of taxes in money. This tribute rice heretofore had been taken to Peking by flat-bottom boats, via the Grand Canal. Thousands of these boats were built expressly for this rice transportation, which supported a large population all along the whole route of the Grand Canal.

On account of the great evils arising from this mode of transportation, such as the great length of time it took to take the rice to Peking, the great percentage of loss from theft, and from fermentation, which made the rice unfit for food, part of the tribute rice was carried by sea in Ningpo junks as far as Tientsin, and from thence transhipped again in flat-bottom boats to Peking. But even the Ningpo junk system was attended with great loss of time and much damage, almost as great as by flat-bottom scows. My proposition was to use steam to do the work, supplanting both the flat-bottomed scows and the Ningpo junk system, so that the millions who were dependent on rice for subsistence might find it possible to get good and sound rice. This is one of the great benefits and blessings which the China Merchant Steamship Co. has conferred upon China.

【Second Proposal】 The second proposition was for the government to send picked Chinese youths abroad to be thoroughly educated for the public service. The scheme contemplated the education of one hundred and twenty students as an experiment. These one hundred and twenty students were to be divided into four installments of thirty students each, one installment to be sent out each year. They were to have fifteen years to finish their education. Their average age was to be from twelve to fourteen years. If the first and second installments proved to be a success, the scheme was to be continued indefinitely. Chinese teachers were to be provided to keep up their knowledge of Chinese while in the United States. Over the whole enterprise two commissioners were to be appointed, and the government was to appropriate a certain percentage of the Shanghai customs to maintain the mission.

【Third Proposal】 The third proposition was to induce the government to open the mineral resources of the country and thus in an indirect way lead to the necessity of introducing railroads to transport the mineral products from the interior to the ports.

I did not expect this proposition to be adopted and carried out, because China at that time had no mining engineers who could be depended upon to develop the mines, nor were the people free from the Fung Shui superstition.[1] I had no faith whatever in the success of this proposition, but simply put it in writing to show how ambitious I was to have the government wake up to the possibilities of the development of its vast resources.

【Fourth Proposal】 The encroachment of foreign powers upon the independent sovereignty of China has always been watched by me with the most intense interest. No one who is at all acquainted with Roman Catholicism can fail to be impressed with the unwarranted pretensions and assumptions of the Romish church in China. She claims civil jurisdiction over her proselytes, and takes civil and criminal cases out of Chinese courts. In order to put a stop to such insidious and crafty workings to gain temporal power in China, I put forth this proposition: to prohibit missionaries of any religious sect or denomination from exercising any kind of jurisdiction over their converts, in either civil or criminal cases. These four propositions were carefully drawn up, and were presented to Governor Ting for transmission to Peking.

Of the four proposals, the first, third and fourth were put in to chaperone the second, in which my whole heart was enlisted, and which above all others was the one I wanted to be taken up; but not to give it too prominent a place, at the suggestion of my Chinese teacher, it was assigned a second place in the order of the arrangement. Governor Ting recognized this, and accordingly wrote to Prime Minister Wen Seang and forwarded the proposals to Peking. Two months later, a letter from Ting, at Suchau, his headquarters, gave me to understand that news from Peking had reached him that Wen Seang's mother had died, and he was obliged, according to Chinese laws and customs, to retire from office and go into mourning for a period of twenty-seven months, equivalent to three years, and to abstain altogether from public affairs of all kinds. This news threw a cold blanket over my educational scheme for the time being. No sooner had one misfortune happened than another took its place, worst than the first —— Wen Seang himself, three months afterwards, was overtaken by death during his retirement. This announcement appeared in the Peking "Gazette," which I saw, besides being officially informed of it by Governor Ting. No one who had a pet scheme to

---

1   The doctrine held by the Chinese in relation to the spirits or genii that rule over winds and waters, especially running streams and subterranean waters. This doctrine is universal and inveterate among the Chinese, and in a great measure prompts their hostility to railroads and telegraphs, since they believe that such structures anger the spirits of the air and waters and consequently cause floods and typhoons. *Standard Dictionary*.

promote or a hobby to ride could feel more blue than I did, when the cup of joy held so near to his lips was dashed from him. I was not entirely disheartened by such circumstances, but had an abiding faith that my educational scheme would in the end come out all right. There was an interval of at least three years of suspense and waiting between 1868 and 1870. I kept pegging at Governor Ting, urging him to keep the subject constantly before Viceroy Tsang's mind. But like the fate of all measures of reform, it had to abide its time and opportunity.

The time and the opportunity for my educational scheme to materialize finally came. Contrary to all human expectations, the opportunity appeared in the guise of the Tientsin Massacre. No more did Samson, when he slew the Timnath lion, expect to extract honey from its carcass than did I expect to extract from the slaughter of the French nuns and Sisters of Charity the educational scheme that was destined to make a new China of the old, and to work out an oriental civilization on an occidental basis.

The Tientsin Massacre took place early in 1870. It arose from the gross ignorance and superstition of the Tientsin populace regarding the work of the nuns and Sisters of Charity, part of whose religious duty it was to rescue foundlings and castaway orphans, who were gathered into hospitals, cared for and educated for the services of the Roman Catholic church. This beneficent work was misunderstood and misconstrued by the ignorant masses, who really believed in the rumors and stories that the infants and children thus gathered in were taken into the hospitals and churches to have their eyes gouged out for medical and religious purposes. Such diabolical reports soon spread like wild-fire till popular excitement was worked up to its highest pitch of frenzy, and the infuriated mob, regardless of death and fearless of law, plunged headlong into the Tientsin Massacre. In that massacre a Protestant church was burned and destroyed, as was also a Roman Catholic church and hospital; several nuns or Sisters of Charity were killed.

At the time of this occurrence, Chung Hou was viceroy of the Metropolitan province. He had been ambassador to Russia previously, but in this unfortunate affair, according to Chinese law, he was held responsible, was degraded from office and banished. The whole imbroglio was finally settled and patched up by the payment of an indemnity to the relatives and friends of the victims of the massacre and the rebuilding of the Roman Catholic and Protestant churches, another Catholic hospital, besides a suitable official apology made by the government for the incident. Had the French government not been handicapped by the impending German War which threatened her at the time, France would certainly have made the Tientsin Massacre a "casus belli", and another slice of the Chinese Empire would have been annexed to the French possessions in Asia. As it was, Tonquin, a tributary state of China, was afterwards unscrupulously wrenched from her.

In the settlement of the massacre, the Imperial commissioners appointed were: Viceroy Tsang Kwoh Fan, Mow Chung Hsi, Liu * * * [2]and Ting Yih Chang, Governor of Kiang Su. Li Hung Chang was still in the field finishing up the Nienfi rebellion, otherwise he, too, would have been appointed to take part in the proceedings of the settlement. I was telegraphed for by my friend, Ting Yih Chang, to be present to act as interpreter on the occasion, but the telegram did not reach me in time for me to accompany him to Tientsin; but I reached Tientsin in time to witness the last proceedings. The High Commissioners, after the settlement with the French, for some reason or other, did not disband, but remained in Tientsin for several days. They evidently had other matters of State connected with Chung Hou's degradation and banishment to consider.

---

2   Yung Wing forgot the name of this person. He only recalled his surname as "Liu".

Chapter 17
The Chinese Educational Mission

Taking advantage of their presence, I seized the opportunity to press my educational scheme upon the attention of Ting Yih Chang and urged him to present the subject to the Board of Commissioners of which Tsang Kwoh Fan was president. I knew Ting sympathized with me in the scheme, and I knew, too, that Tsang Kwoh Fan had been well informed of it three years before through Governor Ting. Governor Ting took up the matter in dead earnest and held many private interviews with Tsang Kwoh Fan as well as with the other members of the Commission. One evening, returning to his headquarters very late, he came to my room and awakened me and told me that Viceroy Tsang and the other Commissioners had unanimously decided to sign their names conjointly in a memorial to the government to adopt my four propositions. This piece of news was too much to allow me to sleep any more that night; while lying on my bed, as wakeful as an owl, I felt as though I were treading on clouds and walking in air. Two days after this stirring piece of news, the memorial was jointly signed with Viceroy Tsang Kwoh Fan's name heading the list, and was on its way to Peking by pony express. Meanwhile, before the Board of Commissioners disbanded and Viceroy Tsang took his departure for Nanking, it was decided that Chin Lan Pin, a member of the Hanlin College, who had served twenty years as a clerk in the Board of Punishment, should be recommended by Ting to co-operate with me in charge of the Chinese Educational Commission. The ground upon which Chin Lan Pin was recommended as a co-commissioner was that he was a Han Lin and a regularly educated Chinese, and the enterprise would not be so likely to meet with the opposition it might have if I were to attempt to carry it out alone, because the scheme in principle and significance was against the Chinese theory of national education, and it would not have taken much to create a reaction to defeat the plan on account of the intense conservatism of the government. The wisdom and the shrewd policy of such a move appealed to me at once, and I accepted the suggestion with pleasure and alacrity. So Chin Lan Pin was written to and came to Tientsin. The next day, after a farewell dinner had been accorded to the Board of Commissioners before it broke up, Governor Ting introduced me to Chin Lan Pin, whom I had never met before and who was to be my associate in the educational scheme. He evidently was pleased to quit Peking, where he had been cooped up in the Board of Punishment for twenty years as a clerk. He had never filled a government position in any other capacity in his life, nor did he show any practical experience in the world of business and hard facts. In his habits he was very retiring, but very scholarly. In disposition he was kindly and pleasant, but very timid and afraid of responsibilities of even a feather's weight.

In the winter of 1870, Tsang Kwoh Fan, after having settled the Tientsin imbroglio, returned to Nanking, his headquarters as the viceroy of the two Kiangs. There he received the imperial rescript sanctioning his joint memorial on the four proposals submitted through Ting Yih Chang for adoption by the government. He notified me on the subject. It was a glorious piece of news, and the Chinese educational project thus became a veritable historical fact, marking a new era in the annals of China. Tsang invited me to repair to Nanking, and during that visit the most important points connected with the mission were settled, viz.: the establishment of a preparatory school; the number of students to be selected to be sent abroad; where the money was to come from to support the students while there; the number of years they were to be allowed to remain there for their education.

The educational commission was to consist of two commissioners, Chin Lan Pin and myself. Chin Lan Pin's duty was to see that the students should keep up their knowledge of Chinese while in America; my duty was to look after their foreign education and to find suitable homes for them. Chin Lan Pin and myself were to look after their expenses conjointly. Two Chinese teachers were provided to keep up their studies in Chinese, and an interpreter was provided for the Commission. Yeh Shu Tung and Yung Yune Foo were the Chinese teachers and Tsang Lai Sun was the interpreter. Such was the composition of the Chinese Educational Commission.

As to the character and selection of the students: the whole number to be sent abroad for education was one hundred and twenty; they were to be divided into four installments of thirty members each, one installment to be sent each year for four successive years at about the same time. The candidates to be selected were not to be younger than twelve or older than fifteen years of age. They were to show respectable parentage or responsible and respectable guardians. They were required to pass a medical examination, and an examination in their Chinese studies according to regulation —— reading and writing in Chinese —— also to pass an English examination if a candidate had been in an English school. All successful candidates were required to repair every day to the preparatory school, where teachers were provided to continue with their Chinese studies, and to begin the study of English or to continue with their English studies, for at least one year before they were to embark for the United States.

Parents and guardians were required to sign a paper which stated that without recourse, they were perfectly willing to let their sons or protégés go abroad to be educated for a period of fifteen years, from the time they began their studies in the United States until they had finished, and that during the fifteen years, the government was not to be responsible for death or for any accident that might happen to any student.

The government guaranteed to pay all their expenses while they were being educated. It was to provide every installment with a Chinese teacher to accompany it to the United States, and to give each installment of students a suitable outfit. Such were the requirements and the organization of the student corps.

Immediately upon my return to Shanghai from Nanking after my long interview with the Viceroy, my first step was to have a preparatory school established in Shanghai for the accommodation of at least thirty students, which was the full complement for the first installment. Liu Kai Sing, who was with the Viceroy for a number of years as his first secretary in the Department on Memorials, was appointed superintendent of the preparatory school in Shanghai. In him, I found an able coadjutor as well as a staunch friend who took a deep interest in the educational scheme. He it was who prepared all the four installments of students to come to this country.

Thus the China end of the scheme was set afloat in the summer of 1871. To make up the full complement of the first installment of students, I had to take a trip down to Hong Kong to visit the English government schools to select from them a few bright candidates who had had some instruction both in English and Chinese studies. As the people in the northern part of China did not know that such an educational scheme had been projected by the government, there being no Chinese newspapers published at that time to spread the news among the people, we had, at first, few applications for entrance into the preparatory school. All the applications came from the Canton people, especially from the district of Heang Shan. This accounts for the fact that nine-tenths of the one hundred and twenty government students were from the south.

In the winter of 1871, a few months after the preparatory school had begun operations, China suffered an irreparable loss by the death of Viceroy Tsang Kwoh Fan, who died in Nanking at the ripe age of seventy-one years. [1]Had his life been spared even a year longer, he would have seen the first installment of thirty students started for the United States, —— the first fruit of his own planting. But founders of all great and good works are not permitted by the nature and order of things to live beyond their ordained limitations to witness the successful developments of their own labor in this world; but the consequences of human action and human character, when once their die is cast, will reach to eternity. Sufficient for Tsang Kwoh Fan that he had completed his share in the educational line well. He did a great and glorious work for China and posterity, and those who were privileged to reap the benefit of his labor will find ample reason to bless him as China's great benefactor. Tsang, as a statesman, a patriot, and as a man, towered above his contemporaries even as Mount Everest rises above the surrounding heights of the Himalaya range, forever resting in undisturbed calmness and crowned with the purity of everlasting snow. Before he breathed his last, I was told that it was his wish that his successor and protégé, Li Hung Chang, be requested to take up his mantle and carry on the work of the Chinese Educational Commission.

Li Hung Chang was of an altogether different make-up from his distinguished predecessor and patron. He was of an excitable and nervous temperament, capricious and impulsive, susceptible to flattery and praise, or, as the Chinese laconically put it, he was fond of wearing tall hats. His outward manners were brusque, but he was inwardly kind-hearted. As a statesman he was far inferior to Tsang; as a patriot and politician, his character could not stand a moment before the searchlight of cold and impartial history. It was under such a man that the Chinese Educational Commission was launched forth.

In the latter part of the summer of 1872 the first installment of Chinese students, thirty in number, were ready to start on the passage across the Pacific to the United States. In order that they might have homes to go to on their arrival, it devolved upon me to precede them by one month, leaving Chin Lan Pin, the two Chinese teachers and their interpreter to come on a mail later. After reaching New York by the Baltimore and Ohio, via Washington, I went as far as New Haven on my way to Springfield, Mass., where I intended to meet the students and other

---

1   Tsang Kwoh Fan died in 1872. He was born in 1811.

members of the commission on their way to the East by the Boston and Albany Railroad. At New Haven, the first person I called upon to announce my mission was Prof. James Hadley. He was indeed glad to see me, and was delighted to know that I had come back with such a mission in my hands. After making my wants known to him, he immediately recommended me to call upon Mr. B. G. Northrop, which I did. Mr. Northrop was then Commissioner of Education for Connecticut. I told him my business and asked his advice. He strongly recommended me to distribute and locate the students in New England families, either by twos or fours to each family, where they could be cared for and at the same time instructed, till they were able to join classes in graded schools. This advice I followed at once. I went on to Springfield, Mass., which city I considered was the most central point from which to distribute the students in New England; for this reason I chose Springfield for my headquarters. This enabled me to be very near my friends, Dr. A. S. McClean and his worthy wife, both of whom had been my steadfast friends since 1854.

But through the advice of Dr. B. G. Northrop and other friends, I made my permanent headquarters in the city of Hartford, Conn., and for nearly two years our headquarters were located on Sumner Street. I did not abandon Springfield, but made it the center of distribution and location of the students as long as they continued to come over, which was for three successive years, ending in 1875.

In 1874, Li Hung Chang, at the recommendation of the commission, authorized me to put up a handsome, substantial building on Collins Street as the permanent headquarters of the Chinese Educational Commission in the United States. In January, 1875, we moved into our new headquarters, which was a large, double three-story house spacious enough to accommodate the Commissioners, teachers and seventy-five students at one time. It was provided with a school-room where Chinese was exclusively taught; a dining room, a double kitchen, dormitories and bath rooms. The motive which led me to build permanent headquarters of our own was to have the educational mission as deeply rooted in the United States as possible, so as not to give the Chinese government any chance of retrograding in this movement. Such was my proposal, but that was not God's disposal as subsequent events plainly proved.

Chapter 18
Investigation of the Coolie Traffic in Peru

In the spring of 1873, I returned to China on a flying visit for the sole purpose of introducing the Gatling gun —— a comparatively new weapon of warfare of a most destructive character. I had some difficulty in persuading the Gatling Company to give me the sole agency of the gun in China, because they did not know who I was, and were unacquainted with my practical business experience. In fact, they did not know how successfully I had carried on the Taiping Green Tea Expedition in 1860-1, in the face of dangers and privations which few men dared to face. However, I prevailed on the president of the company, Dr. Gatling himself, the inventor of the gun, to entrust me with the agency. Exactly a month after my arrival in Tientsin, I cabled the company an order for a battery of fifty guns, which amounted altogether to something over $100,000, a pretty big order for a man who it was thought could not do anything. This order was followed by subsequent orders. I was anxious that China should have the latest modern guns as well as the latest modern educated men. The Gatling Company was satisfied with my work and had a different opinion of me afterwards.

While I was in Tientsin, attending to the gun business, the Viceroy told me that the Peruvian commissioner was there waiting to make a treaty with China regarding the further importation of coolie labor into Peru. He wanted me to call on the commissioner and talk with him on the subject, which I did. In his conversation, he pictured to me in rosy colors how well the Chinese were treated in Peru; how they were prospering and doing well there, and said that the Chinese government ought to conclude a treaty with Peru to encourage the poorer class of Chinese to emigrate to that country, which offered a fine chance for them to better themselves. I told him that I knew something about the coolie traffic as it was carried on in Macao; how the country people were inveigled and kidnapped, put into barracoons and kept there by force till they were shipped on board, where they were made to sign labor contracts either for Cuba or Peru. On landing at their destination, they were then sold to the highest bidder, and made to sign another contract with their new masters, who took special care to have the contract renewed at the end of every term, practically making slaves of them for life. Then I told him something about the horrors of the middle passage between Macao and Cuba or Peru; how whole cargoes of them revolted in mid-ocean, and either committed wholesale suicide by jumping into the ocean, or else overpowered the captain and the crew, killed them and threw them overboard, and then took their chances in the drifting of the vessel.

Such were some of the facts and horrors of the coolie traffic I pictured to the Peruvian Commissioner. I told him plainly that he must not expect me to help him in this diabolical business. On the contrary, I told him I would dissuade the Viceroy from entering into a treaty with Peru to carry on such inhuman traffic. How the Peruvian's countenance changed when he heard me deliver my mind on the subject! Disappointment, displeasure and anger were visible in his countenance. I bade him good morning, for I was myself somewhat excited as I narrated what I had seen in Macao and what I had read in the papers about the coolie traffic. Indeed, one of the first scenes I had seen on my arrival in Macao in 1855 was a string of poor Chinese coolies tied to each other by their cues and led into one of the barracoons like abject slaves. Once, while in Canton, I had succeeded in having two or three kidnappers arrested, and had them put into wooden collars weighing forty pounds, which the culprits had to carry night and day for a couple of months as a punishment for their kidnapping.

Returning to the Viceroy, I told him I had made the call, and narrated my interview. The Viceroy, to make my visit short, then said, "You have come back just in time to save me from cabling you. I wish you to return to Hartford as quickly as possible and make preparations to proceed to Peru at once, to look into the condition of the Chinese coolies there."

On my return to Hartford, I found that Chin Lan Pin had also been instructed by the government to look after the condition of the Chinese coolies in Cuba. These collateral or side missions were ordered at Li Hung Chang's suggestion. I started on my mission before Chin Lan Pin did. My friend, the Rev. J. H. Twichell, and Dr. E. W. Kellogg, who afterwards became my brother-in-law, accompanied me on my trip. I finished my work inside of three months, and had my report completed before Chin started on his journey to Cuba. On his return, both of our reports were forwarded to Viceroy Li, who was in charge of all foreign diplomatic affairs.

My report was accompanied with two dozen photographs of Chinese coolies, showing how their backs had been lacerated and torn, scarred and disfigured by the lash. I had these photographs taken in the night, unknown to anyone except the victims themselves, who were, at my request, collected and assembled together for the purpose. I knew that these photographs would tell a tale of cruelty and inhumanity perpetrated by the owners of haciendas, which would be beyond cavil and dispute.

The Peruvian Commissioner, who was sent out to China to negotiate a treaty with Viceroy Li Hung Chang to continue the coolie traffic to Peru, was still in Tientsin waiting for the arrival of my report. A friend of mine wrote me that he had the hardihood to deny the statements in my report, and said that they could not be supported by facts. I had written to the Viceroy beforehand that he should hold the photographs in reserve, and keep them in the background till the Peruvian had exhausted all his arguments, and then produce them. My correspondent wrote me that the Viceroy followed my suggestion, and the photographs proved to be so incontrovertible and palpable that the Peruvian was taken by surprise and was dumbfounded. He retired completely crestfallen.

Since our reports on the actual conditions of Chinese coolies in Cuba and Peru were made, no more coolies have been allowed to leave China for those countries. The traffic had received its death blow.

Chapter 19
End of the Educational Mission

In the fall of 1875 the last installment of students arrived. They came in charge of a new commissioner, Ou Ngoh Liang, two new Chinese teachers and a new interpreter, Kwang Kee Cheu. These new men were appointed by Viceroy Li Hung Chang. I knew them in China, especially the new commissioner and the interpreter. These changes were made at the request of Chin Lan Pin, who expected soon to return to China on a leave of absence. He was going to take with him the old Chinese teacher, Yeh Shu Tung, who had rendered him great and signal service in his trip to Cuba on the coolie question the year before. Tsang Lai Sun, the old interpreter, was also requested to resign and returned to China. These changes I had anticipated some time before and they did not surprise me.

Three months after Chin Lan Pin's arrival in Peking, word came from China that he and I were appointed joint Chinese ministers to Washington, and that Yeh Shu Tung, the old Chinese teacher, was appointed secretary to the Chinese Legation. This was great news to me to be sure, but I did not feel ecstatic over it; on the contrary, the more I reflected on it, the more I felt depressed. But my friends who congratulated me on the honor and promotion did not take in the whole situation as it loomed up before my mind in all its bearings. As far as I was concerned, I had every reason to feel grateful and honored, but how about my life work —— the Chinese educational mission that I had in hand —— and which needed in its present stage great watchfulness and care? If, as I reflected, I were to be removed to Washington, who was there left behind to look after the welfare of the students with the same interest that I had manifested? It would be like separating the father from his children. This would not do, so I sat down and wrote to the Viceroy a letter, the tenor of which ran somewhat as follows: I thanked him for the appointment which I considered to be a great honor for any man to receive from the government; and said that while I appreciated fully its significance, the obligations and responsibilities inseparably connected with the position filled me with anxious solicitude that my abilities and qualifications might not be equal to their satisfactory fulfilment. In view of such a state of mind, I much preferred, if I were allowed to have my preference in the matter, to remain in my present position as a commissioner of the Chinese mission in Hartford and to continue in it till the Chinese students should have finished their education and were ready to return to China to serve the State in their various capacities. In that event I should have discharged a duty to "Tsang the Upright," and at the same time fulfilled a great duty to China. As Chin Lan Pin had been appointed minister at the same time, he would doubtless be able alone to meet the expectations of the government in his diplomatic capacity.

The letter was written and engrossed by Yung Yune Foo, one of the old Chinese teachers who came over with the first installment of students at the same time Yeh Shu Tung came. In less than four months an answer was received which partially acceded to my request by making me an assistant or associate minister, at the same time allowing me to retain my position as Commissioner of Education, and in that capacity, to exercise a general supervision over the education of the students.

Ou Ngoh Liang, the new commissioner, was a much younger man than Chin. He was a fair Chinese scholar, but not a member of the Hanlin College. He was doubtless recommended by Chin Lan Pin. He brought his family with him, which consisted of his second wife and two children. He was a man of a quiet disposition and showed no inclination to meddle with settled conditions or to create trouble, but took rather a philosophical view of things; he had the good sense to let well enough alone. He was connected with the mission but a short time and resigned in 1876.

In 1876 Chin Lan Pin came as minister plenipotentiary and brought with him among his numerous retinue Woo Tsze Tung, a man whom I knew in Shanghai even in the '50's. He was a member of the Hanlin College, but for some reason or other, he was never assigned to any government department, nor was he ever known to hold any kind of government office. He showed a decided taste for chemistry, but never seemed to have made any progress in it, and was regarded by all his friends as a crank.

After Ou's resignation, Chin Lan Pin before proceeding to Washington to take up his official position as Chinese minister, strongly recommended Woo Tsze Tung to succeed Ou as commissioner, to which Viceroy Li Hung Chang acceded without thinking of the consequences to follow. From this time forth the educational mission found an enemy who was determined to undermine the work of Tsang Kwoh Fan and Ting Yih Cheong, to both of whom Woo Tsze Tung was more or less hostile. Woo was a member of the reactionary party, which looked upon the Chinese Educational Commission as a move subversive of the principles and theories of Chinese culture. This was told me by one of Chin's suite who held the appointment of charge d'affaires for Peru. The making of Woo Tsze Tung a commissioner plainly revealed the fact that Chin Lan Pin himself was at heart an uncompromising Confucian and practically represented the reactionary party with all its rigid and uncompromising conservatism that gnashes its teeth against all and every attempt put forth to reform the government or to improve the general condition of things in China. This accounts for the fact that in the early stages of the mission, I had many and bitter altercations with him on many things which had to be settled for good, once and for all. Such as the school and personal expenses of the students; their vacation expenses; their change of costume; their attendance at family worship; their attendance at Sunday School and church services; their outdoor exercises and athletic games. These and other questions of a social nature came up for settlement. I had to stand as a kind of buffer between Chin and the students, and defended them in all their reasonable claims. It was in this manner that I must have incurred Chin's displeasure if not his utter dislike. He had never been out of China in his life until he came to this country. The only standard by which he measured things and men (especially students) was purely Chinese. The gradual but marked transformation of the students in their behavior and conduct as they grew in knowledge and stature under New England influence, culture and environment produced a contrast to their behavior and conduct when they first set foot in New England that might well be strange and repugnant to the ideas and senses of a man like Chin Lan Pin, who all his life had been accustomed to see the springs of life, energy and independence, candor, ingenuity and open-heartedness all covered up and concealed, and in a great measure smothered and never allowed their full play. Now in New England the heavy weight of repression and suppression was lifted from the minds of these young students; they exulted in their freedom and leaped for joy. No wonder they took to athletic sports with alacrity and delight!

Doubtless Chin Lan Pin when he left Hartford for good to go to Washington carried away with him a very poor idea of the work to which he was singled out and called upon to perform. He must have felt that his own immaculate Chinese training had been contaminated by coming in contact with Occidental schooling, which he looked upon with evident repugnance. At the same time the very work which he seemed to look upon with disgust had certainly served him the best turn in his life. It served to lift him out of his obscurity as a head clerk in the office of the Board of Punishment for twenty years to become a commissioner of the Chinese Educational Commission, and from that post to be a minister plenipotentiary in Washington. It was the stepping stone by which he climbed to political prominence. He should not have kicked away the ladder under him after he had reached his dizzy elevation. He did all he could to break up the educational scheme by recommending Woo Tsze Tung to be the Commissioner of Education, than whom he could not have had a more pliant and subservient tool for his purpose, as may be seen hereinafter.

Woo Tsze Tung was installed commissioner in the fall of 1876. No sooner was he in office than he began to find fault with everything that had been done. Instead of laying those complaints before me, he clandestinely started a stream of misrepresentation to Peking about the students; how they had been mismanaged; how they had been indulged and petted by Commissioner Yung; how they had been allowed to enjoy more privileges than was good for them; how they imitated American students in athletics; that they played more than they studied; that they formed themselves into secret societies, both religious and political; that they ignored their teachers and would not listen to the advice of the new commissioner; that if they were allowed to continue to have their own way, they would soon lose their love of their own country, and on their return to China, they would be good for nothing or worse than nothing; that most of them went to church, attended Sunday Schools and had become Christians; that the sooner this educational enterprise was broken up and all the students recalled, the better it would be for China, etc., etc.

Such malicious misrepresentations and other falsehoods which we knew nothing of, were kept up in a continuous stream from year to year by Woo Tsze Tung to his friends in Peking and to Viceroy Li Hung Chang. The Viceroy called my attention to Woo's accusations. I wrote back in reply that they were malicious fabrications of a man who was known to have been a crank all his life; that it was a grand mistake to put such a man in a responsible position who had done nothing for himself or for others in his life; that he was only attempting to destroy the work of Tsang Kwoh Fan who, by projecting and fathering the educational mission, had the highest interest of China at heart; whereas Woo should have been relegated to a cell in an insane asylum or to an institution for imbeciles. I said further that Chin Lan Pin, who had recommended Woo to His Excellency as commissioner of Chinese Education, was a timid man by nature and trembled at the sight of the smallest responsibilities. He and I had not agreed in our line of policy in our diplomatic correspondence with the State Department nor had we agreed as commissioners in regard to the treatment of the Chinese students. To illustrate his extreme dislike of responsibilities: He was requested by the Governor to go to Cuba to find out the condition of the coolies in that island in 1873. He waited three months before he started on his journey. He sent Yeh Shu Tung and one of the teachers of the Mission accompanied by a young American lawyer and an interpreter to Cuba, which party did the burden of the work and thus paved the way for Chin Lan Pin and made the work easy for him. All he had to do was to take a trip down to Cuba and return, fulfilling his mission in a perfunctory way. The heat of the day and the burden of the labor were all borne by Yeh Shu Tung, but Chin Lan Pin gathered in the laurel and was made a minister plenipotentiary, while Yeh was given the appointment of a secretary of the legation. I mention these things not from any invidious motive towards Chin, but simply to show that often in the official and political world one man gets more praise and glory than he really deserves, while another is not rewarded according to his intrinsic worth. His Excellency was well aware that I had no axe to grind in making the foregoing statement. I further added that I much preferred not to accept the appointment of a minister to Washington, but rather to remain as commissioner of education, for the sole purpose of carrying it through to its final success. And, one time in the heat of our altercation over a letter addressed to the State Department, I told Chin Lan Pin in plain language that I did not care a rap either for the appointment of an assistant minister, or for that matter, of a full minister, and that I was ready and would gladly resign at any moment, leaving him free and independent to do as he pleased.

This letter in answer to the Viceroy's note calling my attention to Woo's accusations gave the Viceroy an insight into Woo's antecedents, as well as into the impalpable character of Chin Lan Pin. Li was, of course, in the dark as to what the Viceroy had written to Chin Lan Pin, but things both in the legation and the Mission apparently moved on smoothly for a while, till some of the students were advanced enough in their studies for me to make application to the State Department for admittance to the Military Academy at West Point and the Naval Academy in Annapolis. The answer to my application was: "There is no room provided for Chinese students." It was curt and disdainful. It breathed the spirit of Kearnyism and Sandlotism with which the whole Pacific atmosphere was impregnated, and which had hypnotized all the departments of the government, especially Congress, in which Blaine figured most conspicuously as the champion against the Chinese on the floor of the Senate. He had the presidential bee buzzing in his bonnet at the time, and did his best to cater for the electoral votes of the Pacific coast. The race prejudice against the Chinese was so rampant and rank that not only my application for the students to gain entrance to Annapolis and West Point was treated with cold indifference and scornful hauteur, but the Burlingame Treaty of 1868 was, without the least provocation, and contrary to all diplomatic precedents and common decency, trampled under foot unceremoniously and wantonly, and set aside as though no such treaty had ever existed, in order to make way for those acts of congressional discrimination against Chinese immigration which were pressed for immediate enactment.

When I wrote to the Viceroy that I had met with a rebuff in my attempt to have some of the students admitted to West Point and Annapolis, his reply at once convinced me that the fate of the Mission was sealed. He too fell back on the Burlingame Treaty of 1868 to convince me that the United States government had violated the treaty by shutting out our students from West Point and Annapolis.

Having given a sketch of the progress of the Chinese Educational Mission from 1870 to 1877-8, my letter applying for their admittance into the Military and Naval Academies might be regarded as my last official act as a commissioner. My duties from 1878 onwards were chiefly confined to legation work.

When the news that my application for the students to enter the Military and Naval Academies of the government had proved a failure, and the displeasure and disappointment of the Viceroy at the rebuff were known, Commissioner Woo once more renewed his efforts to break up the Mission. This time he had the secret co-operation of Chin Lan Pin. Misrepresentations and falsehoods manufactured out of the whole cloth went forth to Peking in renewed budgets in every mail, till a censor from the ranks of the reactionary party came forward and took advantage of the strong anti-Chinese prejudices in America to memorialize the government to break up the Mission and have all the students recalled.

The government before acceding to the memorial put the question to Viceroy Li Hung Chang first, who, instead of standing up for the students, yielded to the opposition of the reactionary party and gave his assent to have the students recalled. Chin Lan Pin, who from his personal experience was supposed to know what ought to be done, was the next man asked to give his opinion. He decided that the students had been in the United States long enough, and that it was time for them to return to China. Woo Tsze Tung, the Commissioner, when asked for his opinion, came out point blank and said that they should be recalled without delay and should be strictly watched after their return. I was ruled out of the consultation altogether as being one utterly incompetent to give an impartial and reliable opinion on the subject. Thus the fate of the educational mission was sealed, and all students, about one hundred in all, returned to China in 1881.

The breaking up of the Chinese Educational Commission and the recall of the young students in 1881, was not brought about without a strenuous effort on the part of some thoughtful men who had watched steadfastly over the development of human progress in the East and the West, who came forward in their quiet and modest ways to enter a protest against the revocation of the Mission. Chief among them were my lifelong friend, the Rev. J. H. Twichell, and Rev. John W. Lane, through whose persistent efforts Presidents Porter and Seelye, Samuel Clemens, T.F. Frelingbuysen, John Russell Young and others were enlisted and brought forward to stay the work of retrogression of the part of the Chinese. The protest was couched in the most dignified, frank and manly language of President Porter of Yale and read as follows:

To The Tsung Li Yamun or Office for Foreign Affairs,

"*The undersigned, who have been instructors, guardians and friends of the students who were sent to this country under the care of the Chinese Educational Commission, beg leave to represent:*

"*That they exceedingly regret that these young men have been withdrawn from the country, and that the Educational Commission has been dissolved.*

"*So far as we have had opportunity to observe, and can learn from the representations of others, the young men have generally made a faithful use of their opportunities, and have made good progress in the studies assigned to them, and in the knowledge of the language, ideas, arts and institutions of the people of this country.*

"*With scarcely a single exception, their morals have been good; their manners have been singularly polite and decorous, and their behavior has been such as to make friends for themselves and their country in the families, the schools, the cities and villages in which they have resided.*

"In these ways they have proved themselves eminently worthy of the confidence which has been reposed in them to represent their families and the great Chinese Empire in a land of strangers. Though children and youths, they have seemed always to understand that the honor of their race and their nation was committed to their keeping. As the result of their good conduct, many of the prejudices of ignorant and wicked men towards the Chinese have been removed, and more favorable sentiments have taken their place.

"We deeply regret that the young men have been taken away just at the time when they were about to reap the most important advantages from their previous studies, and to gather in the rich harvest which their painful and laborious industry had been preparing for them to reap. The studies which most of them have pursued hitherto have been disciplinary and preparatory. The studies of which they have been deprived by their removal, would have been the bright flower and the ripened fruit of the roots and stems which have been slowly reared under patient watering and tillage. We have given to them the same knowledge and culture that we give to our own children and citizens.

"As instructors and guardians of these young men, we should have welcomed to our schools and colleges the Commissioners of Education or their representatives and have explained to them our system and methods of instruction. In some cases, they have been invited to visit us, but have failed to respond to their invitations in person or by their deputies.

"We would remind your honorable body that these students were originally received to our homes and our colleges by request of the Chinese government through the Secretary of State with the express desire that they might learn our language, our manners, our sciences and our arts. To remove them permanently and suddenly without formal notice or inquiry on the ground that as yet they had learned nothing useful to China when their education in Western institutions, arts and sciences is as yet incomplete, seems to us as unworthy of the great Empire for which we wish eminent prosperity and peace, as it is discourteous to the nation that extended to these young men its friendly hospitality.

"We cannot accept as true the representation that they have derived evil and not good from our institutions, our principles and our manners. If they have neglected or forgotten their native language, we never assumed the duty of instructing them in it, and cannot be held responsible for this neglect. The Chinese government thought it wise that some of its own youth should be trained after our methods. We have not finished the work which we were expected to perform. May we not reasonably be displeased that the results of our work should be judged unfavorably before it could possibly be finished?

"In view of these considerations, and especially in view of the injury and loss which have fallen upon the young men whom we have learned to respect and love, and the reproach which has implicitly been brought upon ourselves and the great nation to which we belong, —— we would respectfully urge that the reasons for this sudden decision should be reconsidered, and the representations which have been made concerning the intellectual and moral character of our education should be properly substantiated. We would suggest that to this end, a committee may be appointed of eminent Chinese citizens whose duty it shall be to examine into the truth of the statements unfavorable to the young men or their teachers, which have led to the unexpected abandonment of the Educational Commission and to the withdrawal of the young men from the United States before their education could be finished."

Chapter 20
Journey to Peking and Death of My Wife

The treatment which the students received at the hands of Chinese officials in the first years after their return to China as compared with the treatment they received in America while at school could not fail to make an impression upon their innermost convictions of the superiority of Occidental civilization over that of China —— an impression which will always appeal to them as cogent and valid ground for radical reforms in China, however altered their conditions may be in their subsequent careers. Quite a number of the survivors of the one hundred students, I am happy to say, have risen to high official ranks and positions of great trust and responsibility. The eyes of the government have been opened to see the grand mistake it made in breaking up the Mission and having the students recalled. Within only a few years it had the candor and magnanimity to confess that it wished it had more of just such men as had been turned out by the Chinese Educational Mission in Hartford, Conn. This confession, though coming too late, may be taken as a sure sign that China is really awakening and is making the best use of what few partially educated men are available. And these few accidentally educated men have, in their turn, encouraged and stimulated both the government and the people. Since the memorable events of the China and Japan war, and the war between Japan and Russia, several hundreds of Chinese students have come over to the United States to be educated. Thus the Chinese educational scheme which Tsang Kwoh Fan initiated in 1870 at Tientsin and established in Hartford, Conn., in 1872, though rolled back for a period of twenty-five years, has been practically revived.

Soon after the students' recall and return to China in 1881, I also took my departure and arrived in Tientsin in the fall of that year on my way to Peking to report myself to the government after my term of office as assistant minister had expired. This was the customary step for all diplomatic officers of the government to take at the close of their terms. Chin Lan Pin preceded me by nearly a year, having returned in 1880.

While paying my visit to Li Hung Chang in Tientsin, before going up to Peking, he brought up the subject of the recall of the students. To my great astonishment he asked me why I had allowed the students to return to China. Not knowing exactly the significance of the inquiry, I said that Chin Lan Pin, who was minister, had received an imperial decree to break up the Mission; that His Excellency was in favor of the decree, so was Chin Lan Pin and so was Woo Tsze Tung. If I had stood out alone against carrying out the imperial mandate, would not I have been regarded as a rebel, guilty of treason, and lose my head for it? But he said that at heart he was in favor of their being kept in the States to continue their studies, and that I ought to have detained them. In reply I asked how I could have been supposed to read his heart at a distance of 45,000 lis, especially when it was well known that His Excellency had said that they might just as well be recalled. If His Excellency had written to me beforehand not to break up the Mission under any circumstances, I would then have known what to do; as it was, I could not have done otherwise than to see the decree carried out. "Well," said he, in a somewhat angry and excited tone, "I know the author of this great mischief." Woo Tsze Tung happened to be in Tientsin at the time. He had just been to Peking and sent me word begging me to call and see him. Out of courtesy, I did call. He told me he had not been well received in Peking, and that Viceroy Li was bitter towards him when he had called and had refused to see him a second time. He looked careworn and cast down. He was never heard of after our last interview.

On my arrival in Peking, one of my first duties was to make my round of official calls on the leading dignitaries of the government —— the Princes Kung and Ching and the presidents of the six boards. It took me nearly a month to finish these official calls. Peking may be said to be a city of great distances, and the high officials live quite far apart from each other. The only conveyances that were used to go about from place to place were the mule carts. These were heavy, clumsy vehicles with an axle-tree running right across under the body of a box, which was the carriage, and without springs to break the jolting, with two heavy wheels, one at each end of the axle. They were slow coaches, and with the Peking roads all cut up and seldom repaired, you can imagine what traveling in those days meant. The dust and smell of the roads were something fearful. The dust was nothing but pulverized manure almost as black as ink. It was ground so fine by the millions of mule carts that this black stuff would fill one's eyes and ears and penetrate deep into the pores of one's skin, making it impossible to cleanse oneself with one washing. The neck, head and hands had to have suitable coverings to keep off the dust. The water is brackish, making it difficult to take off the dirt, thereby adding to the discomforts of living in Peking.

I was in Peking about three months. While there, I found time to prepare a plan for the effectual suppression of the Indian opium trade in China and the extinction of the poppy cultivation in China and India. This plan was submitted to the Chinese government to be carried out, but I was told by Whang Wen Shiu, the president of the Tsung Li Yamun (Foreign Affairs), that for want of suitable men, the plan could not be entertained, and it was shelved for nearly a quarter of a century until recently when the subject became an international question.

I left Peking in 1882. After four months' residence in Shanghai, I returned to the United States on account of the health of my family.

I reached home in the spring of 1883, and found my wife in a very low condition. She had lost the use of her voice and greeted me in a hoarse low whisper. I was thankful that I found her still living though much emaciated. In less than a month after my return, she began to pick up and felt more like herself. Doubtless, her declining health and suffering were brought on partly on account of my absence and her inexpressible anxiety over the safety of my life. A missionary fresh from China happened to call on her a few days before my departure for China and told her that my going back to China was a hazardous step, as they would probably cut my head off on account of the Chinese Educational Mission. This piece of gratuitous information tended more to aggravate a mind already weighed down by poor health, and to have this gloomy foreboding added to her anxiety was more than she could bear. I was absent in China from my family this time nearly a year and a half, and I made up my mind that I would never leave it again under any conditions whatever. My return in 1883 seemed to act on my wife's health and spirit like magic, as she gradually recovered strength enough to go up to Norfolk for the summer. The air up in Norfolk was comparatively pure and more wholesome than in the Connecticut valley, and proved highly salubrious to her condition. At the close of the summer, she came back a different person from what she was when she went away, and I was much encouraged by her improved health. I followed up these changes of climate and air with the view of restoring her to her normal condition, taking her down to Atlanta, Georgia, one winter and to the Adirondacks another year. It seemed that these changes brought only temporary relief without any permanent recovery. In the winter of 1885, she began to show signs of a loss of appetite and expressed a desire for a change. Somerville, New Jersey, was recommended to her as a sanitarium. That was the last resort she went to for her health, for there she caught a cold which resulted in her death. She lingered there for nearly two months till she was brought home, and died of Bright's disease on the 28th of June, 1886. She was buried in Cedar Hill Cemetery in the home lot I secured for that purpose. Her death made a great void in my after-life, which was irreparable, but she did not leave me hopelessly deserted and alone; she left me two sons who are constant reminders of her beautiful life and character. They have proved to be my greatest comfort and solace in my declining years. They are most faithful, thoughtful and affectionate sons, and I am proud of their manly and earnest Christian characters. My gratitude to God for blessing me with two such sons will forever rise to heaven, an endless incense.

The two blows that fell upon me one after the other within the short span of five years from 1880 to 1886 were enough to crush my spirit. The one had scattered my life work to the four winds; the other had deprived me of a happy home which had lasted only ten years. The only gleam of light that broke through the dark clouds which hung over my head came from my two motherless sons whose tender years appealed to the very depths of my soul for care and sympathy. They were respectively seven and nine years old when deprived of their mother. I was both father and mother to them from 1886 till 1895. My whole soul was wrapped up in their education and well-being. My mother-in-law, Mrs. Mary B. Kellogg, assisted me in my work and stood by me in my most trying hours, keeping house for me for nearly two years.

Chapter 21
My Recall to China

In 1894-5 war broke out between China and Japan on account of Korea. My sympathies were enlisted on the side of China, not because I am a Chinese, but because China had the right on her side, and Japan was simply trumping up a pretext to go to war with China, in order to show her military and naval prowess. Before the close of the war, it was impossible for me to be indifferent to the situation —— I could not repress my love for China. I wrote to my former legation interpreter and secretary, two letters setting forth a plan by which China might prosecute the war for an indefinite time.

My first plan was to go over to London to negotiate a loan of $15,000,000, with which sum to purchase three or four ready built iron-clads, to raise a foreign force of 5,000 men to attack Japan in the rear from the Pacific coast —— thus creating a diversion to draw the Japanese forces from Korea and give the Chinese government a breathing spell to recruit a fresh army and a new navy to cope with Japan. While this plan was being carried out, the government was to empower a commission to mortgage the Island of Formosa to some Western power for the sum of $400,000,000 for the purpose of organizing a national army and navy to carry on the war. These plans were embodied in two letters to Tsai Sik Yung, at that time secretary to Chang Tsze Tung, viceroy of Hunan and Hupeh. They were translated into Chinese for the Viceroy. That was in the winter of 1894. To my great surprise, Viceroy Chang approved of my first plan. I was authorized by cable to go over to London to negotiate the loan of $15,000,000. The Chinese minister in London, a Li Hung Chang man, was advised of my mission, which in itself was a sufficient credential for me to present myself to the minister. In less than a month after my arrival in London, I succeeded in negotiating the loan; but in order to furnish collaterals for it, I had to get the Chinese minister in London to cable the government for the hypothecation of the customs' revenue. I was told that Sir Robert Hart, inspector-general of customs, and Viceroy Li Hung Chang refused to have the customs' revenue hypothecated, on the ground that this revenue was hardly enough to cover as collateral the loan to meet the heavy indemnity demanded by Japan. The fact was: Viceroy Li Hung Chang and Chang Chi Tung were at loggerheads and opposed to each other in the conduct of the war. The latter was opposed to peace being negotiated by Li Hung Chang; but the former had the Dowager Empress on his side and was strenuous in his efforts for peace.

Hence Sir Robert Hart had to side with the Court party, and ignored Chang Chi Tung's request for the loan of $15,000,000; on that account the loan fell through, and came near involving me in a suit with the London Banking Syndicate.

I returned to New York and cabled for further instructions from Chang Chi Tung as to what my next step would be. In reply he cabled for me to come to China at once.

After thirteen years of absence from China, I thought that my connections with the Chinese government had been severed for good when I left there in 1883. But it did not appear to be so; another call to return awaited me, this time from a man whom I had never seen, of whose character, disposition and views I was altogether ignorant, except from what I knew from hearsay. But he seemed to know all about me, and in his memorial to the government inviting me to return, he could not have spoken of me in higher terms than he did. So I girded myself to go back once more to see what there was in store for me. By this recall, I became Chang Chi Tung's man as opposed to Li Hung Chang.

Before leaving for China this time, I took special pains to see my two sons well provided for in their education. Dr. E. W. Kellogg, my oldest brother-in-law, was appointed their guardian. Morrison Brown Yung, the older son, had just succeeded in entering Yale, Sheffield Scientific, and was able to look out for himself. Bartlett G. Yung, the younger one, was still in the Hartford High School preparing for college. I was anxious to secure a good home for him before leaving the country, as I did not wish to leave him to shift for himself at his critical age. The subject was mentioned to my friends, Mr. and Mrs. Twichell. They at once came forward and proposed to take Bartlett into their family as one of its members, till he was ready to enter college. This is only a single instance illustrative of the large-hearted and broad spirit which has endeared them to their people both in the Asylum Hill church and outside of it. I was deeply affected by this act of self-denial and magnanimity in my behalf as well as in the behalf of my son Bartlett, whom I felt perfectly assured was in first-class hands, adopted as a member of one of the best families in New England. Knowing that my sons would be well cared for, and leaving the development of their characters to an all-wise and ever-ruling Providence, as well as to their innate qualities, I embarked for China, this time without any definite and specific object in view beyond looking out for what opening there might be for me to serve her.

On my arrival in Shanghai, in the early part of the summer of 1895, I had to go to the expense of furnishing myself with a complete outfit of all my official dresses, which cost me quite a sum. Viceroy Chang Chi Tung, a short time previous to my arrival, had been transferred from the viceroyalty of the two Hoos to the viceroyalty of the two Kiangs temporarily. Instead of going up to Wu Chang, the capital of Hupeh, I went up to Nanking, where he was quartered.

In Viceroy Chang Chi Tung, I did not find that magnetic attraction which at once drew me towards Tsang Kwoh Fan when I first met him at Ngan Khing in 1863. There was a cold, supercilious air enveloping him, which at once put me on my guard. After stating in a summary way how the loan of $15,000,000 fell through, he did not state why the Peking government had declined to endorse his action in authorizing the loan, though I knew at the time that Sir Robert Hart, the inspector-general of the Chinese customs, put forward as an excuse that the custom dues were hardly enough to serve as collateral for the big loan that was about to be negotiated to satisfy the war indemnity demanded by the Japanese government. This was the diplomatic way of coating over a bitter pill for Chang Chi Tung to swallow, when the Peking government, through the influence of Li Hung Chang, was induced to ignore the loan. Chang and Li were not at the time on cordial terms, each having a divergent policy to follow in regard to the conduct of the war.

Dropping the subject of the loan as a dead issue, our next topic of conversation was the political state of the country in view of the humiliating defeat China had suffered through the incompetence and corruption of Li Hung Chang, whose defeat both on land and sea had stripped him of all official rank and title and came near costing him his life. I said that China, in order to recover her prestige and become a strong and powerful nation, would have to adopt a new policy. She would have to go to work and engage at least four foreigners to act as advisers in the Department for Foreign Affairs, in the Military and Naval Departments and in the Treasury Department. They might be engaged for a period of ten years, at the end of which time they might be re-engaged for another term. They would have to be men of practical experience, of unquestioned ability and character. While these men were thus engaged to give their best advice in their respective departments, it should be taken up and acted upon, and young and able Chinese students should be selected to work under them. In that way, the government would have been rebuilt upon western methods, and on principles and ideas that look to the reformation of the administrative government of China.

Such was the sum and substance of my talk in the first and only interview with which Chang Chi Tung favored me. During the whole of it, he did not express his opinion at all on any of the topics touched upon. He was as reticent and absorbent as a dry sponge. The interview differed from that accorded me by Tsang Kwoh Fan in 1863, in that Tsang had already made up his mind what he wanted to do for China, and I was pointed out to him to execute it. But in the case of Chang Chi Tung, he had no plan formed for China at the time, and what I presented to him in the interview was entirely new and somewhat radical; but the close of the Japan War justified me in bringing forward such views, as it was on account of that war that I had been recalled. If he had been as broad a statesman as his predecessor, Tsang Kwoh Fan, he could have said something to encourage me to entertain even a glimpse of hope that he was going to do something to reform the political condition of the government of the country at the close of the war. Nothing, however, was said, or even hinted at. In fact, I had no other interview with him after the first one. Before he left Nanking for Wu Chang, he gave me the appointment of Secretary of Foreign Affairs for Kiang Nan.

On the arrival of Liu Kwan Yih, the permanent viceroy of the two Kiang provinces, Chang Chi Tung did not ask me to go up to Wu Chang with him. This I took to be a pretty broad hint that he did not need my services any longer, that I was not the man to suit his purposes; and as I had no axe to grind, I did not make any attempt to run after my grind-stone. On the contrary, after three months' stay in Nanking under Viceroy Liu Kwan Yih, out of regard for official etiquette, I resigned the secretaryship, which was practically a sinecure —— paying about $150 a month. Such was my brief official experience with Viceroys Chang Chi Tung and Liu Kwan Yih.

I severed my official connection with the provincial government of Kiang Nan in 1896, and took up my headquarters in Shanghai —— untrammeled and free to do as I pleased and go where I liked. It was then that I conceived the plan of inducing the central government to establish in Peking a government national bank. For this object I set to work translating into Chinese the National Banking Act and other laws relating to national banks from the Revised Statutes of the United States with Amendments and additional Acts of 1875. In prosecuting this work, I had the aid of a Chinese writer, likewise the co-operation of the late Wong Kai Keh, one of the Chinese students who was afterwards the assistant Chinese commissioner in the St. Louis Exposition, who gave me valuable help. With the translation, I went up to Peking with my Chinese writer, and, at the invitation of my old friend, Chang Yen Hwan, who had been Chinese Minister in Washington from 1884 to 1888, I took up my quarters in his residence and remained there several months. Chang Yen Hwan at that time held two offices: one as a senior member of the Tsung Li Yamun (Office for Foreign Affairs); the other, as the first secretary in the Treasury Department of which Ung Tung Hwo, tutor to the late Emperor Kwang Su, was the president. Chang Yen Hwan was greatly interested in the National Banking scheme. He examined the translation critically and suggested that I should leave out those articles that were inapplicable to the conditions of China, and retain only such as were important and practicable. After the translation and selection were completed, he showed it to Ung Tung Hwo, president of the Treasury. They were both highly pleased with it, and had all the Treasury officials look it over carefully and pass their judgment upon it. In a few weeks'time, the leading officials of the Treasury Department called upon me to congratulate me upon my work, and said it ought to be made a subject of a memorial to the government to have the banking scheme adopted and carried out. Chang Yen Hwan came forward to champion it, backed by Ung Tung Hwo, the president.

To have a basis upon which to start the National Bank of China, it was necessary to have the government advance the sum of Tls. 10,000,000; of this sum, upwards of Tls. 2,000,000 were to be spent on machinery for printing government bonds and bank-notes of different denominations and machinery for a mint; Tls. 2,000,000 for the purchase of land and buildings; and Tls. 6,000,000 were to be held in reserve in the Treasury for the purchase of gold, silver and copper for minting coins of different denominations for general circulation. This Tls. 10,000,000 was to be taken as the initiatory sum to start the National Bank with, and was to be increased every year in proportion to the increase of the commerce of the Empire.

We had made such progress in our project as to warrant our appointing a committee to go around to select a site for the Bank, while I was appointed to come to the United States to consult with the Treasury Department on the plan and scope of the enterprise and to learn the best course to take in carrying out the plan of the National Bank. The Treasury Department, through its president, Ung Tung Hwo, was on the point of memorializing for an imperial decree to sanction setting aside the sum of Tls. 10,000,000 for the purpose indicated, when, to the astonishment of Chang Yen Hwan and other promoters of the enterprise, Ung Tung

Hwo, the president, received a telegraphic message from Shing Sun Whei, head of the Chinese Telegraphic Co., and manager of the Shanghai, China Steamship Navigation Co., asking Ung to suspend his action for a couple of weeks, till his arrival in Peking, Ung and Shing being intimate friends, besides being compatriots, Ung acceded to Shing's request. Shing Taotai, as he was called, was well-known to be a multimillionaire, and no great enterprise or concession of any kind could pass through without his finger in the pie. So in this banking scheme, he was bound to have his say. He had emissaries all over Peking who kept him well posted about everything going on in the capital as well as outside of it. He had access to the most powerful and influential princes in Peking, his system of graft reaching even the Dowager Empress through her favorite eunuch, the notorious Li Ling Ying. So Shing was a well-known character in Chinese politics. It was through his system of graft that the banking enterprise was defeated. It was reported that he came up to Peking with Tls. 300,000 as presents to two or three princes and other high and influential dignitaries, and got away with the Tls. 10,000,000 of appropriation by setting up a bank to manipulate his own projects.

The defeat of the National Banking project owed its origin to the thoroughly corrupt condition of the administrative system of China. From the Dowager Empress down to the lowest and most petty underling in the Empire, the whole political fabric was honey-combed with what Americans characterize as graft —— a species of political barnacles, if I may be allowed to call it that, which, when once allowed to fasten their hold upon the bottom of the ship of State were sure to work havoc and ruination; in other words, with money one could get anything done in China. Everything was for barter; the highest bid got the prize. The two wars —— the one with Japan in 1894-5 and the other, the Japan and Russian War in 1904-5 —— have in some measure purified the Eastern atmosphere, and the Chinese have finally awakened to their senses and have come to some sane consciousness of their actual condition.

After the defeat of the national banking project at the hands of Shing Taotai, I went right to work to secure a railroad concession from the government. The railroad I had in mind was one between the two ports of Tientsin and Chinkiang; one in the north, the other in the south near the mouth of the Yangtze River. The distance between these ports in a bee line is about five hundred miles; by a circuitous route going around the province of Shan Tung and crossing the Yellow River into the province of Hunan through Anwhui, the distance would be about seven hundred miles. The German government objected to having this railroad cross Shan Tung province, as they claimed they had the monopoly of building railroads throughout the province, and would not allow another party to build a railroad across Shan Tung. This was a preposterous and absurd pretension and could not be supported either by the international laws or the sovereign laws of China. At that time, China was too feeble and weak to take up the question and assert her own sovereign rights in the matter, nor had she the men in the Foreign Office to show up the absurdity of the pretension. So, to avoid any international complications, the concession was issued to me with the distinct understanding that the road was to be built by the circuitous route above described. The road was to be built with Chinese, not with foreign capital. I was given six months' time to secure capital. At the end of six months, if I failed to show capital, I was to surrender the concession. I knew very well that it would be impossible to get Chinese capitalists to build any railroad at that time. I tried hard to get around the sticking point by getting foreign syndicates to take over the concession, but all my attempts proved abortive, and I was compelled to give up my railroad scheme also. This ended my last effort to help China.

I did not dream that in the midst of my work, Khang Yu Wei and his disciple, Leang Kai Chiu, whom I met often in Peking during the previous year, were engaged in the great work of reform which was soon to culminate in the momentous coup d'état of 1898.

Chapter 22
The Coup d'état of 1898

The coup d'état of September, 1898, was an event memorable in the annals of the Manchu Dynasty. In it, the late Emperor Kwang Su was arbitrarily deposed; treasonably made a prisoner of state; and had his prerogatives and rights as Emperor of the Chinese Empire wrested from him and usurped by the late Dowager Empress Chi Hsi.

Kwang Su, though crowned Emperor when he was five years of age, had all along held the sceptre only nominally. It was Chi Hsi who held the helm of the government all the time.

As soon as Kwang Su had attained his majority, and began to exercise his authority as emperor, the lynx eye of Chi Hsi was never lifted away from him. His acts and movements were watched with the closest scrutiny, and were looked upon in any light but the right one, because her own stand in the government had never been the legitimate and straight one since 1864, when her first regency over her own son, Tung Chi, woke in her an ambition to dominate and rule, which grew to be a passion too morbid and strong to be curbed.

In the assertion of his true manhood, and the exercise of his sovereign power, his determination to reform the government made him at once the cynosure of Peking, inside and outside of the Palace. In the eyes of the Dowager Empress Chi Hsi, whose retina was darkened by deeds perpetrated in the interest of usurpation and blinded by jealousy, Kwang Su appeared in no other light than as a dement, or to use a milder expression, an imbecile, fit only to be tagged round by an apron string, cared for and watched. But to the disinterested spectator and unprejudiced judge, Kwang Su was no imbecile, much less a dement. Impartial history and posterity will pronounce him not only a patriot emperor, but also a patriot reformer —— as mentally sound and sane as any emperor who ever sat on the throne of China. He may be looked upon as a most remarkable historical character of the Manchu Dynasty from the fact that he was singled out by an all-wise Providence to be the pioneer of the great reform movement in China at the threshold of the twentieth century.

Just at this juncture of the political condition of China, the tide of reform had reached Peking. Emperor Kwang Su, under some mysterious influence, to the astonishment of the world, stood forth as the exponent of this reform movement. I determined to remain in the city to watch its progress. My headquarters became the rendezvous of the leading reformers of 1898. It was in the fall of that memorable year that the coup d'état took place, in which the young Emperor Kwang Su was deposed by the Dowager Empress, and some of the leading reformers arrested and summarily decapitated.

Being implicated by harboring the reformers, and in deep sympathy with them, I had to flee for my own life and succeeded in escaping from Peking. I took up quarters in the foreign settlement of Shanghai. While there, I organized the "Deliberative Association of China," of which I was chosen the first president. The object of the association was to discuss the leading question of the day, especially those of reform.

In 1899, I was advised for my own personal safety, to change my residence. I went to Hong Kong and placed myself under the protection of the British government.

I was in Hong Kong from 1900 till 1902, when I returned to the United States to see my younger son, Bartlett G. Yung, graduate from Yale University.

In the spring of 1901, I visited the Island of Formosa, and in that visit I called upon Viscount Gentarō Kodama, governor of the island, who, in the Russo-Japan War of 1904-5 was the chief of staff to Marshal Oyama in Manchuria. In the interview our conversation had to be carried on through his interpreter, as he, Kodama, could not speak English nor could I speak Japanese. He said he was glad to see me, as he had heard a great deal of me, but never had the pleasure of meeting me. Now that he had the opportunity, he said he might as well tell me that he had most unpleasant if not painful information to give me. Being somewhat surprised at such an announcement, I asked what the information was.

He said he had received from the viceroy of Fuhkein and Chehkiang an official dispatch requesting him to have me arrested, if found in Formosa, and sent over to the mainland to be delivered over to the Chinese authorities. Kodama while giving this information showed neither perturbation of thought nor feeling, but his whole countenance was wreathed with a calm and even playful smile.

I was not disturbed by this unexpected news, nor was I at all excited. I met it calmly and squarely, and said in reply that I was entirely in his power, that he could deliver me over to my enemies whenever he wished; I was ready to die for China at any time, provided that the death was an honorable one.

"Well, Mr. Yung," said he, "I am not going to play the part of a constable for China, so you may rest at ease on this point. I shall not deliver you over to China. But I have another matter to call to your attention." I asked what it was. He immediately held up a Chinese newspaper before me, and asked who was the author of the proposition. Without the least hesitation. I told him I was the author of it. At the same time, to give emphasis to this open declaration, I put my opened right palm on my chest two or three times, which attracted the attention of everyone in the room, and caused a slight excitement among the Japanese officials present.

I then said, "With Your Excellency's permission, I must beg to make one correction in the amount stated; instead of $800,000,000, the sum stated in my proposition was only $400,000,000." At this frank and open declaration and the corrected sum, Kodama was evidently pleased and visibly showed his pleasure by smiling at me.

The Chinese newspaper Kodama showed me contained a proposition I drew up for Viceroy Chang Chi Tung to memorialize the Peking government for adoption in 1894-5, about six months before the signing of the Treaty of Shemonashiki by Viceroy Li Hung Chang. The proposal was to have the Island of Formosa mortgaged to a European Treaty power for a period of ninety-nine years for the sum of $400,000,000 in gold. With this sum China was to carry on the war with Japan by raising a new army and a new navy. This proposition was never carried through, but was made public in the Chinese newspapers, and a copy of it found its way to Kodama's office, where, strange to say, I was confronted with it, and I had the moral courage not only to avow its authorship but also a correction of the amount the island was to be mortgaged for.

To bring the interview to a climax, I said, should like circumstances ever arise, nothing would deter me from repeating the same proposition in order to fight Japan.

This interview with the Japanese governor of Formosa was one of the most memorable ones in my life. I thought at first that at the request of the Chinese viceroy I was going to be surrendered, and that my fate was sealed; but no sooner had the twinkling smile of Kodama lighted his countenance than my assurance of life and safety came back with redoubled strength, and I was emboldened to talk war on Japan with perfect impunity. The bold and open stand I took on that occasion won the admiration of the governor who then invited me to accompany him to Japan where he expected to go soon to be promoted. He said he would introduce me to the Japanese emperor and other leading men of the nation. I thanked him heartily for his kindness and invitation and said I would accept such a generous invitation and consider it a great honor to accompany him on his contemplated journey, but my health would not allow me to take advantage of it. I had the asthma badly at the time.

Then, before parting, he said that my life was in danger, and that while I was in Formosa under his jurisdiction he would see that I was well protected and said that he would furnish me with a bodyguard to prevent all possibilities of assassination. So the next day he sent me four Japanese guards to watch over me at night in my quarters; and in the daytime whenever I went out, two guards would go in advance of me and two behind my jinrickisha to see that I was safe. This protection was continued for the few days I spent in Formosa till I embarked for Hong Kong. I went in person to thank the governor and to express my great obligation and gratitude to him for the deep interest he had manifested towards me.